D1526519

Arn's War

Ohio History and Culture

Series on Ohio History and Culture

Arn's War

Memoirs of a World War II Infantryman, 1940–1946

Edward C. Arn

Edited by Jerome Mushkat

The University of Akron Press

LIBRARY OF CONGRESS CATALOGING-IN-PUBLICATION DATA

Arn, Edward C., 1909–

    Arn's war : memoirs of a World War II infantryman, 1940–1946 /
Edward C. Arn & edited by Jerome Mushkat.

        p. cm. — (Ohio history and culture)

    Includes bibliographical references and index.

    ISBN 1-931968-25-X (cloth : alk. paper)

    ISBN 1-931968-32-2 (paperback : alk. paper)

    1. Arn, Edward C., 1909– 2. United States. Army. Infantry
Regiment, 119th. Battalion, 2nd. F, Company. 3. World War,
1939–1945—Regimental histories—United States. 4. World War,
1939–1945—Campaigns—Western Front. 5. World War,
1939–1945—Personal narratives, American. 6. United States.
Army—Officers—Biography. I. Mushkat, Jerome. II. Title.
III. Series.

D769.31119th .A75 2005

940.54'1273'092—dc22

                             2004030355

All illustrations, unless otherwise noted, come from the personal
collection of the author.

To Patricia Rolph Arn, my children and grandchildren, and to the men of F Company, 2nd Battalion, 119th Regiment, 30th Infantry Division, the Army of the United States

Contents

✺ Illustrations

❀ Maps

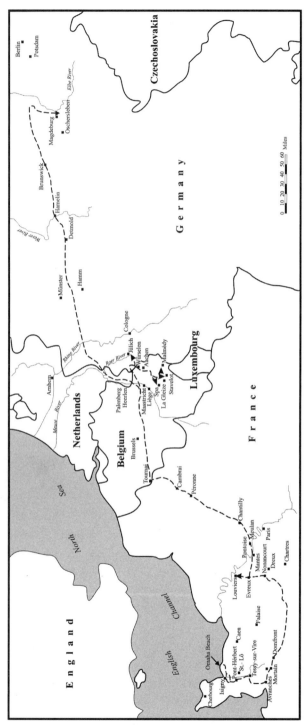

Map 1. Arn's war, 17 July 1944–8 May 1945.

Editor's Preface

ilitary service during World War II marked the most critical period in the lives of millions of young American
men and their families. Edward C. Arn, a highly decorated infantry captain, was among them. Years later, in 1976,
he began a memoir covering his nearly forty-two months of active duty in the Army of the United States, including almost
eleven in continuous combat. Arn had no intention of publishing his recollection. Encouraged by his wife, he wished to
record those long ago events for his own satisfaction, to make
sense out of his wartime activities, and as a record for his six
children and sixteen grandchildren before his memory faded.
Over the years, he added some additional insights, but the
work remained private and unpublished.

In the fall of 2002, Jeffrey D. Musselman, a Wooster, Ohio,
attorney, invited me to assess this memoir. I welcomed the opportunity. Over the next two months, I had the privilege of
meeting Arn, first through his manuscript and then in person.
The more I spoke to this remarkably vital ninety-four-year-
old person, the more I became convinced that his memoir
merited publication. Arn's work falls into five phases: his motivation for enlistment; the cycle of training that turned him
from a civilian into a civilian in uniform; the day-to-day reality
of combat; his adaptability to meet the challenges of battle and
find unsuspected inner resources to survive; and the war's enduring legacy in his personal life.

Arn uses a clear, direct literary style to explain the factors
that made him a first-rate infantryman, especially the psychological necessity to conquer the fears linked to the unspeak-
able horrors of modern war. Basic training and Officer
Candidate School (OCS) gave him the elements of command,

control, tactics, and weaponry. The battlefield tested this instruction when he joined Fox Company, 2nd Battalion, 119th Regiment, 30th Infantry Division, nicknamed "Old Hickory," as a replacement platoon leader. No guarantees existed that Arn would survive, let alone become an efficient combat officer, capable of directing his men against enemy troops, often battle-hardened veterans. He quickly proved his mettle. Arn fought with distinction in the murderous hedgerows of Normandy; at the critical Battle of Mortain, which preserved the Allied breakthrough from the beachhead; in the pursuit of the retreating Wehrmacht across northern France; breaching the Siegfried Line at Aachen; through the arduous Ardennes Campaign, including the Battle of the Bulge; and in the invasion of the Rhineland to the Elbe River and across. After German surrender, Arn's occupation duties took place in a bleak landscape of physical destruction, human desolation, and encounters with the Soviets that anticipated the Cold War.

Arn presents this story in a matter-of-fact, honest voice. He does not glorify war nor offer self-congratulations to embellish his experiences. He realizes that as a front-line soldier, much of the war was beyond his view. Yet he does not accept standard military histories that tell the story from the top down and all too often ignore the contributions small units made to victory. Instead, he makes the point that wars are won on the ground by the life-and-death struggles of determined foot soldiers, no matter their pain, sacrifices, fears, and often capricious deaths. Such combat was an individual experience, an unnerving human turning point in which men reacted in unpredictable ways during minutes, hours, and days of extreme stress. A person could act with heroics in one instance, then succumb to combat fatigue in another. In short, the only standard to measure an infantryman rested in his ability to close with and destroy the enemy.

As a whole, this memoir tells a timeless story. Arn's research technique and perspective further add freshness to this work. He relied primarily on his memory to describe events and reconstruct conversations some forty years later. Arn knew this approach might lead to inaccuracies, chiefly imperfect recall and the tricks that memory played with events that might prove more imagined than real. He had a tool to avoid these pitfalls. Arn consulted and sometimes incorporated sections from 312 letters he wrote to his parents from January 1942 to November 1945. Because of military censorship, most letters held innocuous information and came from unclear locations, such as "Somewhere in France." To add further authenticity and accuracy to these sources, Arn checked facts and events in pertinent secondary works. He had another depository at his disposal. A man who never threw away anything, Arn dug into storage boxes filled with a myriad of reminders. Among these were voluminous scrapbooks, photo albums, maps, newspaper clippings, and souvenirs. Further probing uncovered his personal "201 File"; class papers, tests, and textbooks from Officer Candidate School at Fort Benning, Georgia; special military orders covering assignments, commendations, awards, and promotions; and considerable other data and information about his military career. All this material ensures that his memoir is as accurate and contemporaneous as possible, and allows a reader to become a vicarious participant with Arn in things as they happened.

This memoir has another important quality. Over the last two decades, military historians have engaged in an often contentious debate over the relative superiority of the Wehrmacht's fighting ability and structure compared to its American counterpart, and whether Americans won solely because of their advantages in manpower, industrial output, and technology.[1]

Arn adds his personal perspective to this question. During the invasion's early stages, he concedes, Wehrmacht units, fighting in strong defensive positions, outfought the Americans and inflicted heavy casualties. None of this should have been surprising. The Wehrmacht fielded combat-ready troops, led by professional officers and noncommissioned officers, who sometimes wielded more powerful weapons, mainly armor and artillery. In contrast, American divisions contained civilians in uniform, often reluctant draftees, hardly ready for battle, bound in a replacement system that failed to integrate men in new units, and thrust into battle before they learned basic survival skills. No wonder so many were wounded or died, especially junior infantry officers. Yet as Arn's experience makes clear, American soldiers quickly evened, then changed, the odds in their favor. Arn typified the best of them. He learned and corrected his mistakes. He became an effective company commander with strong leadership skills. He had the human virtues, especially courage, patience, resiliency, and honesty, that turned a green company with constant turnover into a lethal fighting machine. He gained the trust of his men by sharing their dangers. He thrived on competition and had an obsession with winning, but remained an innately decent man who never took gambles that might cost lives. He fostered and nurtured small-unit cohesion and personal loyalty among Fox Company personnel even as casualties mounted and unseasoned replacements took their place. He had the doggedness to persist and the steadfastness to prevail, to bear with and surmount setbacks, and to wear down the enemy through undiluted will. Arn had another singular advantage. He entered combat at thirty-four, an advanced age for a combat infantryman and distinctly older than his "boys," particularly during the fall of 1944. His age provided the maturity, emotional stability, and ultimate self-confidence that proved vital in a company commander responsible for leading his men in battle, keeping them alive, and conquering the enemy.

Arn harbors few illusions. A realist, he admits that Fox Company's ability to fight well fluctuated with casualties, fear, exhaustion, friendly fire, weather conditions, logistics, terrain, disease, and raw replacements. Even so, Arn's wartime record illustrates that the Americans won with the type of men epitomized in his Fox Company, a vital component of the 30th Infantry Division, the "work horse of the Western Front," one of only eight of forty-two combat divisions in the European Theater of Operations that General of the Army Dwight D. Eisenhower designated for a Distinguished Unit Citation.[2]

In editing this manuscript, I followed a few guidelines. I kept the focus on Arn, his words and thoughts, and deleted material that detracted from his personal story. In a few instances, I shifted sentences, began new paragraphs, placed additional information within brackets to maintain the story's thread, clarified points, spelled uncommon military abbreviations, and inserted new punctuation. To familiarize a reader with Arn and his world, a biographic sketch precedes his memoir. I arranged this work in nine topical and chronologic chapters and began each with a short introduction to convey context. Since this work covers a wide variety of topics, I annotated and documented some points Arn raised, not to contradict him, but for more clarity and to provide references to studies available to readers.

I have accumulated a number of scholarly debts I wish to acknowledge. I am grateful to Edward C. Arn for his permission to edit his memoir. The holder of the copyright to the Edward C. Arn's Papers, Institute on World War II and the Human Experience, Florida State University, Tallahassee, Florida, granted me permission to quote from Arn's wartime letters. I am indebted to my colleagues, Professors Alan Hart and James F. Richardson, for their thoughtful criticism. Above all, I wish to thank my wife, Barbara S. Mushkat, for her encouragement. Special thanks are further due to Tiger, my silent friend.

Captain Edward C. Arn

Introduction:

The Saga of a Citizen-Soldier

In June 1990, Edward C. Arn answered an extensive questionnaire from the U.S. Army Military Institute, Carlisle Barracks, about his "service experiences" during World War II as a captain and commanding officer of Company F, 2nd Battalion, 119th Infantry Regiment, 30th Infantry Division. Arn's replies contained a mixture of modesty and pride, especially when he listed his combat record in the major campaigns in the European Theater of Operations: Normandy, Northern France, Ardennes-Alsace, Rhineland, and Central Germany, as well as occupation duty in postwar Germany. In a concluding section probing for any "recollections" the questions might have overlooked, Arn condensed his experiences in a few brief sentences: "I became a true combat infantry officer with all the fears and failings that such men suffered. I became commander of a rifle company not because of my ability but because of casualties. There was no other commissioned man around when my commanding officer died in my arms."[1] Arn was too self-effacing. His contributions to Allied victory exemplified the best qualities this nation has always sought in its citizen-soldiers.

Little in Arn's background indicated that he would become a decorated front-line infantry officer, swept into a war unprecedented in human history for violence.[2] His father, Edward Arn, left a Swiss-American enclave in New Philadelphia, Ohio when he was twenty-one in search of economic opportunity in Cleveland and became a manager of a retail grocery. The teenaged Cora M. Conelly, the eldest of seven Irish-

American children, also moved to Cleveland from the small community of Waverly, Ohio. She met Edward Arn, and they married on 9 May 1907. Edward Conelly Arn, their first son, was born 11 January 1909. His younger brother, John Arthur Arn, came twenty-two months later. A half-sister from his father's first marriage completed Arn's immediate circle.[3]

Arn's parents shaped their son in a number of ways. From his mother he inherited an "energetic, organized, dedicated, [and] intelligent" character. Moreover, he followed the example of community service she set, particularly with the Red Cross during World War II, culminating with her selection as East Cleveland Citizen of the Year in 1958. Arn's father was equally influential. Although his family "never starved," Edward Arn spent most of his adult life in jobs "he didn't like" and considered "demeaning." This example gave his son a competitive drive for upward mobility.

Arn grew to adolescence in this loving but economically constricted family environment. A bright, gregarious, and articulate child who made friends easily, he attended East Cleveland public schools, and graduated from Shaw High School in 1927. He was an above-average student, much involved in extracurricular activities, mainly dramatics and journalism. His peers recognized his abilities. In addition to being chosen editor of the school paper, Arn became senior class president, and was honored as the "outstanding boy" in his class. With that award came a $250 scholarship to a college of his choice.

That fall Arn enrolled at the College of Wooster, a private institution in Wooster, Ohio. Times were hard. Even with another scholarship from the college's Cleveland alumni club, he arrived on campus with "less than $100 in cash." Although long accustomed to holding a variety of jobs, Arn recalled that "I never worked any harder than I did when I got to college." He washed dishes and waited tables in the womens' dormitory. By his senior year, he "became head waiter in charge of the dining hall." During the football season, he "operated the concession." Off campus, he solicited customers for a dry cleaner on commission, labored as a handyman for a local family at thirty-five cents an hour, and spent summers as a truck driver, asphalt mixer, school furniture cleaner, magazine salesman, floral shop clerk, and landscape gardener. All these efforts fell short. "I graduated from college in debt to the institution," Arn wrote, "but I have paid it all back I am proud to say."

Even with this demanding schedule, Arn found time to continue his interests in the stage and literature. He majored in English, edited the college yearbook, and joined Kappa Theta Gamma, the honorary dramatic society. With his remaining time, he pledged one of the three social fraternities on campus. Arn's peers again acknowledged his attributes. They elected him president of his 1931 graduating class.

This impressive college record meant little when Arn entered the job market. Like other young and hopeful graduates, he faced limited opportunities in a nation caught in the throes of the Great Depression. Arn was persistent. After a three-month search, he found a place, even if it fell below his aspirations. For two years, he worked as a department manager and buyer, at a top salary of $18 a week, in the "Epicure Shop, fancy and imported foods" at the May Company, one of Cleveland's major department stores. In the winter of 1934, he met Eleanore C. Richards, a dental assistant. They were married on 3 February 1935. Shortly afterward, Arn made his own luck. Through a friend, he became a member of the Firestone Tire and Rubber Company's sales training program in Akron, Ohio. Arn made swift progress. In his first four years with Firestone, he rose from a local service manager to regional service manager to "Midwest Salesman of the Year" in 1938. This life kept the Arns on the move. They lived briefly in Chicago, Indianapolis, and Terre Haute, Indiana.

In May 1939, an even better economic opportunity beckoned. Arn joined the American Seating Company of Grand Rapids, Michigan, an organization that manufactured and sold a variety of chairs to schools, churches, transportation companies, and entertainment businesses. After training for several months, Arn and his wife relocated to Evanston, Illinois. He was good at this work. By 1942, Arn's territory covered parts of three states, and he lived a comfortable life based on his salary and commissions from sales.

By late 1941, Arn stood on the threshold of success. Now mature physically, he stood slightly under six feet. His round face, strong jaw,

We put the farm on rubber, 1937. Author is second from left.

bright eyes, and the perpetual smile around his lips showed the confidence and the promise for the future he felt. At the same time, Arn had an uneasy feeling about himself. Too many meals on the road and too little exercise had made his body soft. More serious, his marriage was deteriorating. Establishing homes in so many places in so short a period, coupled with the large blocks of time he spent traveling on business, left his wife with pangs of loneliness and neglect. Turning increasingly to drink for solace, she gradually succumbed to alcoholism.

At this critical juncture, events overseas reshaped Arn's world in unexpected ways. When the nation's first peacetime conscription act went into operation on 16 September 1940, Arn registered for the draft and received a deferment as a married man. The Japanese attack on Pearl Harbor, followed by the United States' formal entry into World War II, electrified Arn's patriotism and anger against Japan, Germany, and Italy. He wanted to contribute to the war effort, but thought his age and physical condition precluded his prospects as a combat soldier. Too, he had finally achieved monetary comfort, which allowed him to ease his parents' shaky finances. Yet his wife's escalating drinking and erratic behavior made his private life increasingly uncomfortable. Moreover, Arn felt pangs of guilt as he watched his brother and nephew join the military. Caught in this ambiguity, Arn drifted along until the late summer of 1942 when two events resolved his emotional turmoil. New military manpower calls changed his status and meant he would be drafted, and his marriage became irreparable after his mother's futile attempts to cure his wife's alcoholism.

Determined to enter the war on his own terms, Arn found his opening in the U.S. Army's Volunteer Officer Candidate (VOC) program, which the Department of War had authorized in March 1942. Under its terms, the VOC offered men with a deferment for dependents the opportunity to become officers. Once an applicant received permission to enter and passed basic training, he moved on to Officer Candidate School. If he succeeded, he received a commission as a second lieutenant. If he failed, he reverted to his civilian status and his prior draft category. Furthermore, Arn's company promised him a place once the war ended.[4]

Arn's course of action now came into focus. He decided to join the VOC. This decision led to another move. He filed the necessary legal papers to dissolve his marriage and in July 1944, the Court of Common Pleas in Cleveland dissolved his childless marriage.

On 7 September 1942 Arn entered the United States Army at Fort Sheridan, Illinois. In the months that followed, the military, with all its physical, technical, and psychological demands, plus its social and disciplinary acculturation, challenged Arn in new and harrowing ways. Equally daunting, the program's high attrition rate made him fearful of "washing out." Yet his desire to excel and nervous energy, along with his educational background, maturity, intelligence, and unsuspected aptitude in weaponry, eased his transition into this new "civilian army." He underwent basic training at the infantry replacement training center at Camp Croft, near Spartanburg, South Carolina, and received a promotion to corporal, 13 February 1943. Advanced infantry training followed at Fort Benning, Georgia. On 26 May 1943 Arn received his commission as a second lieutenant.

Still convinced that his age ruled out actual combat, Arn became an infantry basics instructor at Fort McClellan, Alabama. He proved a demanding, conscientious, but fair teacher, who relished his ability to mold recruits into effective troops. Despite his contributions, Arn gradually grew restless and began to investigate a transfer to an infantry division preparing for combat. His wish came true 28 January 1944. He received orders to join the 106th Infantry Division, currently on rugged maneuvers in the Tennessee mountains, as a rifle platoon leader. In March, the Department of War transferred the 106th to Camp Atterbury, Indiana, to prepare for overseas duty. Within days, the army reversed itself by detaching some seven thousand enlisted men and six hundred officers from the division as replacements for the looming invasion of Nazi German-controlled France. Arn was among them. Assigned to Fort Meade, Maryland, as a platoon leader replacement officer, he then transferred to Camp Shanks on the Hudson River, a port of embarkation to the European Theater of Operations, and shipped out 9 June 1944.

The D-Day invasion of Normandy was more than a month past when Arn reported on 17 July 1944 for combat duty to the 30th Infantry Division.[5] Service in the 30th left Arn with friendships and memories that left an indelible mark on his soul, symbolized by his lifelong attachment to its distinctive shoulder patch, a blue "H" within a blue "O" against an oval-shaped red background with a Roman numeral "XXX" in blue inside the double crossbar of the "H."

The 30th, originally a national guard unit from the Carolinas and Tennessee, nicknamed "Old Hickory" in honor of President Andrew Jackson, had carved a distinguished record in World War I. The full division, under Major General Leland S. Hobbs, with Brigadier General William K. Harrison as its executive officer, had landed in Normandy by 17 June 1944, D+11 days after the invasion. When Arn joined Fox Company under Captain Frank J. Parlavecchia, the division had bloodied itself in savage but inconclusive hedgerow fighting in the Vire-et-Taute Canal and the Vire River area near St.-Lô, about fifteen miles south of Omaha Beach.[6]

To regain the initiative, Lieutenant General Omar N. Bradley devised Operation Cobra. This plan to punch through German lines, prevent their reformation, encircle their forces, and score a breakthrough into France and Germany itself, began with saturation carpet bombing. General Hobbs pulled the 30th about two thousand yards from the front to avoid "friendly fire." Allied fighters and bombers, however, hit the division twice on 25 July and 26 July. They inflicted 133 casualties in the 119th Regiment, and 814 in the total division, also killing Lieutenant General Lesley J. McNair, who was inspecting troops he had earlier trained. Arn never forgave the "fly boys" for their mistakes.[7]

Despite this coordination failure, the 30th, one of three divisions in this assault, with the 119th leading the way, launched Operation Cobra on its most eastern flank. After rolling back the German 2nd Panzer Division, Fox Company drove toward its objectives, taking heavy losses in the process, including Captain Parlavecchia. He died of his wounds on 31 July. First Lieutenant Melvin L. Riesch took over. Arn was a less serious victim. Hit by a glancing bullet in his lower stomach, he earned the first of his two Purple Hearts, but quickly returned to his "boys."

By 2 August, Operation Cobra was a clear success. As for Arn, he learned firsthand the psychological terrors of war and the full horrors of combat. Initially, most enlisted men in Fox Company, and even Captain Parlavecchia, literally veterans overnight, distrusted this newcomer as just another callow "shavetail," unlikely to survive. Not surprisingly, Arn admitted that he was "scared to death" and "temporarily forgetful of being an American soldier of any worth at all." He underwent a range of emotions, running from excitement, fear, and revulsion to self pity. With the practical issue of life or death facing him, Arn adjusted "fast largely from keen survival instincts," a sense of duty, responsibility to his men, and the pragmatic desire to "bring my derrière" home safe. As this process unfolded, Arn lost any moral qualms about embracing his role as a killer. He considered the enemy a "stubborn, arrogant people, particularly their officers," and thought Chancellor Adolf Hitler "maniacal." Though Arn grudgingly respected the professionalism of German troops, he believed that "they had killed too many of our people." By the first week of August, Arn had transformed himself from novice to veteran. He had learned how to endure, how to command, how to live with himself. All these, along with a promotion to first lieutenant, the award of a Silver Star, a decoration recognizing his "gallantry in action" in the hedgerows, and an appointment as Fox Company's new executive officer, allowed Arn to conquer his insecurities and to certify his transition from a bewildered replacement to a seasoned front-line soldier.[8]

Arn had little time to digest these developments or even to shave and shower. Late in the night of 6 August and early the next morning, a surprise German counterattack at Mortain threatened to undo everything the Allies had accomplished. Only the 30th, which had abruptly shifted to the Mortain area, blocked the way of three Panzer divisions, notably the some seven hundred tenacious GIs of the 2nd Battalion, 120th Regiment, who controlled Hill 314, a critical observation point which became pivotal to American resistance and eventual victory. Arn played a minor role in the battle. Ordered to use his undermanned platoon in support of a tank advance, he faced the almost impossible task of moving across a field under fierce German artillery shelling while trying to integrate thirty-six frightened replacements into Fox Company. Arn's men suffered heavy losses until finding safety in foxholes. When curious enemy troops came out of their positions to look at destroyed American tanks, Fox Company fired back, exacting their own toll of deaths.[9]

The War Department awarded the Distinguished Unit Citation to six groups in the 30th for their conduct at Mortain, and Old Hickory emerged as one of the premier divisions in the Army of the United States (AUS). Eventually, the full division received the French Croix de Guerre with Palm in recognition of the "outstanding part" it played "in the liberation of France." By contrast, enemy troops paid a stiff price for their failure. Their headlong retreat across France opened the way to a direct land invasion of Germany. The 30th, including Fox Company, joined the pursuit.

Over the next month, the division pushed northeast for some 520 miles against intermittent resistance. By mid-September, Old Hickory's forward units reached into Belgium, then moved through the southern area of the Netherlands, crossed the Meuse River, and reached the northern end of the German Siegfried Line. Despite their rapid advance, few Allied troops relished the prospect of attacking this position. Considered by the Germans as invincible, the Siegfried Line bristled with thick concrete pillboxes, emplacements, and minefields, nine miles deep in some places, and stretched from Belgium to Switzerland.[10]

Arn enjoyed these days, despite a number of distractions. Liberated and welcoming French citizens caused disciplinary problems among his battle-weary men, mainly due to their overindulgence of Calvados, the fiery liqueur friendly crowds thrust in their hands. Long supply lines created logistic snarls. Marching mostly on foot proved exhausting. Short but sharp encounters with the enemy led to inevitable casualties. Orienting younger and younger replacements, many from the "elite" Army Specialized Training Program, who resented being assigned to the infantry, demanded great nurturing. Yet with his front relatively quiet, Arn relaxed. He wrote letters, and watched in early September as the high command tried and failed another breakthrough through Operation Market Garden, a complex plan to avoid a direct attack on the Siegfried Line by crossing the Rhine in Holland and thrusting into Germany.[11]

The 30th's "honeymoon" ended on 2 October when the division, spearheaded by the 117th Regiment on the left and 119th on the right, crossed the Wurm River and sought to punch its way through the Siegfried Line north of Aachen.[12] As Company F moved ahead, the overconfident Captain Riesch took one chance too many and died of a sniper's shot. Arn became company commander, but Riesch had not prepared him for such an eventuality. Worse, Arn went against his instincts by following orders in sending some of his troops to capture enemy pillboxes. He watched helplessly when counterattacking Germans captured some of them. Arn managed to rally his men, held his position with the aid of artillery, mortars, and air attacks, and regained lost ground. For this performance, Arn received another Silver Star. Yet he also learned valuable though bitter lessons about effective leadership amid the "maddening situations that enemy fire could create." In particular, he understood the need to gain "the confidence of one's platoon and squad leaders"; the importance of establishing clear channels of communication with "rear echelon support"; and the necessity of somehow creating "some form of order out of chaos." Even more, he realized the futility of sending raw recruits into battle. From these experiences, he "resolved to attain objectives with as little personnel loss as possible." His men were not expendable.[13]

Fox Company made progress slowly, hindered by land mines and booby traps. In the early evening of 16 October, Arn's men made a vital contribution to the Allied victory. One of his patrols east of Aachen linked with the 1st Division's 18th Infantry Regiment and completed the city's encirclement. Some days later, Major General Clarence R. Heubner, the 1st Division's commander, recognized this feat. In making an unannounced visit to 119th Regiment, he especially praised their role in closing the Aachen Gap.[14]

Under the Army's table of organization, a captain normally headed an infantry company. No matter his accomplishments, Arn remained a first lieutenant. Battalion command indeed replaced him with a captain. Within days, his replacement suffered a nervous breakdown. Arn regained his position, and led the company as it pushed toward the west bank of the Roer River through increasingly wintry weather. Allied command recognized that the steady combat since Normandy had weakened the 30th, both psychologically and physically. In rupturing the Siegfried Line, the division, especially Fox Company, had lost far too many men and needed replenishment. On 30 November, the 119th rotated off line for a short recuperation, new uniforms, and clean beds and hot food. Twelve days later, Fox Company gained an added three-day leave for similar purposes and to integrate and train replacements. Although Arn welcomed this "seventy-two-hour break," he did not think the time improved morale, because it "gave soldiers time to think and realize what an abnormal situation they were in."

Nothing in Arn's experience had prepared him for the sheer ghastliness of what came next. On 16 December, massive German tank and infantry forces pounded slack, unprepared, and thinly manned Allied lines in the opening round of the Ardennes Campaign. As bewildered and panicked American troops retreated, Old Hickory shifted to counter the Germans. When in place, the 30th held in a line from Malmédy west to Stoumont on the north shoulder of the growing "Bulge."[15]

The 119th Regiment, with Fox Company at the point, hurried through the night by truck over dark and snowy roads in this southward redeployment. Still lacking firm intelligence about the enemy's strength and troop disposition, Arn found himself in a perilous spot. Fox Company was essentially isolated, ahead of all units in the division, and faced Lieutenant Colonel Jochen Peiper's 1st SS Panzer Division, the spearhead of the German attack. At once, Arn took a defensive position, and his men repulsed an enemy attack in a firefight that lasted through the night.[16]

The ensuing Battle of the Bulge, with Fox Company locked in merciless face-to-face bloodbaths with the enemy, left Arn with enduring memories. His men helped stem the German tide in a series of costly fights in towns and villages that took their places in American military history: Neumoulin, Stavelot, Stoumont, La Gleize, Malmédy, St. Vith. As momentum slowly shifted toward the Allies, Fox Company still took heavy losses inflicted by enemy armor and infantry. Worse, the lack of supplies, cold, cloudy weather, sleep deprivation, and "much snow" created "abominable living conditions" and pervasive "trench foot." This "misery" did not end when the skies opened and medium bombers strafed and bombed the enemy. Over three consecutive days, the Air Corps misjudged troop locations and again battered the 30th Division, mainly in the Malmédy area.[17]

Arn also showed initiative in ways contrary to accepted miliary protocol. Based on his experience, judgment, and reading of the terrain, he either refused or delayed orders to sacrifice his men in what he believed were needless frontal assaults. Arn was lucky. In the press of combat, a court martial was not an option. Rather, he reaped the gratitude of his men and earned promotion to captain.

As 1945 began, all signs indicated that "Hitler's last gamble" had failed and that the 30th Division deserved much credit for turning the tide by blocking the Germans on the Bulge's northern flank. Army command restarted the policy of relieving hard-pressed units, including Fox Company, for rest and reorganization. This once more proved short-lived. The Ardennes Campaign was not over. Arn and his men went back on the offensive in mid-January. The weather remained atrocious. Sleet, rain, and falling temperatures froze clothes and equipment. As the Allies increased pressure, a growing number of German troops began to surrender. Fox Company did not celebrate. At Malmédy, they saw firsthand the bodies of American prisoners of war executed by the Germans. By month's end, the 30th Division again pulled back, this time to prepare for crossing the Roer River and the coming "Battle of Germany."[18]

Fox Company braced for this new phase of the war by intensive training in river-crossing techniques. On 18 February, Arn's luck ran out. While on reconnaissance to assess one of his platoon's position, fragments from an enemy shell struck his leg and knee. Though his entire body ached, he refused medical help and tried to remain in the field. That proved impossible. Becoming increasingly immobile, Arn was hospitalized in Liége, Belgium, and then transferred to Paris. While he recuperated, Arn received a second Purple Heart and chafed at the delay in rejoining Fox Company. His behavior contradicted the much-cherished infantryman's dream of receiving a "million-dollar wound," the honorable way front-line troops avoided further combat. This sense of obligation to his "boys" led to his return on 15 April. While he was gone, they had crossed the Roer and Rhine rivers. The 30th then linked with the 2nd Armored Division and pushed toward the Elbe River near Magdeburg.

In contrast to previous campaigns, the 119th had a comparatively easy task. Diehard SS troops still resisted, along with Hitler Youth, but most Wehrmacht troops surrendered in wholesale lots. By 19 April, Magdeburg fell, and Fox Company dug in on the bank of Elbe, watching and waiting for enemy retaliation. None came. Ordered to probe enemy strength across the river, the ever-cautious Arn picked a squad and reached the far side. When nothing materialized, he moved ahead, ignoring General Dwight D. Eisenhower's orders for American troops to halt at the Elbe. To his surprise, Arn's men finally reached Soviet soldiers. He found little about them appealing. They were undisciplined, drunk, and many had raped German women. In disgust, Arn returned to the west bank.[19]

V-E Day, 8 May 1945, found Arn in the same position. As he recalled, victory in Europe left him in "stunned silence with no desire to celebrate at all." Whatever elation he might have felt masked the realization that war still raged in the Far East. Arn thought the 30th Division might return stateside for a short furlough and then be reassigned to a Pacific staging area preliminary to invading Japan. For the moment, he busied himself with occupation assignments in central and southwestern Germany, mostly dealing with the perplexing problems created by unclear denazification programs, restless GIs eager for home, and brutalized displaced persons and concentration camp survivors. Even so, Arn took pride in Fox Company's selection as an honor guard in a ceremonial exchange of medals with Soviet troops.

By the end of July, all probabilities pointed toward Old Hickory being transferred to the Pacific. Arn believed that he had already served his nation well and had no desire to tempt the law of averages. Under the army's system for "Redeployment and Discharge," which calculated points for discharge on length of service, overseas duty, combat record, age, and medals earned, Arn had eighty-eight points, more than sufficient to be released from additional active service.[20]

For those reasons, Arn rejected an offer from the regimental commanding officer to make the army his career and left his beloved Old Hickory. He joined the 75th Division, an outfit the War Department designated for deactivation, and awaited processing home. Japan's formal surrender on 2 September changed his calculations. Ironically, the 30th Division, which no longer faced any further duty, reached the United States before the 75th and deactivated on 25 November 1945. Arn returned to Cleveland and a low-key family homecoming two weeks later. After a sixty-day terminal leave, he moved into the active reserve on 2 February 1946, followed by stints in the inactive reserve and the standby reserve at his captain's rank until he received his honorable discharge, 23 September 1957, completing fourteen years and four months of service to his nation.

After his almost eleven months of continuous combat, Arn had every reason for satisfaction. The medals and campaign ribbons he wore testified to his individual service, bravery in combat, resourcefulness, personal achievements, and plain luck: the Silver Star with Cluster; Purple Heart with Cluster; Bronze Star; Combat Infantry Badge; World War II Victory Medal; American Campaign Medal; Army of Occupation, World War II, Germany; Good Conduct Badge; and European Theater of Operations Campaign Badge with five Clusters. Better, he had survived. The number of men dead, wounded, maimed, and missing in the 30th Division came to a proportion unimaginable three years earlier. Old Hickory had suffered 26,038 total casualties during 282 days of actual fighting, a ratio of 184.5 percent. Survivors could only count their blessings, not seek logical explanations.[21]

Like many other veterans, Arn had no wish to look backward or seek praise for his service. Rather, he sought privacy and security in a life disrupted by war. He did so rather quickly by returning to the American Seating Company in 1946 and continued in sales until he resigned in 1958. Arn found even greater stability after he married Patricia J. Rolph in 1948. Finding the happiness that had escaped him in his first marriage, Arn moved his family, which eventually numbered six children and sixteen grandchildren, back to the familiar area of Wooster after he left the American Seating Company. He joined the college's administrators, initiated a number of innovative programs for alumni, took a strong interest in the intercollegiate sports programs, and remained active in the college's many functions until his retirement in 1974. He also kept close tabs on former comrades in the 30th Division through periodic reunions, exchanges of letters, and a return to Normandy battlefields and military cemeteries. He also became an active member in multiple veterans' organizations and a much sought-after figure in local affairs, often as a speaker at countywide patriotic events and in high school and college classes. His community and state honored him in a number of ways in selecting him to a number of halls of fame, most notably the Ohio Veterans Hall of Fame in 2003.

Arn found continuity in other ways he did not appreciate. The war left him with scars, some visible, some not. Physically, his injured knee remained a painful reminder of his service, resulting in a veteran's dis-

Edward C. Arn, April 2005.

ability payment. Shelling left him with a hearing problem. Enclosed spaces led to claustrophobia. Other echoes of the war lurked below the surface. Loud noises, a car backfire, or a passing plane would make him cringe or seek cover. Nightmares disrupted sleep. With his wife's aid and sympathy, Arn managed to cope with these demons.

When he allowed himself the luxury of introspection, Arn pondered the meaning of his World War II experiences. As he sought to recapture his younger self, the more he thought about what lessons the war held for future generations of Americans, especially his children and grand-children. One afternoon in 1976, he decided to "browse leisurely through old mementos of my military tour of duty during World War II" for answers. From them came this memoir.[22]

1. A Wrenching Decision

16 October 1940–7 September 1942

*Under the new Selective Training and Service Act, all males
in the United States, including aliens, between the ages of 21
to 36, were eligible, if chosen, for one year's active service
followed by ten years in the reserve. After Arn registered in the
early fall of 1940, he received a 3-A classification as a married
man with a dependent. His local draft board, like many of the
nation's 6,400 others, believed young, single men made the
best soldiers and called them first. Based on this procedure, his
age, and draft category, Arn had ample reasons to think that
he would not be drafted, let alone become a combat soldier.
The Japanese attack on Pearl Harbor changed his life in ways
he never anticipated. With his personal life at a crossroads,
however, American entry into World War II came at a
propitious time for Arn.*

I have always found it difficult to ascertain the prime explanation for my decision to enlist in the Army in 1942. As I
look back on the situation now, many influences seem to
emerge. Some were prominent and some were not.

My 1935 marriage was rapidly approaching an unhappy
and unavoidable termination. We were living in Evanston, Illinois in a pleasant apartment not too far west of the blue-green
waters of Lake Michigan on the famous North Shore of
Chicago. The area snuggled rather pridefully into that noted
contour. It was known as a good address in 1940 when we arrived there. There were no children of this marriage, and my

I am placed in "3-A" classification, 19 February 1941.

position as a sales representative for the American Seating Company often required several days of each week to be out of town on business. Loneliness, frustration, our social activities, and various emotional problems were assisting my wife into becoming a serious alcoholic. I shall not dwell at length on this long-ago disaster, but my disgust and embarrassment were proliferating almost daily.

Enlistment might be a way out of the dilemma. Adolf Hitler's European and African invasions were reaching out in all directions. Only England seemed to have a chance against his mechanized legions. Even the beleaguered British would need America's help. I possessed a foreboding conviction that my country would be in the thick of things in the not too distant future. Should I attempt to get into Uncle Sam's uniform now? I had registered for the draft in Evanston on 16 October 1940.[1] A 3-A classification followed, 19 February 1941. As I recall, a 3-A was only an eyelash above a 1-A. Once placed in 1-A, an individual had more than a nodding acquaintance with his draft board. I was placed in 1-A soon after the United States entered the war in December 1941.[2]

Why wait for the draft board to send a notice to report? All sorts of things were happening, beyond those already mentioned to influence my decision. My younger brother, Jack, was drafted on 14 March 1941. I had an inner urge to join him in uniform. The War Department was literally seizing all new tires, and we who made a living on the road were forced to use recapped or retreaded tires on our company-owned cars. As a former Firestone salesman, I didn't care for that requirement at all. To add to the dilemma, we were ordered to use our company cars as little as possible in order to save wear and tear on them. I guess we were to resort to cabs, trains, buses, streetcars, or horse and buggy. Commercial airlines were nonexistent [in my area].

The American Seating Company was becoming more and more involved with millions of dollars worth of war materials contracts. In my sales work, I was concentrating on the various military installations in my territory and doing rather well. I recall nearly $20,000 worth of military orders in December 1941.[3] Most of that volume related to Uncle Sam's burgeoning war machine. On the other hand, the demand for civilian products was plummeting. Eventually, my company would have little need for field representatives. I would certainly be in that phased-out category.

Our Evanston radio on a late Sunday afternoon burst forth with the startling news of the "Day of Infamy," 7 December 1941. The Japanese Air Force had attacked and just about destroyed the United States Naval Base at Pearl Harbor, Hawaii. Overnight a country torn apart between intervention and isolation was united. I felt a sincere surge of patriotism, a desire to help in some way. President Franklin D. Roosevelt declared war the next day, and World War II began for this nation.[4]

I reached my thirty-third birthday the following January. I had worked hard since my graduation from college in 1931, always facing the challenges and obstacles of the Great Depression. At long last, I was becoming accustomed to the good life, by that day's standards. I had earned it. Nevertheless, I seemed to be getting closer to making a decision that would return me to the rough road once again as the pangs of guilt over not being in the service increased.

In late January 1942, I made a business call at Camp Grant, Rockford, Illinois, where I discovered the new Volunteer Officer Candidate (VOC) program. This plan was designed specifically to attract men of

Author, brother T/Sgt. John A. (Jack) Arn, sister Helen A. Pender, and father Edward Arn.

talent and ability who might not be drafted for a variety of reasons, but had the potential pointing to officer qualifications. If the volunteer candidate "washed out," he returned to his home and awaited the fortunes of the draft. I was attracted to the program at once. I secured literature and studied carefully the various features. It would be a gamble at my age, and then I knew what I had to do. Not right away, but soon. At least the stage was being set and I was about to pick up my script covering my role in the greatest conflict of the twentieth century.[5]

I accumulated more information about the VOC plan. It would be difficult mentally and physically, and the chance for failure at my age would be considerable. I also realized that it would be difficult to sell my disturbed wife on joining up. It would be necessary to approach that challenge cautiously. She would have to sign a waiver of dependency to permit me to pursue the matter further.

In February 1942, Bob Hope was entertaining troops personally and broadcasting on the radio. I listened, and wrestled with my inner thoughts. The pressures increased. The American Seating Company announced that there would be little or no steel available for the manufacture of civilian products. If the company made such items at all, they would have to be made of wood. That meant the company was about to stop manufacturing its regular lines.

Our social life in Evanston hurried on, unchecked, often resulting in embarrassment and despair as my wife continued her disastrous bouts with alcohol. A visit to the famous Empire Room in the Palmer House in Chicago one evening resulted in a total cost of "over $16 for two." Horrendous. I was really living it up, but to what purpose?

About 23,000 men were now stationed at Chanute Field in Rantoul, Illinois. I had sold the authorities there all the seating equipment they would need. This was also the case on other military bases in my sales territory. I worried about my dwindling sales volume, my marriage, my future, and a host of other bothersome problems.

Those who held a draft classification of 3-A were being interviewed by their draft boards in some areas of the country. These officials often determined that many were 3-A for flimsy reasons. They were reclassified rapidly. Single men had to be basket cases to stay out of a uniform.

I wondered why my own draft board in Evanston wasn't calling up some of its 1-As. Maybe they would, soon. Was my age a factor?[6]

"If I were single and had no responsibilities, I would have enlisted in the Navy long ago," I wrote in a letter to my parents. "There are now 100,000 men in training within seventy-five miles of Chicago, and I keep thinking what I should or should not do." Excerpts from my letters to my folks during this period seem to emphasize the depth of my confusion and indecision. "All 3-A men will be reevaluated before the end of 1942, and here I am holding a 1-A card." "I can't see where I am doing anything at all that is vital to the war effort." There "are 35,000 miles on my company car. I must take good care of it for there won't be another." "My sales are getting further and further apart. If I do go I'll give it everything I've got." "Of course, I could get a deferment by working in our factory on war contracts for the duration, as management has already indicated."

It was quite evident that this latter option was my wife's wish, particularly when the weather in the apartment was turbulent and wild. I often regretted the fact that I had shared the company's deferment proposal with her, because I just didn't believe the policy could be adhered to forever. To me, the war would be long and frightful. The effort would call for men, men, and more men.

Meanwhile, I was traveling widely seeking increasingly hard-to-obtain business. One day, on State Street, in the heart of Chicago's Loop, an elderly lady blocked my way. "When are they going to get you, young man?" I sidestepped her, but not my conscience. By early summer, I had 8,000 miles on those retreaded tires. Over 3.5 million men were now in uniform, and Arn was running around in civvies.

To ease the situation a bit, but not to solve my dilemma, my wife, by mutual agreement, left for Cleveland on a trial basis and for an indefinite period of time. The enlistment challenge and confronting her husband was becoming a handy excuse for all-out consumption of liquor. I was at my wit's end coping with her problem. I reminded my people that "I am doing plenty of thinking."

In June I assured everyone, "I am getting along fine as a bachelor." But I was getting no closer to a decision. Suddenly, the American Seating Company announced still another policy: employees who would enlist or be drafted would be given a leave of absence by the company and would be rehired after the war was over. Said policy didn't erase my burden.

I recall my bitterness seemed almost to overwhelm me. All that hard work pushing myself financially and academically through college; suffering the hardship of low income during the Great Depression; finally getting my teeth into something that seemed promising and exciting with a reputable company; and then domestic problems and the war. I groped for an answer, alone.

About this time, an occupational questionnaire from my draft board indicated to me that the board would not consider my present job as essential to the war effort. I had really become a tottering 1-A. In July, I studied further angles to the VOC program, for I was becoming convinced that I was wasting time. I so informed my wife, who had returned to Evanston, unchanged and in bad shape. She refused to accept my viewpoint. I tried employment agencies and the civil service to no avail. I realized that the draft board was delaying things because of my age. There were men available in my particular area who were much younger than I.

Startlingly, one evening the opening came that I assume I had been seeking all along. In a drunken mood of complete detachment and oblivious to what she was doing, my sodden wife signed the "Waiver of Dependency" and I was free to move forward in the direction I wished to go. In truth, my desperation had obliterated any feeling of guilt on my part.

On 28 July 1942 I took the physical examination as a prospective VOC, for my hastily submitted application had been approved. The Department of War had further clarified the VOC system during the past few months. If one failed as a VOC and did not get to Officer Candidate School, or washed out at Officer Candidate School, he could leave the military service and return to civilian life where he could wait for his draft board's decision. The one thing the plan did guarantee was an officer's commission, *if* the candidate earned it according to requirements.

On 6 August 1942 I was ordered to Camp Grant for further tests and still another physical examination. My age must have concerned the army medical people. Here I was told that, if accepted, I would have about ten days to settle my affairs.[7]

Some discouraging news now developed. Only about thirty to forty percent of the candidates were actually accepted for the plan, because most of the aspirants were either too old or simply not officer material. I recall that I took this news in stride. I was involved in this venture now and what was to be was to be, and that was that. In a sense I was running and breathing hard.

On 11 August 1942 I was notified that I had passed all of the qualification tests and the second physical examination. My induction into the service was now assured as a bona fide VOC. I was elated and a profound awareness of pride surged through me. Not bad for an old geezer of thirty-three, I said smugly to myself. I was told to report or be ready to report either the latter part of August or the first week in September.[8]

My concerned Mother and Dad visited us in Evanston. I was not too happy about the situation. I wanted to see them before entering this new phase of my existence, but, quite frankly, I didn't want them exposed to the conditions that existed in our wretched home. On the other hand, I would be able to explain to them in person what I was about to do and why. My beloved parents understood almost immediately. Their tolerance and patience were inspirational. It was a good visit, and it would be several months before I would see them again.

Shortly afterward, I drove to Grand Rapids and turned in my company car. There I received the best wishes of my colleagues. Ironically, three of the four men in my sales training class of 1939 took occupational deferments, reported for duty in Grand Rapids, and when I returned four years later, all were in promising management positions. The other chap went into the Coast Guard and served with distinction. I have never made much of a point of this and I'm not bitter. Too many years have passed. I do permit myself to wonder, now and then, if they were ever troubled with a guilty conscience. I suspect not.

It would be totally dishonest if I did not confess that, at this time, I did not anticipate getting into actual combat. I hated the "Japs," as they were called then, for their sneak attack on Pearl Harbor. I despised Hitler and all that he represented. I can't lay claim to a burning desire to meet the enemy face-to-face. I was confident that there were millions of American men in uniform who were younger, braver, and far more able than I. I just wanted to help, somehow, and in some way. At thirty-three and overweight at about 190 pounds, I didn't in any fashion consider myself a hell-bent-for-leather combat trooper. I was certain the Army would discover that obvious trait early. "Everything will be okay and don't worry," I wrote my apprehensive parents.

Anxiety over how to settle our domestic affairs as efficiently as possible, under the strained circumstances, was reduced significantly when we were able to rent our leased apartment to an army captain. He was to be stationed in the Chicago area for the extent of the war. To this day I do not know what happened to the household furnishings, my many books, and so forth. My parents recovered my civilian wardrobe, which awaited me when I was discharged from the service. Nothing else.

"I probably will go direct from Ft. Sheridan to the Officer Candidate School at Ft. Benning," I wrote my parents. I either forgot all about basic training or simply disregarded it. I don't really know. Basic training was the lot of all recruits. I was to be reminded of my stupidity, rather emphatically, a bit later. Before leaving, a letter arrived from the American Seating Company enclosing a check for two weeks' pay as a special "going away bonus."[9]

Orders came instructing me to report to Fort Sheridan, Illinois, for induction on 7 September 1942. My ordeal was over, and yet I sensed that there was an even more potent one just ahead. Would I meet the pending challenges triumphantly or plunge further into a chasm of uncertainty and indecision?

2. The Gauntlet of Readiness

7 September 1942–23 May 1943

The military training that Arn and similar men underwent indicated the nation's unpreparedness for war and why the Army needed such efforts to get them ready to confront the enemy on equal terms. In Arn's case, the Volunteer Officer Candidate program prepared him for infantry duty in ways unlike anything he had experienced. Stringent regulation, drill, conformity, discipline, and harassment became daily staples in his life during the first phase of basic training at Camp Croft, South Carolina. Demanding cadre began to tear and reassemble Arn from an overweight, rather insecure civilian into an effective future officer. The Army shaped this grueling regimen in physical fitness, psychological conditioning, military courtesy, and weaponry usage to test the capabilities of potential combat officers and to weed out the unfit. More awaited him in the program's second phase at Fort Benning, Georgia, for those who had survived this initial process. Instructors refined the physical strength, technical mastery, personal confidence, instinctive habits, and leadership qualities necessary to lead men in battle. Arn passed these tests and earned his commission. No longer an anxious recruit, he radiated pride in his newfound military skills, physicality, and mental toughness.

I left the apartment early on the morning of 7 September 1942. Perhaps a portent of things to come greeted me at the draft board headquarters. Twelve other draftees were going to Sheridan with me and I was appointed "leader" of the group. I soon discovered that my leadership assignment was bestowed upon me because my name began with A. The illusion of superiority vanished quickly. The train arrived in Sheridan from Evanston. I had no difficulty with "my" men.

We were sworn into the service and my serial number as Pvt. Edward C. Arn was to be 36 607 066. I signed for $10,000 worth of GI Insurance. I left the beneficiary option open until a final decision could be made about my dissolving marriage. Then came a surprise. "We are so loaded here with inductees to be processed, we are sending you men back home on a furlough of four days. Report back here on 11 September," snarled a sweating sergeant. Back I went to that miserable apartment to be greeted by a totally and helplessly inebriated wife. The army captain who had rented the apartment would occupy it on 12 September 1942. My wife was on the train to Cleveland on the tenth, for I was moving decisively now. I had my mind set at last and suddenly I was free.

I reported to Sheridan on the eleventh as ordered. I received uniforms, shoes, hats, fatigues, the whole bit, and was told that I would ship out in, at least, three days. "To Fort Benning?" I asked stupidly. "Are you in your right mind, soldier? You people take thirteen weeks of basic training just like everyone else." The non-commissioned officer (NCO) was obviously disgusted, and I was astounded. There was very little I could do about army regulations. I was in, maybe for the duration.

I was assigned a bunk in a barracks in the Recruit Reception Center. Fifteen September came and went. Nineteen days passed and I was still in Sheridan languishing away. Fifth October was checked off the calendar by my bunk. By now, I had spent twenty-four days in Sheridan. How could the military do this to me? Maybe to some yardbird in books or movies but surely not to me.[1] I was finally informed that my VOC records had been misdirected between Camp Grant and Fort Sheridan, and were only now arriving at their proper destination. I was to eventually become accustomed to military "SNAFUS" (Situation Normal—All Fouled Up).

On 9 October 1942, after almost one month's delay, I received my shipping orders. I left on a jam-packed troop train for Camp Croft near

Spartanburg, South Carolina. Croft was an Infantry Replacement Training Center. The center was named in honor of Major General Edward Croft, former Chief of Infantry, U.S. Army.[2]

I was assigned to Company D, 32nd Infantry Training Battalion, Building number 166. There were four infantry rifle companies in each battalion. Typically the scuttlebutt (rumors) had it that our cadre (officers and NCOs) had the toughest and most efficient reputation in the entire camp. We would soon know.

I obtained, as ordered, a GI (General Issue) "butch" haircut for 30 cents. Movies, the very latest, cost 15 cents and were shown in theaters right on the post. My laundry would run $1.50 per month. Only one soldier in all of D Company was older than I. The average age was under twenty. The men nicknamed me "Old Folks." I discovered, to my astonishment and concern, that VOCs were being trained right along with all the other recruits. There would be no special privilege or treatment. Would I be able to stay with the program physically? I didn't really know, nor would I hazard a guess.

Basic training began. Up at 5:45 every morning and back in your cot with lights out—and sighs of intense fatigue on my part—every night at ten. The first week we hiked to the rifle range, one and a half hours one way. We learned how to pitch pup tents, miserable little pieces of canvas, a half-shelter per man, for they were supposed to provide shelter for two men. We each carried one of the canvas half-shelters together with the required number of tent pegs, ropes, and the like. Time was also spent on the art of properly packing forty pounds of gear into a compact haversack. My traveling experiences helped me with this latter process rather handily, except as a civilian I never had a sergeant screaming at me when I packed my bag for an out-of-town trip.

Physical stamina exercises took place almost every day mostly on the hellish obstacle courses, designed by the devil and put into operation by the devil's friends. The course consisted of high wooden walls, ten feet high, straight up; parallel hand-over-hand ladder walks at least ten feet off the ground and ladder bars about thirty inches apart; water hazards requiring at least a ten-foot running broad jump, or off in the drink you would go; vertical rope climbs and in nets; crawling under

Mess hall, Camp Croft.

close-to-the-earth barbed wire; and much more. The whole course had to be done within a certain time limit or back you went until you did comply with the time requirement. The high walls, hell, the whole damned layout, gave my soft body more punishment than I thought I could possibly endure. With the encouragement of the kids around me, I managed to perform well enough to make the course time limit. My performance would not qualify me for the next Olympics, but it was respectable.

We began to live with our M-1 Garand rifles even though we had not yet fired them. Strangely, when we did get around to firing the rifle, I could do better than most in the company. I had never fired a deadly weapon of any type, and some of my buddies refused to believe me. But I scored a 165 out of 250 out on the rifle range from four different positions and at varying distances. According to platoon ratings, I was in the upper half. I was considered a "qualified marksman." It was gratifying to accomplish something with which I had no previous experience.

Meanwhile, we plugged away at map reading, personal hygiene, hand grenades, camouflage, calisthenics, bayonet, and a myriad of other skills important to the infantry soldier. Mentioning personal hygiene recalls to me a lad from Kentucky who was in our platoon. He could neither read nor write. Said his folks owned about "three acres of tobacco." It was quite apparent that he did not know how to keep clean. It just wasn't that important where he came from. Consequently, he never showered, and I had reason to believe that he probably didn't know how to manipulate the shower plumbing. The odor in the vicinity of his bunk was not pleasant.

One late afternoon we came in from the field to discover that our Kentuckian's bunk, odorous clothes, filthy socks, and practically all of his other equipment had been tossed outside into a rear area behind the barracks building. With tears of frustration in his eyes, he turned to Old Folks—me—for help. We both missed chow that evening. We retrieved his belongings and put things back into some semblance of order. I told him I would help him make out the army's laundry slip each week and show him where to take it. A lesson in showering technique was next. It was indeed a busy evening but "Kain-tuck" and I became warm friends. There were many children in his family, but only a fourteen-year-old sister could write. She wrote badly and her spelling was atrocious. For the remainder of basic training, I read her letters to him and I wrote to his family. Finally, the other members of the platoon decided that he belonged. When he proved to be the best man in the platoon with the M-1 rifle on the firing range, he acquired real stature and respect.

On one night problem, I sprained my ankle badly. As I look back on the accident, I am certain that I must have torn some tendons. I refused sick call, not because I didn't want to report to the dispensary, for I was in real pain, but because I knew how the cadre looked with disdain upon gold bricks, especially elderly gold bricks (men who pretend ills or hurts to get into a comfortable hospital bed).

The following week we marched to the rifle range every day. I managed to make all of the painful treks, on one leg. The jaunt was four miles one way. I have trouble with that ankle to this day. The physical impact on my healthy but out-of-shape body was tremendous. I wrote home, "It takes a detail of four men to get me into my bunk at night and out again in the morning." I was trying to be funny, but it wasn't a hilarious situation. Creaking joints responded slowly, but, as I was to learn as time wore on, respond they did.

In addition, the cadre instructed us in close order marching drill. Close order drill consisted of learning how to march to a shouted cadence on the proper foot and the correct execution of right face, left face, position of attention, to-the-rear march, on-the-double, a proper military salute, and a host of other tidbits emerging from the bellowing commands of impatient, sweating NCOs.

Tauntingly and with biting scorn in his voice, our platoon sergeant ordered me to take command of a squad one day in close order drill. A training platoon consisted of four such squads with fifteen men in each squad. I had listened and learned. I knew I had the necessary deep voice because seven years in high school and college dramatics had developed that talent. The men were impressed and responded to my commands readily. Even my blistered feet felt better. "Not bad, Old Folks," chirped the sergeant with reluctance.

The Manual of Arms was something else. We learned how to maneuver or handle a rifle in response to various commands and positions. We would go through Manual of Arms so often and for such lengthy periods of time that at first my arms, legs, and hands ached. Then one day there were no more strained muscles and hurting limbs. I was getting closer and closer to a finely-tuned physical condition. "I am now down to 168 pounds and I have 32-inch waist," the statistics rang with pride. I had also qualified on all the basic infantry weapons. I was promoted to full-time squad leader. I led my men in close order drill, field maneuvers, and everything else they threw at us.

The rifles we used had been badly treated by those who had gone before. I was getting "gigged" (a gig was a first cousin to a demerit) constantly for having a rusty bore in my rifle, no matter how hard I cleaned the damned piece, the army's name for a rifle. I never did get all the little rust marks out of that weapon's barrel. I learned later that no one else before me had succeeded either. The situation allowed the cadre to continue constant goading.

By the middle of November 1942, we had advanced to the Browning Automatic Rifle (BAR). It weighed twenty-one pounds and could fire 550 rounds per minute. During training a forward bipod was used to support the barrel and it was usually fired from the prone position under close supervision. Later, and I was to have good reason to know, there would be men who could fire the BAR from the hip as they advanced forward. It was an awesome weapon, indeed, when handled with skill.

One night we went out into the woods for battalion maneuvers. For a chap who had spent most of his life on sidewalks and pavements, this was still another demanding challenge. All I can recall now is experiencing much stumbling and falling over one another in the dark. Our fatigues were soaked with sweat and torn from the bushes and trees when we returned to camp the next morning. I can't explain it but I enjoyed the feel and purpose of the whole maneuver. I was to learn later that night fighting could become a terrible experience.

Eight- and ten-mile hikes with sixty pounds of equipment on our backs, plus that old rifle (twelve pounds) in our hands or on our tired shoulders were now quite common. "I used to be a bit rotund around the middle. 'Member? Well, it's all gone now, out there, somewhere on this red Carolina clay," I boasted to Mom and Dad.

We all took physicals at this point and I passed mine easily and, if I may say so, proudly. A week of foxhole digging in all sorts of places followed. I began to know, hate, and then love that little trench shovel (the name a holdover from World War I), that I carried affectionately in a special holder in my pistol belt. It became quite worn and shiny. There was to be another like it later, more worn and shinier. If I was engaged to the first one, I married the latter.

We spent several days in training with the 60-mm and 81-mm mortars, followed by the .30 caliber, light, air-cooled machine guns. A bit later, we worked with the heavy, water-cooled machine guns. The 60-mm mortars and light machine guns were used in the weapons platoon

(Fourth) of a combat rifle company. The 80-mm mortars operated in a heavy weapons company of an infantry regiment.[3]

On Sunday 14 December 1942 a busload of Croft's soldiers journeyed to Tryon, North Carolina. Pvt. Brady of Boston teamed up with Pvt. Arn. Miss Austin Wilcox was our hostess. This gracious and charming southern lady, a woman of quality and breeding, took us to dinner. On that December day, we had a good, good time. I also inaugurated a lasting friendship with Austin Wilcox until her death in 1974.

A few days later I wrote my parents, "I shall miss being with you at Christmas time. It'll be my first Christmas away from home." I had been home for thirty-three Christmases in a row. I was to miss the next three. My treasured present from home was a pocketknife. I carried it throughout my military career. I still have it.

I had about two weeks to go. Rumor had it that some of the VOCs would get to Fort Benning in January. By 3 January 1943 only VOCs were left in C Company. I had said goodbye to my young infantry replacement buddies forever, for I never saw any of them again. We were told that we might have to attend NCO school at Croft for a time. Apparently, VOCs were washing out at Benning in wholesale lots. Doubt was even being cast upon the true value of the program. I fretted and worried as always. I was eight days from my thirty-fourth birthday.

"My chances of getting into combat are very slim," I wrote home. "Thirty-four is just too old. I may end up as an Infantry Basics Instructor somewhere, if I make it through Benning. So, don't worry, please." The rumors started to fly all over the place. "Ft. Benning is tough and the wash-out rate is quite high."

Another delay was upon me. About two hundred VOCs, including Pvt. Arn, were transferred to Officer Candidate Preparatory School at Camp Croft. In this new program with new training, we lectured, led calisthenics, worked on voice commands, led plenty of close order drills, and a host of other demanding leadership assignments. Another three weeks passed. We drilled and we drilled, and we grumbled and grumbled to one another. Nevertheless, we were also becoming soldiers in every sense of the word as each day passed.[4]

It now became clear after five more weeks that I would know by 5

February 1943 if I had passed the Camp Croft Officer Candidate
Preparatory School requirements. "We are down to 137 men now.
That's all we have, numbers. No one knows which category he is in. I
am in excellent shape. My stomach is flat as a board." I should have said
that inside that stomach there were millions of butterflies.[5]

Then I received good news. I had qualified and was headed for Fort
Benning, the Infantry Officer Candidate School. On 13 February 1943 I
was promoted to a corporal in the Army of the United States. Yet I was
still not on shipping order for Benning. A friend of mine at Camp Croft
Headquarters gave me the information that only a certain quota could
be shipped to Officer Candidate School, as they were now bringing
back qualified combat people from overseas for enrollment. These candidates were often given priority over VOCs. Men over thirty-eight
were being flunked out fast for a wide variety of reasons. "But I am only
thirty-four," I muttered to myself. Orders came at last, and I left Camp
Croft for Fort Benning, 16 February 1943. I had spent over seventeen
weeks at Croft. But wait a minute. I had been in a uniform for only five
months. What in the world was I complaining about?

It took over twenty-four hours for the troop train to travel the 310
miles. We arrived at 0200 (2:00 A.M.) during the morning of 18 February 1943. Entrance processing went on right away. There were over
20,000 men in Benning at that time. The entire cadre was working
overtime, often twenty-four hours a day.

The program had started at Benning more than two years before.
There were four platoons of fifty men each in my company. Sixty-six of
our two hundred people were from Camp Croft. The rest were Reserve
Officer Training Corps (ROTC) personnel just out of college, plus a
small percentage of combat NCOs from overseas. Some tough stateside
NCOs were also in the company seeking commissions. Average age
ranged from twenty-one to twenty-three. Once again I would be moving
in fast company right down to the wire. I managed to know most of them.

We were told that the men in our training unit would be commissioned on 27 May 1943. But we were also told, in simple terms, that only
about half of us would become second lieutenants. During the following thirteen weeks, we took sixteen examinations on sixteen military

subjects, thirty to forty questions on each test. A failure in three and the candidate packed his duffel bag. We went to work. Our platoon leaders were first and second lieutenants, called tactical officers (TOs), men who possessed solid military backgrounds. We had other names for them also, but not to their faces.

One of my vivid memories was the regimental obstacle course. It was a sophisticated version of the worrisome one that had caused me so much trouble at Croft. The whole challenge had to be completed in less than ten minutes, or, well, that was it: either finish or one's candidacy was in peril. We practiced and practiced.

Consistently, I failed to clear that damned water hazard and would land, just as consistently, in the muddy "drink" that was about four feet deep and, maybe, ten to twelve feet long. Since I had learned to jump the one at Croft successfully, I was quite confident that I could conquer this one. After awhile it reminded me of Lake Erie in size. It had to be much longer than Croft's. At this hateful spot in the obstacle course, a tactical officer would yell out, by habit, "Okay, Corporal Arn, show us how gracefully you enter the water." I would proceed to accommodate him. I was desperate; I knew that "lake" was adding to my total time for the course and preventing me from qualifying.

A friend in need came along just in time in the person of a huge, broad-shouldered redhead by the name of Patterson, who had played varsity football for "Ole Miss." "Arn, I think you're taking off on the wrong foot," said he. "You should start your jump at the very edge of the hazard on your right foot, not your left. Let's try it tonight after chow." Patterson was correct. He instructed and I jumped, and I finally began to sail over that pesky ditch. The next day the tactical officer said, "Okay, Arn, give us your usual demonstration." I can still see the look of astonishment on that tactical officer's face as I launched a beautiful jump over the damned thing and landed a good two feet in the clear. I still root for "Ole Miss"!

A great many of the infantry courses were somewhat repetitive, only now the level of instruction was considerably more advanced and more severe. The competitive atmosphere permeated everything we did. You could feel it in the air. "We want brains, leadership, and example," said they. They meant it. Tactical officers were everywhere, checking everything day and night. We even had compulsory study periods four evenings a week. There was little or no time for recreation. As a matter of fact, I never left the base the whole time I was stationed there.

We trained in infantry weapons all over again, as well as camouflage and concealment, the rifle company in the attack, night maneuvers, the battalion in the attack, booby traps, company administration, proper control of supplies, map reading, attack orders, defensive tactics, village and city street fighting, what to do in a bombing raid, correct use of artillery support and air support, and so on. We also learned how to teach by performing with one another. No NCOs helped for hours on end. The candidates performed various functions by physical or verbal communication.

They jammed it at us as fast as was humanly possible. I worked. I studied. I prayed. Each of us was graded as we performed. Presently I was called upon to put the whole company (200 men) through close order drill out on the area parade grounds. Again the voice helped, and I passed the "voice and command" requirements rather handily.

I did equally well in map reading, the written exam on the light machine gun, scored 160 on the heavy machine gun (140 qualified), and I was squad leader for three days. I got a demerit on my rifle. Again, they were well-used weapons and the rust was in the barrels permanently. From a high wooden platform, I led the company in calisthenics. Then I was told that I was not giving the calisthenics exercises' calls fast enough. Actually, I knew the candidates were tired so I deliberately put them through the commands slowly. No excuse. A "C" in calisthenics. Amazingly, we also had a writing test that consisted of composing our autobiographies.[6] We took an Army IQ test. I scored 141. I was amazed and decided quickly that the Army version of an IQ test must be somewhat different from any other IQ test. However, my score did not hurt my army records one bit. Battle Indoctrination verged as closely as possible on the real thing. The whine of bullets above our heads did not please me at all. But it did encourage my love affair with Mother Earth. Too, a four-day bivouac maneuver proved to be as rugged as any yet experienced. I lectured the whole company on the BAR, and then scored 160 out of 175 for an expert classification with that weapon. The BAR and I got along well. I still remember the value of that infantry combat piece in certain situations that were to develop later.[7]

We were then exposed to the importance of an Infantry Rifle Company's rifle squads. Each rifle company had three rifle platoons (First, Second, and Third) and one weapons platoon (the Fourth). Each of the rifle platoons had three squads of twelve men each. Each squad had a leader, his assistant, one BAR man, two assistant BAR men, and seven riflemen. The squads were given a chance to develop their fire-power during the training session. "Our squad broke a camp record for effective fire," I wrote home. "My ears are still ringing."[8]

In the same letter I commented at some length on how "the folks back home should see the looks on men's faces when they don't get mail during the evening mail call. It is often heartbreaking and I witness it all too often." Fortunately for me, my family wrote often. Friends, too. I was envied.[9]

My Son

I wish I had the power to write
The thoughts wedged in my heart tonight.
As I sit watching that small star,
And wondering how and what you are?
You know son, it's a funny thing
How close a war can always bring
Your Dad, who for years with pride,
Has kept emotion deep inside.
I realize you are quite small,
And that sea between us is like a wall.
If I tell you that real men never cried,
And it was Moms who always dried
your tears, and smoothed the hurt away,
So that you soon can go back to play.
But son, deep down within my heart,
I long to have some little part

In drying your small tear-strained face,
Instead of being in this—darn ole place.
For suddenly, I find a son
A reality, with childhood begun.
Tonight you're far across the sea,
While I'm waging war with the Infantry.
Well somehow, pride and what is right,
Just doesn't seem to go tonight.
I find my eyes won't stay quite dry;
I find that sometimes men do cry,
And if we stood here face to face,
I'd hold you tight in my embrace.
Son, Dads are quite a funny lot,
And if I should fail you in some spot
It's not because I love you less,
For it might be—the wrong guess;
And if I do . . I wish I may,
Straighten it Son—during the same day.
For if I had the power to write,
The thoughts wedged in my heart tonight,
The words would ring out loud and true,
I'm proud Son; I'm proud of YOU.
        My Dad Sent This to Me While Overseas. Ah—Men!!

Forty-two men were soon called before the Examining Board. I was not one of them. Twenty-five of the candidates in our company were washed out. I cried out in a letter, "The men who bunk on each side of me are gone. That's getting close isn't it?" Wham. I got a "D" in a mortar exam. First one. Two more would earn a visit before the Examining Board. But I ran the obstacle course in one minute and fifty-five seconds. The qualifying time limit was two minutes and fifteen seconds. I had come a long way. I also qualified on the 37-mm antitank gun. The instructors indicated that it was a formidable weapon. Unfortunately, that was just not so. Against German tanks, I later found out, it was about as effective as a peashooter.

I was ordered one morning to put the whole company, all four platoons, through close order drill. "Very good," murmured the hardbitten commanding officer (CO). I felt a little better. I was most confident and comfortable when I was handling people. I found out later that those in charge sensed that trait also.

We were told to order our officers' uniforms. The orders would be held up until the "final trial period is over." No one seemed to know what that "period" was. We were allowed $250 to purchase everything. I ordered a Hickey-Freeman dark green blouse that cost $55. Florsheim low-quarter shoes sold for $12. Nothing chintzy about me.

We were impressed when President Franklin D. Roosevelt visited Benning in early May. I read about it in the post newspaper. I was never a Roosevelt enthusiast anyway. He did say that things looked better in the Pacific theater and that the African campaign held "great promise." A glance at the casualty total made us wonder about that.

It was evident according to my letters that my fellow soldiers had come to the conviction that "Arn takes this whole program seriously." Well, if I were to get into actual combat I wanted to perform by instinct, through conscientious attention to training, in order to bring my rear end home safely and in one piece. Said instinct, it seemed to me at the time, could come from listening, learning, doing, and trying to remember. Such a philosophy should help in teaching also.[10]

"Three weeks to go and then I will know whether I am to be an officer and a gentleman, or a failure." Then I wrote cautiously, "Forty-seven men in the company are doubtful. I don't think I'm one of them. I just may be a second lieutenant in about nineteen days." "I think I've gone stale." "I still don't know. I'll write you one or the other, or maybe send you a wire. If I make it, we'll proceed according to plan."

The plan was that I would be on the 6:10 P.M. train out of Atlanta, on 27 May, the day after being commissioned. I even had a Pullman reserved, for there was nothing too good for a new shavetail. I would arrive in the Terminal Tower in Cleveland at 3:10 P.M. on the twenty-eighth. In the same letter I remarked, "There are empty bunks all around me." Paranoid? Yes, sir. Well, I was granted my commission as a second lieutenant in the Army of the United States in an impressive

Cora Conelly Arn in her
Red Cross uniform.

ceremony at Fort Benning, Georgia on 26 May 1943, a little over eight
and a half months after I had entered military service.[11]

This entire effort had been difficult. I am certain now that had I been
ten years younger and engaged in a civilian occupation that demanded
more physical effort than mental, it would have been far less of a strain
on my whole system. Nevertheless, I would also be unfair to myself if I
did not indicate the pride that I felt when the gold bars were pinned on
me. I would continue in service to my country at a time when I was
most needed. One was mustered out as an enlisted man and then "pa-
pered back in" as an officer. So, from corporal to second lieutenant for
a fellow named Arn, new serial number O-1320396. That "O" stood for
"Officer."[12]

The reunion at home was warm and pleasant. I was welcomed by
my immediate family, which did not include my wife. I had engaged my
cousin, William R. Conelly, as my lawyer, and though it was to take
months of correspondence and negotiation, divorce proceedings were
underway. I stayed with my parents during the furlough.

The family was proud of all of its military people, for it was a time when families were close and the war brought them even closer. People showed their pride and pleasure on many occasions during my leave and I loved it. I was equally proud of my Mother for the commendatory job she was doing with the East Cleveland Red Cross and also as founder and president of the town's Blue Star Mothers' Club.[13]

3. Merciless Reality Emerges

5 June 1943–27 May 1944

As a newly-minted second lieutenant, Arn initially enjoyed his first assignment in passing on to green recruits the skills he had so assiduously learned. Arn also liked the perquisites and privileges of being an officer, a bachelor at that, free from worries about earning a living and his failed marriage. Yet he felt ambivalent about the situation. Because of his age, Arn still did not expect overseas combat duty. Nor did he have a false notion of heroics. Rather, an awakening sense of adventure, the tedium, monotony, and repetition of training troops, perhaps along with a gnawing subconscious sense that he should join the men he had prepared, made Arn restless. By the early winter of 1944, the Department of War's manpower needs made the decision for him. The recruits he had molded joined one of the Army's ninety divisions, or became replacements in units already on-line. While Allied commanders were still in the early stages of their plan to invade Normandy, their experiences in the Mediterranean Theater of Operations indicated that front-line divisions inevitably took heavy losses. Infantry units could not remain effective without sustained replacements. Despite his expectations, Arn became one of these men.

My orders were to report after furlough to the Infantry Replacement Training Center at Fort McClellan, Alabama. I would be an Infantry Platoon Instructor in infantry basic subjects. I arrived there at 3:00 P.M., on 5 June 1943. Second Lieutenant Arn, with his shining single brass bar on each shoulder, was delivered by jeep to D (DOG) Company, 6th Battalion.[1]

It was hot in Alabama. The camp was five miles from the town of Anniston. The southern summer was really blazing away. The raw recruits we trained at McClellan were to become infantry replacements for overseas casualties. It was as uncomplicated as that and the recruits knew it. The program was quite similar to the one at Camp Croft. Thirteen weeks of basic training, ten days delay en route, which meant that the new soldiers had that much time to get home, say goodbye (meaning a brief stay only), and then make their way to a port of embarkation (POE). Usually, but not always, their lot would be cast with rifle companies on-line in various theaters of operation.

It was a damned responsible teaching assignment and nobody sensed it more acutely than I. It became my custom to say at the beginning of a training cycle, "Men, no one wants to die, particularly at your age. So, here at McClellan the more you listen, learn, and remember, the longer you'll stay alive, wherever you're going." It wasn't an eloquent, or even a kindly way to say it, but I believed with all my heart those words of advice. I still do. Too often, peace-loving America fights her wars with partially trained civilian-soldiers. The early cost is horrendous, for our foes are usually composed of expert professionals. I would try to do my best to help form these inexperienced youngsters into competent fighting people.

There were two hundred recruits in D Company. It was necessary to instruct them in a wide variety of infantry subjects. Usually, mornings were devoted to fieldwork of a very physical nature. It was Croft and Benning all over again but with me instructing and using NCOs to demonstrate and help maintain discipline. Every afternoon, if the schedule were so arranged, we would devote our attention to lectures on one subject or another. Portable chalkboards were taken right out into the maneuver areas.

I gained a reputation for a no-nonsense attitude. We were in a serious business dealing with the lives of men. I would never tolerate any shabby indifference. However, we were attempting to make soldiers out of draftees. Most of them were in uniform because they were forced to be and not necessarily for patriotic reasons. That fact did not make our tasks any easier. It proved to be an uphill mission to inspire and motivate disgruntled captives of a compulsory system. I worked at it with a fervor that attracted attention. I suspect I made many a GI unhappy because of my gung ho methods, but I know that I soon earned their respect.[2] Generally, most of them became oriented to their situation within a few days, and that made the undertaking a little bit easier.

It wasn't long until I became acquainted with Remington Hall, the famous officers' club at McClellan, a permanent brick and stone building. It was really something: swimming pool, plush bar, and large dinner and dance area. My Saturday nights there after days in the field were memorable ones.[3]

At first, I was an assistant platoon leader. My immediate superior was First Lieutenant Verne Leffel of Springfield, Ohio. Verne stayed in the service after the war and retired as a full colonel. He was about my age and a likeable guy. We liked each other. I soon discovered that he was having a torrid love affair with an attractive gal in a nearby post exchange (PX). The relationship was so fervent he was debating about asking his wife for a divorce.

The Bachelor Officers Quarters (BOQ) at McClellan consisted of large tents with half-wood sides and floors, about three feet off the ground. When the weather was chilly, we resorted to good old potbelly stoves burning wood or coal. My "hut mates" were both young second lieutenants: Johnny Morrison from Princeton, Indiana, McClellan's welterweight boxing champion and coach of the post's boxing team, and Mat Beck from somewhere in the state of Washington. Johnny was a wiry, tough devil who cared for nobody actually, except women, and those for entertainment only. Beck was a tall, bug-eyed, blond chap, an indifferent type who seemed to sense that eventually he would be in combat and adopted a sort of what-the-hell attitude.

Morrison had an old car that was serviceable. These two strange young characters took a liking to me, and I must confess we three created a never-dull social good time. I was known as "Dad" to both of them. It was one weekend in Birmingham and the next in Atlanta. We had a sort of a social seesaw and one of considerable magnitude.

One incident calmed down my two young roughnecks considerably. We had checked into a hotel in Atlanta. We showered, shaved, and started to leave the hotel. The elevator was not working for some reason or another, so we used the stairs. Several floors down, I noticed a room door almost wide open next to the stairwell. As I passed by, I peeked into the room, to be greeted by one of the most tragic and hectic scenes I had ever witnessed up to that time. A young woman of about eighteen had apparently been gang-raped, I suspect by soldiers, for they were all over the place. She was barely alive, and her nude body was bruised and beat-up to the point that I wanted to vomit. Both Beck and Morrison wanted to get the hell out of there. But not old Dad. I reported the whole thing to the desk clerk. He alerted the police and ordered an ambulance. I stayed around until I saw the girl placed aboard that ambulance. I've never forgotten the incident. I was to see much worse, but that was tops at the time. The three of us spent a relatively quiet evening. My two friends were not as tough as they would like to have me believe they were.[4]

Johnny's resourceful mind hit upon an idea. He suggested we bootleg liquor into McClellan from Rome, Georgia. Anniston was dry, and the bellhops at the Anniston Hotel were highway robbers, asking as much as ten dollars for a fifth of bourbon. It could be purchased for much less than that over the border in Rome. His plan was to buy it cheap and sell in McClellan at prices lower than the Anniston bellhops. I knew his plan was illegal and that we would be subject to severe penalties if we were caught. I had no desire to be a part of such a harebrained scheme. My two reckless friends went ahead anyway, and got caught red-handed by the Military Police (MPs) at the post's gate with a trunk load of liquor. They were soon on their way to other outfits scheduled for combat duty.

The relentless sun shimmered in out-of-focus oscillations above the red dust of the Alabama territory. We labored on, absorbed with the exasperating task of making soldiers out of civilians in a too-limited time period. I held forth on the virtues of the light, air-cooled machine gun. Long hikes of the toughest variety left brow sweat in drip dabs on the toes of our heavy GI shoes. Ambulances brought up the rear of the long, tired columns for those who could not stay with it. The officers and NCOs, on the other hand, did not dare to even glance in the direction of the lumbering vehicles.

I was issued a .30 caliber carbine as a replacement for the .45 automatic pistol with the assurance that I would possess improved accuracy at greater ranges. I didn't like the carbine. I believed it was cumbersome and inaccurate. To me, the required change was an error. I proved to be right later on in more precarious situations. For example, when one has to live with a situation map and is involved in issuing orders, one cannot tuck a carbine into a holster and have it with him when he moves on. A carbine could be propped into the corner of a bombed-out building, while its user is engaged in other activities. It often remained behind, forgotten. I returned to the snug feeling of that pistol in its holster against my body, regulations or not, early in my combat career.

August was upon us. I taught classes in camouflage and concealment. Tragedy marred the one in the "Rifle Company in the Attack." A violent thunderstorm hit the area. A soldier, name long forgotten, was standing under a tree when an incoming bolt struck the tree. I recall seeing his body bounce into the air and out into the field. We tried all sorts of revival methods to no avail. I remember that he was from Flint, Michigan. I cannot explain why I remember the lad's city and not his name. It was a sobering experience for all of us.

Field problems were accompanied by chiggers, mosquitos, and heat rash. No showers, no clean laundry, and only cold water added to the infantryman's misery. Some ingenious GI long before had discovered that fingernail polish when applied to the bite would smother the chigger. Usually, post exchanges were sold out of the product when an area unit moved into the field.

At home, my cousin, lawyer Bill Conelly, was having some difficulty with my request for a divorce. My wife was drinking heavily and was incoherent most of the time. I had indicated previously that I would do the suing, but now I suggested a change in strategy: that she sue me for alienation of affection or desertion or whatever. I would not contest ownership of property and so forth. Otherwise, I indicated to Bill, I would drag her through the courts in the muck and mire of her own miserable conduct. Bill promised to pursue my suggested plan.

I was transferred to B Company, and I was informed that I would be at McClellan for at least six more months. I became leader of the Second Platoon. We went into the Talladega National Forest area on a six-day company maneuver.[5] It was hot, humid, and miserable. The men groaned and bitched to the high heavens. Of course, that meant to those of us in charge that they were really shaping up as normal "doughfeet." I led a platoon during the entire time, and my unit led the company in efficiency, accomplishments, etc. Captain Boyle, the CO, was pleased and said so.

The thirteen-week training period was now over, and I was in charge of shipping out our "finished products." I processed over 200 men in three days, whereupon the battalion command officer placed me in charge of receiving 812 recruits at the Reception Center and getting them assigned to the unit's four training companies.

How green and bewildered they looked. Four of my own new platoon recruits received medical discharges in the first week. Outwardly, I was much the stern and demanding officer. Inwardly, I asked myself, "Why?" Hundreds of them had never been away from home before. Many were just out of high school. The cycle this time would be for seventeen weeks, instead of thirteen. The army had decided to expose its "meat hunks" to a more in-depth training program.

I spent a weekend in Birmingham, and phoned Major General Ludwig S. Conelly, my mother's first cousin, who was headquartered there. His assignment was to inspect periodically the infantry training camps over a certain area. We had a friendly conversation. A few days later I was out on the hand grenade course with my platoon. A cloud of red dust approached and out of it sputtered a camp headquarters jeep. An excited sergeant leaped out, and saluted me with the kind of alacrity and respect due General Douglas MacArthur. "Sir," he panted, "there is a two-star general at post headquarters asking for you. I suggest you come with me at once." I knew who it was, and dusty fatigues, sweat, dirt, and all we took off. Major General Conelly was waiting for me in the post commander's office. I threw both of them a high ball (a formal, full salute) that came from somewhere under the office floor.

"At ease, Lieutenant Arn," grinned General Conelly. "Let me introduce you to General So-and-so (I cannot recall the post commander's name). Since I am pressed for time, I'd like to take him over to Remington Hall for a drink." You would have thought I was General Dwight D. Eisenhower in the flesh from the reaction. Immediate permission was granted, and I enjoyed an hour with a man who had risen from the enlisted ranks and had served proudly and well in two world wars. General Conelly was proud of me. I could tell. I am sure he had checked my officer's file from the nature of the questions he asked me. He urged me to "keep up the good work." I came away considerably encouraged.[6]

Our new group of "doggies" moved into its third week as the autumn leaves fell and were hoarded in the low areas and under the trees of the abundant forests. Out of the forty-seven men in my platoon, I had only four bolos. A "bolo" was a soldier who failed to qualify on the rifle range. I still remember one bolo. One brisk morning out on the rifle range, a sergeant came up to me on the double. "Sir, I have a problem at my station." "What is that problem, sergeant?" "One of our soldiers is refusing to fire his weapon. Mumbles something about his religious beliefs. It's my job to get these men qualified, and he's holding things up."

I moved to the station where the lad was in the prone position and to all intents and purposes prepared to fire. I looked down and met the most determined pair of eyes I had witnessed in a long time. "Soldier, are you aware that I am about to issue you an order to fire that weapon." "I assume you are, sir." "Why are you disobeying?" "I have certain religious beliefs that prevent me from firing a weapon that is designed to kill or wound human beings." "You must have had this belief long ago." "That I did, sir, and no one would listen to me. I have been ridiculed and scorned ever since the training started, sir. So, I made up my mind that when I got to this point on the range, I would have to resist." "Very well, soldier. It's your decision. The sergeant will please act as a witness of what I am about to do. I command you to fire that rifle." "I refuse, sir."

I repeated the order two more times. He refused to obey two more times. "Sergeant, place this man under arrest for insubordination and disobedience. Remove him to the post guardhouse. I shall file charges when we return from the range this afternoon." They took him away. He never once looked back. He just held his head high and his shoulders erect. I had a brief feeling that I may have trod upon the Lord's work but only briefly.

That evening at Remington Hall, over a bit of libation, I shared the story with some of my fellow officers. One spoke up. "That's the same conscientious objector I had a few days ago in my hand-to-hand fighting session. I had heard he was a conscientious objector, and would declare himself in a definite way sooner or later. In my opinion, these bastards are real phonies. So I called the SOB out in front of the platoon and ordered my sergeant to demonstrate some of the hand-to-hand techniques to the platoon, using this bastard in the demonstration. He damned near killed the yardbird. Tossed him all over the place. I had informed the sergeant of the soldier's yellow streak beforehand." This officer seemed pleased with the whole incident, although he did admit with wonder that the lad "never even whimpered."

I pressed charges. Eventually, the young man was mustered out of the service with an honorable discharge based on religious beliefs. Somehow, I don't believe that particular soldier was a phony. I think he believed in God and the law of Moses, "Thou shalt not kill." This incident shows how some people felt about conscientious objectors during World War II. I blamed the Army for allowing him to get as far as he did in the service. I had to enforce the regulations in my own role as an Army officer.[7]

"As I acquire experience and confidence in myself," I wrote my parents, "I am getting more and more in the mood for an overseas assignment. I'll probably never make it for as you two well know I will be thirty-five next January. A boat ride at least in one direction or another would be an experience. We are now in our sixth week with this particular group of trainees, and they are moving second lieutenants out of here like ants."

On 11 October 1943 I was transferred to battalion headquarters. My first reaction was one of dejection. "They evidently don't think I'm doing well with troops in the field." Actually, a Colonel Hamlett had asked for me, and did he load me with paperwork, especially special stuff in which he needed decisions and help right now. He said he wanted an officer with gumption, one who wasn't afraid to make some decisions and to carry them out. One of my titles was Assistant S-3 (Training).

I introduced new ideas as a result of my field experience into the training curriculum. I also got involved with S-1 (Personnel), and recommended promotions as well as transfers. Much to my distaste, I was ordered to conduct two-hour inspections of the whole battalion area every morning. I missed nothing: mess halls, barracks, supply depots, parade grounds, enlisted men's quarters, and those of the officers. All came under my searching methods and no-nonsense reports.

It was a great experience. The colonel had given me full authority and I had used it. I had made many people unhappy, but Hamlett was pleased because he had a cleaner and better-organized battalion at the level in which I was involved, and that's what he wanted. "Things have happened around here since you've been raising so much hell, Arn," the colonel observed. "I'd much rather be with the men in the field," I reported in a letter home. Apparently, I had forgotten all too quickly the misery of fieldwork.

On 9 November 1943 I was transferred back to B Company and my old platoon. Colonel Hamlett said, "Thank you, Lieutenant, for a job well done." I hadn't been with him long. Maybe he was afraid I'd get shot by some irate NCO or something. The report he placed in my officer's file was most gratifying. The men were glad to see me.

We were given the unwelcome news that the battalion would be in the field on maneuvers in December. I came as close to a demerit on my record as I ever did about this time. There was a girl named Mary (I have long since forgotten her last name) who worked at one of the post exchanges. Her face reminded me of an old "artillery impact area" but she could dance like Ginger Rogers, if not better. Mary and I assaulted Remington Hall one Saturday evening. The music was great, and the cocktails were flowing. Mary was getting lighter than a feather. I often danced backwards in those days. A waiter came across the floor with his tray loaded with drinks. Before Mary could get a syllable of warning out, we hit that waiter hard. The tray performed a graceful arc in the air and came down right in the middle of a table of high-ranking officers and their wives. I apologized profusely, but the damage was done. Mary and I sneaked out, I think, through a rear door.

I was ordered to report to Colonel Williams, the regimental CO, the next Monday morning. After studying my record, he decided not to give me a demerit. I did receive a real dressing down, however. I promised to be more careful in the future. The session ended with the colonel asking me where I had learned to dance like that. I told him I had never taken a lesson in my life. It was a close call indeed. I wonder whatever happened to Mary.

We moved into the cold and the rain of Talladega National Forest. Reilly and I shared a pup tent that leaked badly. In disgust one bad night, after the men had bedded down as best they could in what had become a freezing rain, Reilly and I made for the nearest town by bumming a ride on a supply truck. We checked into a small hotel for a shower, shave, and then a look-around of the town. We managed to get back to the company area just before daylight, feeling somewhat better although tired. It was against regulations, and thank goodness we were not caught in the act.[8]

We were in the field on Christmas Day, 1943. We were miserable and forlorn. What did all this discomfort prove? It seemed to me there was only one person in the whole wide world in a worse position than I, and that person was Adolf Hitler. His dreams of an empire were, seemingly, disintegrating everywhere. Allied Air Forces were reducing Germany and German-held positions into shambles, and the Kremlin was pressing for a Second Front. In the Pacific, the Japs were beginning to feel the Allied might.[9]

Yes, Hitler was having his problems. My problems were eased considerably when, on 14 January 1944 I left for a ten day furlough. I can recall little about the leave. I do recollect that I again contacted Bill Conelly. Divorce proceedings were moving ahead, but slowly. I urged speed at all costs. I wanted out. When I returned to McClellan, I received a letter of commendation with a superior rating for handling the transfer of 1,500 men from McClellan to Fort Meade, Maryland and Fort Ord, California.[10]

Lieutenant Leffel was still having a bit of a time with that comely lass in one of the camp post exchanges. He asked me to take a strange assignment. "My wife is coming here for a visit of a few days. I want to make a comparison of my wife and my sweetheart. Would you be kind enough to double date with my wife and me? You take my girl, and I'll bring my wife. I would like to observe the two women at close hand." It was a screwball project, but I had no axe to grind. Leffel said he'd pick up the tab, so we went. Leff's girl was a good dancer and a jovial sort. So was his wife. I was glad that I didn't have to make the choice. Leff chose the post exchange clerk. He divorced his wife and married the girl after the war. They had several children and lived happily ever after. I had played the part of Cupid's helper with some measure of success.

About this time, a passage in a pamphlet entitled *The Infantry Lieutenant and His Platoon* [made a strong impression on Arn]. An infantry lieutenant "must draw on his common sense, his cool courage, determination, ingenuity, cunning, and patience. If he destroys the enemy, he has done his job. A first class Infantry Officer looks after his men, loves his weapons, and his job. He is proud of his platoon and its skills, as well as his own. Every healthy man is afraid. Not afraid of death or wounds but afraid of being afraid. Once it starts he won't have time to be anything but cool and efficient. He cannot be an individual in battle. He is a commander of soldiers. When men are killed or wounded, the others will look at him to see how he reacts. Make sure the dead are properly marked with bayonet, rifle, and helmet. He will write the relatives later. Now, he is at the head of a team, wanting revenge, perfect soldiers all."[11]

When I first read those ideas, I thought, how cold, professional, and even heartless. Later, I was to remember parts of this passage about the infantry officer, a true line officer. It was now a business in a sense: get the job done, soldier. I never measured up 100 percent. I did try, though, to be at least a reasonable facsimile of that infantry officer.

The long days and nights in the field came to an end at last. There was a dance one Saturday evening at the Battalion Officers' Club. One of the training companies had a private by the name of King. In civilian life, he and his wife had formed a professional ballroom dance team. They were billed around the country as "King and King—Dancing to the King's Taste." That was sort of corny, but vaudeville in those days was on the corny side as we measure things today. King's wife lived in Anniston.

The battalion's Special Services Officer asked the Kings to entertain at this dance. I was fascinated with the young lady's grace and skill, a real professional. Strengthened by several trips to the bar, plus the fact that I thought I was Fred Astaire's first cousin, I went up to Pvt. King after their performance was over and asked if I might dance with his wife. I was much out of order, they told me later, but gosh, what could he say to an officer? Did we dance. The crowd stopped dancing to watch, with all eyes upon us. I'm bragging, but she was something else. It wasn't ballroom. It was just plain old jitterbug with some Arn innovations. I had a ball. This gal even followed my mistakes. Suddenly, I realized that I was probably in deep trouble, and I danced the girl back to her husband and made for the bar in a sweat-soaked uniform. A battalion staff officer found me and ordered me to report to battalion headquarters the next Monday morning. This was a second visit, also for disciplinary reasons.[12]

Several days before, I had talked with a friend in headquarters about the possibilities of a transfer to an infantry division preparing for combat. He had said he would investigate and get back to me one way or the other. I was getting restless, and I am unable to explain why. There was another gentle reprimand from the colonel. He was, I suspect, a bit of a fun lover himself. But the dancing incident, innocent as it was, coupled with my already-expressed desire for a change, helped to hurry my departure from McClellan, my home for nearly eight months.

On 28 January 1944 I was transferred to Camp Forrest, Tennessee and ordered to join the 106th Division currently engaged in the famous "Tennessee Maneuvers." I reported to L Company, 3rd Battalion, 423rd Regiment. The 106th was known as the "Lion's Head Division," and was often referred to as the "diaper division" of Uncle Sam's army. At the time, it was the youngest and highest-numbered division in service. It had been activated about eleven months.[13]

"These Tennessee Maneuvers are rough, but so what else is new? I am a platoon leader in a rifle company at last. All the rest of my background has been preparation." That's all I bothered my folks with, and I added "this 106th will be in the States for a long time." It was, but I wasn't.[14]

Lieutenant Binder, a young, arrogant, and not-too-knowledgeable native of New Jersey, commanded L Company. This dodo I didn't like.[15] We didn't click from the start. Anyway, soldiering was getting very rugged. I remember crawling into an old barn in the dead of night during a violent thunderstorm. I checked the place out as well as I could, and then ordered my whole platoon in there with me. It seemed utterly stupid to expose those men to any further hardship, even though the platoon was an integral part of the training problem in which we were engaged. We stayed there all night. I recall being awakened several times during the night by barn rats crawling over my drenched and cold legs. We were several hours late reaching our objective and my procrastinating lost points in the regimental maneuver. I made some excuse about following the wrong compass reading. Binder raved and ranted. But much more important than his wild screaming, no one seemed to notice that my kids were more rested and drier than the others. Incidentally, so was Lieutenant Arn.

I wrote home that, "If you can believe this I have just spent my most miserable time this past week since I joined the Army. Now that I'm into divisional maneuvers, I am becoming less anxious to get into combat. Rain, snow, or shine, it makes no difference. We go—go—go!" "Mud everywhere: in our hair, crotch, between our toes. Fifty to seventy-five miles a week, day and night, on foot, cross country. I don't know how I'd feel without water running down my back and oozing into my shoes. I have been in a bed once since I arrived here. Sixteen hours of continuous hiking in infantry weather. But I just can't let the men know I'm about to drop. I haven't even sat on a toilet in three weeks. Toilet paper? We use the leaves of winter, wet, withered ones that have been on the ground since last fall. Some say that troops and mechanized equipment (tanks, half tracks) have done so much damage around here to farmland that this division may be the last to use this area. If I never see this place again it will be too soon." (20 February 1944)

"We haven't been within fifty miles of Camp Forrest for days. We recently moved thirty-eight miles in three days on foot. Yep, you guessed it, in the rain. But please remember, dear people, 1909 is the magic number at the top of my record and it still should prevent me from going overseas." (27 February 1944)

"They say the 106th Division will be moving to Camp Atterbury, Indiana, at the end of the month, forty miles south of Indianapolis, a rest camp. When did the Army provide rest camps? It'll take two days to move the division by truck." (11 March 1944) "We leave in a couple of days for Atterbury. Will be settled in by 31 March. The kids in my platoon are my concern now. Their average age is eighteen to twenty-two. I am getting attached to the damned yardbirds. The 106th Division is to be a replacement training division, and I have reason to believe we could be in the area for a lengthy period." (18 March 1944)

"Have had another physical. I weigh 170 and declared in top condition. 'If you were a bit younger, we'd have to ship you out' observed one doctor. I'm delighted to hear about divorce proceedings. Looks good. I once again instructing in infantry basics. We have hundreds of replacements now. They took 900 men out of the 423rd Regiment the other day and shipped them overseas. 1,200 recruits are coming in." (2 May 1944)

"Once I become a single officer, I will be cut from $244.50 per month to $163.50. They say this division will never go overseas as a division." [Three days later, a new development changed Arn's thoughts.] "I am concerned. They gave me a book to read yesterday. It's called *A Guide for Replacement Infantry Officers Preparing for Overseas Shipment.* I wonder if something's cooking? My dream is to attain a captaincy some day, but that is only a dream and nothing else. I'm still a second lieutenant and I have been in grade now for almost a year. We had this last batch of men for only seven weeks. There is a strong rumor around here that the brass in Washington is planning a European invasion. That would take lots of men." (12 May 1944)

The time wore on. Lieutenant Arn and a new friend, Lieutenant John Kennedy, spent a weekend in Indianapolis at the Hotel Lincoln. Then it happened. On 19 May 1944 I was presented with an eight-day furlough, and ordered to report at the termination of that leave to Fort Meade. I was now classified as Military Occupational Specialty (MOS) No. 1542, or Infantry Unit Commander. No more; no less. What was the old expression—cannon fodder? I had been in the 106th Division a little over three months. I was to hear more about the division a few months later.[16]

John Kennedy, on the same order as I, went to Cleveland with me because his home was in Santa Rosa, California, and the leave did not provide enough time for him to go back. A good time was had by all, outwardly at any rate. Everyone knew where John and I were headed: overseas and most likely into combat. My two loving parents were as brave as any son could wish under the circumstances. There was no sentimental emotion, just an acute awareness. John and I finally took an eastern train with little or no notice and certainly no bands playing. My dear parents must have surely suffered.[17]

God above! What was to be my destiny?

4. A Tormenting Ordeal

29 May 1944–2 October 1944

After their successful cross-channel invasion of Normandy, American forces bogged down when they sought to enlarge their front. German resistance amid inhospitable and nearly impenetrable hedgerows prevented any open and swift breakout. By the time Arn arrived on 14 July 1944 as a replacement infantry officer, high casualty rates among American units forced such newcomers directly into front-line units. Arn's experiences typified this system's strengths and weaknesses. He joined F Company, 2nd Battalion, 119th Infantry Regiment, 30th Infantry Division, alone, disoriented, anxious, and distrusted by most veterans. Facing either survival or quick death, he matured quickly from a neophyte officer into a steady combat leader and gained self-confidence and the respect of his men and his commanders. These traits were crucial among junior officers who led the small units that were the key to victory on the ground. In continuous combat for seventy-nine days, Arn participated in Operation Cobra, the breakout from Normandy, the failed German counterattack at the Battle of Mortain, and the dash across France into Belgium and the Netherlands. By the end of September, Arn and his men from Fox Company were poised for the invasion of the German heartland.

Evidently, I shall be here in Meade only three or four days. John and I hope to take in Washington, D.C., while we're here. From Meade, we'll be sent to a port of embarkation.

At the most, I would guess that we will be there three or four more days. I suspect, although we never discussed it during my leave, that my predictions about never getting out of the country were quite groundless, even hollow. I am now aware that my physical condition was one factor and my record for handling men was another. The infantry, in the final analysis, will be needed to draw this war to a conclusion. I am an infantryman. So be it. I have changed the beneficiary in my GI Insurance from my about-to-be former wife to you two."[1] (29 May 1944)

On 1 June 1944 John and I were sent to Camp Shanks, New York, which was the port of embarkation for the European Theater of Operations (ETO). Now I knew what my general destination would be.[2]

Five days later, John and I took the train into New York City for one last fling. We made our way to a huge ballroom under the roof of the Hotel Astor. Harry James and his orchestra were playing tunes like "I'll Be Seein' You" and "I'll Walk Alone." I can still see the veins stand out now on James' forehead as he played his heart out on his trumpet for an audience largely composed of military personnel of both sexes. During the evening, Harry James' wife made her appearance. She was Betty Grable, the movie star. She took a bow and received a nice ovation.

John and I didn't have much to say. We were on our way into God knew what. So we got loaded. Late that night, or was it early that morning, I managed my last stateside letter home. "I just wanted you to know that everybody said goodbye very graciously and with a minimum of emotion. For that I am most grateful. Remember my letters will be censored from now on. I will not be able to give you many details as I have in the past. I will not even be able to tell you where I am exactly. Dad, I would suggest that you conduct your usual close reading of the news papers. I have a feeling you'll be able to locate me. They say our mail comes back from overseas promptly, but it doesn't do very well catching up with me. I may ask questions from time to time that you may have answered long ago. I guess all of us will have to be patient. Please use airmail as often as you can. It takes weeks by boat or what they call surface mail. I shall try hard to write as often as humanly possible, for I am well aware of your concern."

I didn't let John Kennedy know, but I recollect a horrible feeling in the pit of my stomach. I kept asking myself: Would I ever see my family and my homeland again? The odds were very much against a safe return. As an infantry unit commander, I knew that with the rank of second lieutenant that I would most likely be assigned to a platoon in an infantry rifle company. That duty would be as far forward as one could get. I was well trained for such an assignment, it seemed to me, but being ready for it mentally? The hardship and the miserable aches and pains of training could be endured with the comfortable knowledge that no one was firing at you. Over there, I would be exposed to the raw atmosphere and roughness of training, but beyond all of that it would be a simple matter of survival. I sealed the envelope, my last letter home before sailing, crawled on my cot, and was still wide-eyed at dawn.[3]

The landings on the Normandy beaches, D-Day, 6 June 1944, were already history when on 9 June 1944 we climbed into one and a half ton trucks and roared down to the harbor of New York City. We passed ship after ship at anchor. We finally halted at Pier 3. Rocking gently in the murky waters of the Hudson River was a small, weather-beaten, obviously old ship. Her cracked letters on her hull read *Santa Marta*. As we used to say when the rigors of training were particularly rough, "Please, someone, put me on a banana boat and get me out of here!" Wouldn't you know, the *Santa Marta* proved to be a converted freighter from the fleet of the United Fruit Lines. It had been used for months to carry replacement troops to combat zones. Prior to her present role, her ladyship had carried tons of bananas all over the world since her maiden voyage out of Belfast, Ireland, in the year, 1909, the year I was born. We were told that the British skipper now at her helm was the same sailor who had taken her on her first voyage, thirty-five years before. I believe there were about 300 enlisted men and 150 officers on board. It was a small ship but sturdy, and when the high seas were raging, her wooden parts below would creak and groan as we lay in our bunks. I've always thought that gallant old ship was trying to tell us something.

There were no bands playing or pretty girls waving as we weighed anchor that early morning long ago, just a few busy and sour-faced dockworkers who could not have cared less. The grey mists and horrible odors of the harbor seemed to say, "Yes, we aren't much but you aren't either. Furthermore, we're glad we are not going where you are going." The Statue of Liberty watched our departure with a sort of gray-green look of pity and perhaps some solicitude.

A few miles out, a huge convoy began to form. I've never really known how many ships were in our convoy. There must have been at least forty or fifty, maybe more. Canadian "baby flat tops" (small airplane carriers) were in our convoy, which meant that we had some form of protection against possible air attack. Corvettes darted hither and yon also. These ships were antisubmarine vessels loaded to the gunwale with explosive "ash cans" (metal missiles).

About ten days out, we went through a U-boat alert. During some particularly rough weather and poor visibility, several ships were separated from the main convoy, the *Santa Marta* among them. During the submarine scare, the Corvettes began "tossing" their "ash cans" into the sea. Such action convinced the disturbed people aboard the "banana boat" that German subs just had to be lurking in the vicinity. We became even more perturbed when the cans exploded under water at controlled depths, causing considerable internal shuddering in our little ship. We never knew whether any subs were sunk or not, but it was an early taste of the urgencies to come. The Navy crewmen on board showed little or no concern.

Two days later we rejoined the convoy. We were under blackout orders throughout the voyage and were allowed on deck for calisthenics only. On 15 June 1944 I managed a letter home, headed "Somewhere at Sea," that I mailed later. "I have lots of time on my hands and I read a lot." Another day, 20 June 1944, I wrote, "Still at sea. Haven't been seasick at all and we've had several good blows. I sang lead in a quartet to relieve the monotony. Must have sounded okay for they asked for an encore. The salt water showers are hard to get used to, as they have a strange influence on the quality and quantity of the soap suds."[4]

Since the maximum speed of the convoy was governed by the maximum speed of the slowest ship, we averaged about eight knots. This is probably why we never sighted the Firth of Clyde in Scotland until we had been at sea for seventeen days. Some four hours later, we docked at

Glasgow. It was 26 June 1944, now D+20, using the military language of tacticians in Normandy.

We were greeted by American Red Cross girls with free coffee and doughnuts. They weren't much to look at, but they were our women anyway. I have always thought highly of the Red Cross organization. These particular women had been greeting arriving GIs for months, and it struck me they were just a little bored. Can't blame them though. We were nothing special to them.[5]

A troop train whisked us south, loaded to the roofs with equipment and men, in a matter of hours to a neat, clean English village named Nantwich near the Welsh border. Officers were bedded down in bedrolls on the straw-covered stone floors of a castle. The bedrolls were warm and comfortable. We slept well into the next day, 27 June 1944. "The English countryside is lovely. Hedge-rimmed houses surrounded by brick or stonewall. Picturesque and winding roads where everybody drives on the left side. Gorgeous flowers everywhere. This castle can get cold and drafty. Thank goodness for our bedrolls. I have been warmer in a pup tent."

"We're doing our own laundry. I passed another physical. I showed no effects from the long ocean voyage. We're still in the castle. Close order drill and plenty of calisthenics help. John Kennedy was given permission to visit his wife, Inez, in London. She is a nurse in an army hospital there." (30 June 1944)

On 2 July 1944 I was still in England and not unhappy with my lot. The invasion was going well, so we were told anyway, along a seventy-five mile front in Normandy. We were informed that the Allied Forces were about fifteen to twenty miles in from the beaches.[6] One thing seemed certain: casualties were high, for replacements were crossing the English Channel into Normandy in ever-increasing numbers. It would be only a matter of time until "the roll would be called up yonder" and I would be there, personally.[7]

"I spent last evening in Nantwich. I had a few warm beers and watched other GIs live it up. I had no desire to. I have received word from Bill Conelly. Notice will be in the mail soon that I am at last a single person, or is that divorced person? As far as soldiering is concerned, I am doing the same things I did in the States." (3 July 1944) That meant marching to the firing range, where it seemed we fired weapons almost incessantly, drilling troops, and lecturing.

By this time we had moved to another bivouac area in southern England. I can't remember where. We lived in small one-room barracks, cold and drafty at night, heated by potbelly stoves. My guess would be that we were not too far north of Southampton, the shove-off point for the American beaches, Omaha and Utah. No one in authority would tell us anything. I never visited London. About this time John Kennedy, the lucky dog, was transferred there to be with his wife. I never saw them again until years later while on a business trip to California.

The rains came, typical English weather. I had time, too much time, to think. How would I react under fire? I knew I would be scared, but how scared? What would my first combat assignment be? "I'm really bored stiff. I would welcome some action, maybe soon." (12 July 1944) Action did come, fast. On 13 July 1944 we left our bivouac area and journeyed south by truck to Southampton. For the first time, since I had been confined to military bases since arriving in England, I witnessed the devastation of enemy bombing. The barrage balloons hovering over Southampton presented a weird sight, but I was told they had all but eliminated low-level bombing and strafing.

There were ships and then more ships crowded into the ancient seaport. Soon I found myself crammed among military people on the deck of one of the vessels. My eyes searched the sky for enemy bombers. None came. Later that night, under the cover of darkness (an expression with which I would become quite familiar), we slipped out of the harbor and into the English Channel headed east toward Normandy. I was getting closer to the ball game. My stomach churned. I attempted to join the noisy and raucous banter that surrounded me. What's with these guys anyway? I turned away. I thought of my home, my dear parents, my friends; a thousand memories crowded into my head.[8]

As dawn was breaking, I could see the rugged outlines of what I was told was now-famous Omaha Beach. It was D+40. The men of the First Army had swarmed over that beach a month ago with paratroopers dropping in ahead of them by a matter of hours. Signs of war were everywhere. Our U.S. Navy skipper skillfully dodged rusting, sunken ships offshore. We boarded LSTs (landing ship, tanks), and were taken ashore. I imagined that these same boats, some of them, were probably used on D-Day. I even looked for dried vomit because I had been told that hundreds of our men were miserably seasick when they hit the beach. There was no sign of their misery.

Omaha Beach was littered, nearly choked with debris. Paths had been bulldozed through the mess to allow men and vehicles to get through. Countless shell craters dotted the shore and the high cliffs beyond. Burned-out, destroyed tanks, upside-down jeeps, ammo carriers, twisted and black from enemy fire, abounded everywhere. Suddenly, I had an impulse to get down on my knees and thank the Good Lord that I had, at least, missed this phase of the holocaust. How in God's name had those valiant men come ashore and climbed those embankments in the face of the heavily armed positions above?[9]

Herculean tasks had already been performed by the combat engineers and the quartermaster corps. Troop trucks greeted us as we mounted the scarred cliffs. We journeyed inland over pockmarked roads once under heavy fire. This was French farm country. I gazed in awe at burned and splintered tree trunks, shattered farm houses, and military vehicles of all types smashed to kingdom come, shoved disdainfully aside so the traffic could move. Now and then I saw parachute shrouds flapping dismally in the wind from the tops of what was left of trees. Mercifully, the men who had used those chutes had long since been cut down and whisked to hospitals in England or buried in Normandy's temporary cemetery in Ste.-Mère-Église.

I cannot recall where we stopped, but it was a Replacement Depot (called "repple depples" by GIs) in the region near Isigny, not far from the Caen-Carentan Highway. We were assigned foxholes over which pup tents had been pitched. I had little confidence in the effectiveness of a pup tent in stopping even small arms fire, let alone fragments from 500-pound bombs. The foxholes would provide some protection if they were deep enough, and these were. I learned that the village of St.-Lô was about twenty miles south of the depot. It was about to become a famous name in American military history. There was no sound of even artillery fire, so we must have been in a fairly quiet sector.[10]

Somehow on 16 July 1944 I managed to write, "I am sitting under a French apple tree that has seen better days. A bloated cow, dead for days with its legs sticking straight up into the air, is, fortunately for me, down wind from where I sit. Evidently, some GIs have used the cow for target practice in the past few days or else shrapnel has taken its toll. Frankly, it's a bovine mess. I am in no danger at this time. What few civilians I have seen seem to like us and why not? A glass of apple cider sells for ten francs, about five cents."

On the Cherbourg-Carentan Highway, the quaint little French village of Ste.-Mère-Église had catapulted into the limelight overnight by being chosen as the site of a temporary American cemetery. At one time as the war progressed, there were as many as 50,000 GIs buried there. This resting place for so many has some significance for me. We replacement officers had heard that Teddy Roosevelt Jr., second-in-command of the 1st Infantry Division, the "Big Red One," had died of a heart attack during the invasion, and after some delay was being buried in Ste.-Mère-Église Cemetery.[11]

The burial ceremony in the cemetery was to take place not too far from our "repple depple." Two or three of us managed to get to the place just as Lieutenant General George Patton arrived on the scene. As he dashed from his command car, I marveled at what a jaunty, devil-may-care figure he cut with his pearl-handled pistols dangling from each hip. It was the first time I had ever seen three stars on a helmet. We didn't dare stay long, but I could always say I had seen General Patton in the flesh while attending the graveside services of a son of one of America's presidents.[12]

On 17 July 1944 I was processed and sent forward with a half-dozen other officers into the combat zone. I was assigned to the 30th Infantry Division, called "Old Hickory" in honor of President Andrew Jackson, one of the best divisions in the European Theater of Operations. Old Hickory contained three infantry regiments, the 117th, 119th, and 120th. The full division had landed in Normandy by 17 June 1944 in the vicinity of Isigny where the Vire River, flowing from the south, empties into

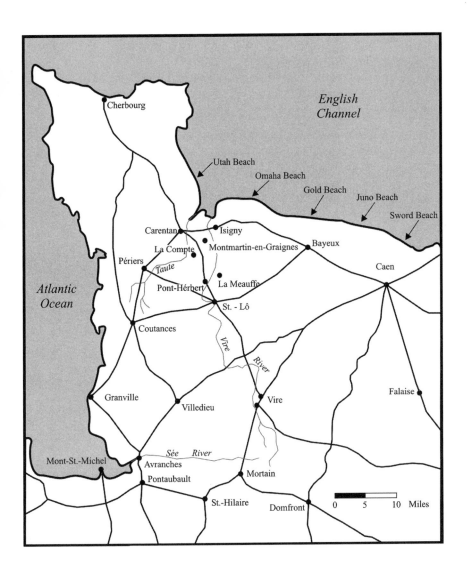

Map 2. Normandy, July 1944. (Hewitt, pg. 9)

the English Channel. The beachhead did not have much penetration in this area, and the invasion troops were stretched along a thin line. Opposing them was the German commander, Field Marshal Gerd von Rundstedt, with powerful and mobile reserves at his disposal.[13]

The invasion area in Normandy was largely dairy and orchard country. The ancient farms were fenced in, not in the conventional American manner, but by gigantic hedgerows: sturdy, thick hedge growing out of a broad, earthen base, often ten to fifteen feet thick. The whole growth, base, and hedge could reach a height of fifteen feet or even more. Moreover, the complicated terrain in Normandy created all sorts of problems for man's modern weapons and his war vehicles. Paralleling the Vire River, on an average of ten to fifteen miles further west, was a smaller river called the Taute. A canal connected the two rivers about three miles south of Isigny, running east and west at a point about fifteen miles south of the Channel coast. The 30th's first assignment was to fight through to that canal, which would require an agonizing advance through the hedgerow country.[14]

Resistance was tough and progress was slow, in some places from hedgerow to hedgerow only. It was difficult to tell whether a Norman concentration of people was a "village" or a "hamlet." The latter was usually only a cluster of houses or a large farm operation consisting of several buildings. Old Hickory's first day of battle ended in places like Montmartin-en-Graignes and La Ray. The costly advance reached a line about one mile south of the Vire-et-Taute Canal, with Old Hickory enduring a bloody lesson while fighting from barnyard to hedgerow, to farmhouse to village, and on to the sunken road. The medics and the field hospitals were busy until far into the night.[15]

By 19 June 1944 the 119th (my eventual regiment), sustaining heavy casualties, had reached the vicinity of the village of La Meauffe. At this point, enemy pressure stiffened, causing the regiment to move several hundred dearly-bought yards backwards. Because of this stubborn resistance, Allied commanders decided to hold up for more replacements and needed supplies. The tired troopers dug deep foxholes behind and at the bases of the thick hedgerows.

A three-week interlude followed, nightmarish in nature. There were no major advances. Reconnaissance patrols roamed about at night getting into all sorts of terrifying and confusing situations. The enemy probed also, and firefights were constant. The small farm orchards and pastures identified by the hedge-topped walls of earth demanded entirely new warfare techniques. American tanks had little room to maneuver. Stateside training had not been conducted with this kind of geographical challenge in mind.[16]

The Germans employed effective small arms. Their "burp gun," which was actually a machine pistol, made a sound when fired like a giant's belch, and had devastating firepower. High-trajectory mortars seemed to walk the shells along the tops of the hedgerows with demoralizing effect. A mortar shell never signals its arrival. One cannot hear them coming due to the sort of high trajectory. It is suddenly there and exploding. Enemy snipers amazed the Americans with their uncanny accuracy.

The division's inexperience was showing, and a bloody stalemate resulted. Infiltrations were so numerous that it was nothing at all to discover enemy behind one's positions and vice versa. The correspondents called it "slow, intermittent progress." Intense artillery fire from the heights beyond the Vire was so deadly that the 119th suffered 50 percent casualties on its flanks during the period of 7 July through 13 July 1944.[17]

The hedgerows were still so high, in spite of the trimming effect of rifle and machine gun fire, that men would have to climb them. An appearance at the top would draw fire at once. The alternative would be to advance in single file along the row until an opening would appear, but enemy fire patterns were zeroed in on all openings. It was rough going. Our own artillery fire was becoming increasingly ineffective, because the artillery forward observers (FOs) were unable to gain good terrain advantages to mark enemy dispositions properly. The casualty rate among our brave forward observers was appalling. They were as expendable as company commanders and platoon leaders. On 17 July the 29th Division took St.-Lô, with the 30th progressing slowly south, west of St.-Lô toward the Terette River.[18]

This was the situation when we replacements reported in the early morning of 17 July 1944 to the division commander, Major General Leland S. Hobbs. He talked to our little group on the spacious lawn of a battered but still elegant French chateau, the general's forward command post. Hobbs' executive officer (second-in-command) was Brigadier General William K. Harrison. General Hobbs eloquently informed us of the greatness of Old Hickory and how fortunate we were to be going into battle with such a distinguished infantry division. I listened nervously, for I did not visualize the situation as a football game with "Knute Rockne" Hobbs asking us to make one more try for the "Gipper" and the glory of old Notre Dame. I could hear the sound of combat fire now, and I was filled with considerable concern as I viewed my uncharted future with the 30th. I was assigned to the 119th Regiment as a replacement infantry platoon officer.

Colonel Edwin M. Sutherland, a wiry, crotchety, hard-bitten sort, was CO of the 119th. A regimental commander had three battalions, the 1st, 2nd, and 3rd, under his command. I can't recall where his command post was located. I do recall that a huge hole had been bulldozed out of a pasture. The hole had been covered with earth, logs, etc. One could stand up in it, and the place was busy as a beehive, with field phone wires running in all directions. I suspect they had no end of trouble with communication wire being constantly torn up by shellfire. A wire crew always faced many dangerous hazards, but I was in no mood to worry about their problems.

I will make a guess that the colonel's command post was in the vicinity of Airel. He talked to each of us individually. "You're a little old to be up here with an MOS 1542 (Military Occupation Specialty, Infantry Officer), aren't you?" "You are right, sir, but I have taken all the required training, and I guess our casualty rates are such that they need us all." What the hell else could I say? "Yes, you are so right, Lieutenant. We need all we can get. Thank goodness, your record with troops is a good one. I'm sending you up to the 2nd Battalion." He looked in the direction of the sound of battle. "All of the 2nd Battalion's rifle companies are on-line now and in contact. They've got sergeants handling platoons. A jeep will be here shortly. Good-bye, and may God bless you." He stalked back into the far recesses of his command post.

In split seconds I had a thousand reservations about my ability. I was now scared as hell. No matter. A jeep arrived, and I was on my way still further forward. We passed artillery batteries firing as fast as they could load. "105-mm sawed-offs," volunteered my filthy driver. "Close-in support artillery." I nodded. Was that my teeth chattering from the jolting of the jeep over the uneven surface of the sunken, hedgerow-lined dirt road, or from apprehension? The din was terrific. I wondered how "those boys in the outfield" (an affectionate GI name for artillerymen) could take that day after day and night after night. I never did find out. The road was now becoming nearly impassable. The driver never hesitated. I clutched my new carbine and my old, worn musette bag with a silent prayer on my lips.

The battalion command post was a huge hole about seven feet deep, much smaller than Colonel Sutherland's but many times larger than a GI foxhole. I cannot for the life of me recall the name of that battalion CO. My main concern at the time was with a guy named Arn. I was informed that I was going to F Company or Company F (Fox). I always preferred Fox Company, but I think it is proper to call it Company F. Take your choice. F Company was on-line and in contact with the enemy. The four companies in the 2nd Battalion were E, F, G, and H, or Easy, Fox, George, and Howe. Fox Company's CO was Captain Frank J. Parlavecchia of New York City.

A company runner was on his way back to fetch miserable Arn forward. I crouched down against the earthen wall of the command post. I waited. The longer I waited, the more nervous I became. A soft voice could be heard at the entrance to the command post. "Is Lieutenant Arn here?" "Yes, soldier, I am Lieutenant Arn." The weary, bloodshot eyes picked me out in the gloom of the hole. He was a dirty, bedraggled GI, and the smell of sweat and other odors permeated my nostrils. Through the grime a soft smile creased his lips. "May I help you with any of your gear, Lieutenant?" "No, I can manage. What is your name, soldier?" "Pfc. Ray Beaudoin, sir." A quiet almost subdued reply, again, the shy smile. "What do you do, Beaudoin?" I was stalling. It was no place for small talk. "Well, sir, a bit of everything. I am a company runner now but I have been with the Second Platoon as a rifleman most of the time."

There was a controlled relaxation about this lad that amazed me. I did not know it at the time, but my first contact with Fox Company was through a soldier who was to become the company's finest. I grew to understand, respect, and like him in the weeks ahead. Be that as it may, I had now exchanged my first words with an honest-to-God front-line trooper.

"Lead the way, Beaudoin, and I'll follow." "Yes, sir." And he looked at me in such a way that he seemed to say, "God bless you, Lieutenant, for you know not where I shall take you." We left the battalion command post at double-time. My newfound colleague went ahead in a semi-crouch, his rifle sling dangling, helmet chin straps unfastened (for a reason I found out later), and swinging wildly from side to side.

I tried to keep close but I had never been over an obstacle course as rough as the terrain we were dashing over now: huge bomb craters, shell holes, downed trees to be circled, abandoned equipment, and the always-present and ominous hedgerows. Here and there a body marked for the burial details by a bayoneted rifle stuck in the ground with the fallen warrior's helmet perched on top of the butt. An almost over-powering stench of the human bodies mingled with that of the bloated cattle.

An enemy artillery shell whistled in. I hit the dirt for the first time in combat. My new carbine, as yet only an ornament, went one way and my helmet with its bright yellow single bar, painted courageously on its front, rolled in another direction. I lay there for what seemed an eternity. Friendly footsteps approached. "Are you okay, Lieutenant?" It was the calm voice of my newfound friend. "I think so, Beaudoin, but that one was really close, wasn't it?" Hesitating only a moment, he replied, "No, sir, that shell hit about a hundred yards to our left."

He squatted and waited while I gathered up my scattered equipment, and made ready to continue our uneasy journey. "After awhile, sir, you'll get used to 'em. You'll even be able to tell when to hit the dirt or a hole or when to ignore 'em completely. 'Course one's judgment isn't always correct," and his voice trailed off. I detected a bit of pleasure in his eyes. He was giving an officer and a gentleman (supposedly) a bit of advice. I thanked him. We moved on.

Shortly thereafter, I spotted a small stream to our front. Without hesitation or even losing stride, Beaudoin slopped right through it, climbed the other bank, and disappeared around and behind a hedgerow. I could do nothing but duplicate his actions. The old familiar feeling of water in my GI boots followed. Up that slippery bank I went, only to slide awkwardly into a shell hole near the top of the rise.

Recovering quickly, I scrambled up the other side of the hole only to bump squarely into two grotesque and quite dead Germans. One torso was headless and the other slouched clumsily against the first with his eyes staring straight at me. The bomb or shell explosion had deposited them very neatly at the top rim of the crater. They had obviously been dead for some time. What was to become a familiar sort of sticky-sweet smell entered my nostrils, the odor of the uncared for departed.

It was too much. A distressed second lieutenant crawled over to a hedgerow and deposited all he had eaten that day on the ancient Norman soil. The new fatigues were stained now, and I must have been a sight. Again, the gentle voice, "Sorry, sir, most of us have gone through the same experience. You won't even notice such things after awhile." A woebegone olive drab handkerchief that had previously performed many other functions for which it had not been designed, was proffered to me. Desperately, I grabbed it and wiped my face. It helped. What was the matter with me? I was supposed to be a well-trained, efficient infantry officer, and I was acting like a yardbird in the rear rank of the third squad. I determined to try to do better.[19]

Moments passed. Beaudoin waited, saying nothing. I dared not glance in the direction of the hole. I signaled to Beaudoin that I was ready to continue. As we moved forward, the whine and swish of small arms fire became increasingly prominent. The impacts seemed to whip across the tops of the hedgerows. I watched Beaudoin warily. When he crouched and waited, so did I. I was learning. Chunks of dirt hit my helmet, dislodged by the relentless anger of the enemy beating a tattoo along the venerable hedges. Unheralded mortar shells were beginning to burst all around us. I could feel the sweat oozing into the leather band of my helmet liner. Even Beaudoin was becoming extremely cautious. The eerie whistle of shrapnel seemed to permeate every inch of space around us. How do people manage to survive in situations like this? I asked myself desperately.

Unexpectedly, Beaudoin disappeared into a foxhole. I huddled against the warm base of the hedge near his refuge. Now what? Slowly his helmet appeared above the rim of the hole. First the lower edge of his helmet and then his tired, darting eyes. Oh, how I longed to crawl in there with him. He emerged further and then pointed to a foxhole a few yards beyond his. I assumed quickly that either the hole was empty or that it might be F Company's command post.[20]

The hole was at the base of what was once a rather large tree that had been growing out of the hedgerow. I made a desperate lunge for the hole just as a mortar shell hit the shattered tree. Frantically, I dove head-first into the hole. My carbine clattered in after me with seemingly only one intent: to find a canteen coffee cup filled to the brim and resting on the bottom of the hole. The carbine's aim was unerring, and coffee spilled all around the hole. I immediately sensed that the other occupant of that blessed foxhole was F Company's CO. The captain had his map spread out on the earthen floor of his command post, studying it by his flashlight. The cascading coffee showed no mercy to the map, the flashlight, or the captain's legs.

Still half in and half out of the hole, I did only what I was able to do. I waited in a state of suspended anticipation. And then it came. "Jesus Christ. Who the hell are you?" "Lieutenant Arn reporting for duty, sir." By this time I was in the hole. "Good God above. What will they send me next?" His contempt bristled, and I felt it down in my very bones. "I am sorry, sir, but that shell hit the tree just above your hole and I re-acted to it; perhaps too hastily," my voice trailed off. "Yes," he replied. "Someone's mortar sights are on this position. This German-made hole is managing pretty well to give me some protection while I figure out what to do next."

We shook hands. Captain Parlavecchia, showing his competence, was all business in an instant. "I want you to take the weapons platoon, Arn (the Fourth Platoon of a rifle company). I will send for the platoon sergeant, and he will show you where the mortars and the machine guns are set up. Check the positions and then get back to me with your opinions as to where they ought to be if you think they should be changed." Just like that, as if we were on a peaceful golf course or some place back home. "We are in a holding situation and have been for several days, receiving lots of stuff, light and heavy. I expect infiltrations tonight so check the positions before dark."

The captain banged away at the field phone. The weapons platoon sergeant came from Hawaii. He was obviously prepared to be scornful, although he exercised careful respect. I spent the rest of the day with him dashing all over the company's sector. Running in a crouched position became second nature. Slowly, I became a little more accustomed to the inherent danger all around me. I ducked and sprawled and listened. I began to understand friend Beaudoin and his words of wisdom. The deafening noise presented still another challenge. It was with us constantly and our own replies to the enemy added to the uproar.

One of the platoon commanders, Lieutenant Melvin L. Riesch, acquainted me with F Company's current situation: the estimated enemy strength confronting us, approximate positions of the Germans' automatic weapons, what type of fire was coming and from where, and so on. From that information and recalling what I had learned in the States, I decided that the weapons platoon sergeant had the platoon's support weapons in the correct positions for not only defensive purposes, but for support fire in the event we went into the attack. My Hawaiian sergeant merely grinned knowingly as I dashed for Parlavecchia's never-to-be-forgotten command post. I am sure the sergeant didn't expect anything brilliant or innovative from me, and neither did the captain. I rose to their expectations.

As near as I can now determine, we were probably in an area near the village of Pont-Hébert, close to the west bank of the Vire River, perhaps three or four miles south of Airel. Strangely, and I'll never know how or why I managed the feat, I wrote home on 20 July 1944. "Mail will be very slow. I like the kids in my platoon a lot. I have learned much already and I'm not nearly as scared as I was. The APO (Army Post office) number in my address might give you a clue." I was referring to "APO 30," a part of my overseas mailing address, which meant the "30th Division." My Dad told me later that from then on he and Mom

were able to follow the feats and progress of the division in the newspapers, guessing correctly that I was in it. No big deal but it did clarify
things for the folks.

A 1944 Infantry Rifle Company contained a headquarters, three rifle
platoons, and a weapons platoon armed with machine guns and mortars. Second lieutenants headed the platoons. A captain served as company commander, with a first lieutenant his executive officer. At full
strength, a rifle company had 188 enlisted men and six officers. This
table of organization describes that combat infantry unit at full-strength
with every position filled.[21] Fox Company was NEVER at full strength
in combat. There were many times when platoon sergeants commanded platoons. I can recall a situation where the first sergeant ("Top
Kick") was one officer away, me, from taking over the entire Company
as CO. There just weren't many officers around most of the time.

In the hectic days that followed my disgraceful arrival on the field of
battle and my taking over as weapons platoon leader for Fox Company,
our forward progress continued to be slow and bloody. One could say
we "sat" and absorbed casualties by simply not moving, much as they
did in the old trench warfare days of WWI. Our tanks were of little help
because of the perplexing nature of the Normandy terrain. The light
tank was still in use, and it resembled a matchbox when hit directly by
the formidable German 88-mm guns. Their Panzerfaust, a handheld
German version of our bazooka antitank weapon, wreaked deadly
havoc. Finally, we began to commit our medium tanks, mounting a 75-
mm gun, and their performance was a decided improvement. Later, the
mediums were to mount a 90-mm gun and that provided even greater
effectiveness. But right now the bigger, heavily armored German tanks
took heart-rending tolls.[22]

I remember several days where our general inexperience showed
vividly. I am referring to all of the combat units of the 30th Division. I
can recall artillery shells crashing into our positions; high-ranking officers screaming frantic orders to no avail from dug-in positions; men
running aimlessly hither and yon: complete pandemonium with no one
seemingly in authority. It was really disgraceful in many respects.

One day I was hugging the base of one of those pesky hedgerows, and, believe me, hugging it with a desperation born of fear and frustration. Several GIs were near me. A shell hit nearby. A GI screamed in pain. The lad was down on the ground and thrashing about. I jumped him, pinned him down, and tried to determine where he had been hit and yelling for a medic at the same time. Then I discovered something: his left hand had been almost severed at the wrist by shrapnel and was merely dangling by one or two sinews or perhaps bits of flesh. The medic arrived, took one look, whipped out his trench knife and severed the hand from the forearm. As he was applying a tourniquet, I said to the wounded lad, "Soldier, I need a watch bad. Mine was destroyed a while back. Could I have your watch?" The soldier nodded, grimacing with pain. I slipped the watch off his bloody stump. I still have that watch, a 17-jewel Hamilton, US Army Ordinance # OD-100489. I never did know what happened to that unfortunate soldier.

The continued confusion amounted to hysteria in a way. Mindless emotions hit me hard. I recall drawing my .45 out of its holster and holding it to my head. Had I pulled the trigger my doubts and fears would have been over forever. However, at this precise moment one of our platoon sergeants crawled over to me displaying a bullet hole right through the palm of his hand. It was bleeding badly. At that time, some of us were still wearing gas mask bags. I ripped mine off, cut the shoulder straps with my faithful pocket knife, and made a tourniquet out of a stick and the straps. The bleeding stopped. A medic crawled over to us and took charge. My pistol went back into its holster and the soldier in me came to the surface once again. How stupid and silly to take one's own life and create a casualty for the enemy.[23]

We became a bewildered unit, milling about in a hailstorm of shot and shell. Another stalemate resulted. We found out later that the enemy, for the moment, had been receiving death-dealing artillery fire from our "Long Toms." The artillery competence of both sides was literally beating up both front lines.[24] We dug deeper. So did the Krauts. Advances, such as they were, and retreats ceased. We went about the welcome business of catching our breath.

Word came through that a "big plan" was in the development stage. It was to be called Cobra, an all-out attempt to break out of the horrible, high-casualty hedgerows of Normandy on a narrow front. If Cobra's mass-bombing technique were successful, soldiers were to attack through the "breakthrough."[25]

The 30th was selected as one of the assault elements. General Hobbs was delighted and proud, we heard. Hebecrevon would be the objective of the 119th Regiment, three miles south of Pont-Hébert. Captain Parlavecchia summoned the four platoon leaders to his command post. Sgt. Jack Beatty reported for Lieutenant Johnson of the Second Platoon. "Where's Johnson, Sgt.?" snapped the CO. "We can't get him out of his hole, sir. I don't know what his trouble is." "Riesch, you and Arn get off your duffs and find out what Johnson's trouble is."

We darted and dodged behind Beatty to Johnson's foxhole. He was alive, unhurt but utterly immobile. He didn't speak, not a muscle moved, only his fear-haunted eyes. Riesch grabbed the platoon-to-command post field phone. The captain ordered Johnson evacuated at once. We never saw him again. Shell shock? Combat fatigue? I really didn't know. Johnson had become a waxen image of what had been a fine, young officer. Sgt. Beatty was now a platoon leader.[26]

The captain informed us to the best of his ability, competing against the constant uproar all around us, what Operation Cobra was all about. The 30th, 4th, and 9th Infantry Divisions making up the VII Corps were to attack south. After breaking through, the 2nd and 3rd Armored Divisions, plus the 1st Infantry Division, would pour through the opening created by the initial assault units. Old Hickory's particular route would be along the west bank of the Vire River to Tessy-sur-Vire, twelve miles from the Line of Departure (LD) and located about midpoint on the Caen-Avranches Highway, just east of the St.-Lô-Vire main road. The 30th would be the easternmost of the attacking divisions and would have the additional task of protecting the left flank of the thrust.

The captain continued that before the ground troops would launch the attack, a saturation bombing was planned of the enemy positions, including heavy, medium, and fighter-bombers that would cover an area from the enemy's front lines back through their artillery locations. "All we have to do, I was told by battalion, is that after the bombing, the greatest of its kind ever attempted, we will get up out of our holes and move forward. The enemy soldiers will be either dead, wounded or so shell-shocked from the devastating effect of the bombing that they will be rendered useless." The platoon leaders, including this writer, must have reacted in such a way that the captain sensed he did not sound convincing. To front-line GIs, all Germans were at least nine feet tall and there were millions and millions of them.[27]

The fly boys were great when it came to the destruction of cities, fortifications, harbors, and what-have-you, but what did they know about working in coordination with ground troops, their own troops? That was another ball game, we muttered among ourselves. The plan called for over two hours of bombing in four waves: 350 fighter-bombers, 1,500 heavy bombers, 350 dive-bombers, and finally 350 mediums. Each wave would have a different mission, over a target area 6,000 yards wide and 2,500 yards deep. Almost 2,600 planes were operating over an area that small. I just couldn't believe it was possible. I wouldn't believe it, but I said nothing.[28]

The captain also told us that the 119th Regiment (all three battalions) would withdraw two thousand yards from its present positions before the bombing attack, better than a mile of precious territory won at a tremendous cost. I couldn't absorb that one either. The dutiful captain continued to the effect that the "bomb line" would be our present front-line positions and would be marked to guide the fly boys by the artillery with pink smoke shells.

We retired to our various platoon command posts and called in the squad leaders, in my case the section leaders. Cobra was explained, and my kids didn't find me credible any more than I did the captain. Nevertheless, they listened carefully. As always, I ordered each to get the information to the last man in each unit. All of this was to become known as the famous "St.-Lô Breakthrough."

On 24 July 1944 we cautiously withdrew under cover of darkness to former positions two thousand yards to the north. Some of us even found old familiar holes from days before, but we still had doubts and misgivings. In a few hours, the pink smoke shells could be heard whizzing south over our heads.

And then we heard it: the thunderous drone of many plane engines. I have never seen or heard anything like it, before or since. The early sun glistened on the silver fuselages against a clear, blue sky. They came in such a fashion that one imagined he was watching an event in a dazzling space age centuries ahead in history. Thousands and thousands, or so it seemed, of planes coming from the east like a gigantic flock of eager birds.

We crawled out of our holes. Tankers unbuttoned and climbed down off their tanks to watch the spectacle. I relaxed; the men relaxed. Boy, were "them Krauts" about to take a pasting. There was no ground fire from the direction of the enemy. We could understand why. They were, no doubt, trying to get as deep in Mother Earth as was humanly possible. The first wave of planes was now distinct. To the rear we could hear the deeper roar of the heavies.

The awesome "crrr. . .umph" of the 500-pounders could now be felt through the tremors in the earth beneath our feet. Instantly, I felt a chill run up and down my spine. Those babies are falling behind us, ten miles behind us, we found out later. We were about to be pounded by OUR OWN AIR FORCE!

The tankers threw their cerise banners at us. Frantically, we spread them along the tops of the hedgerows, over the beat-up apple trees, over the tanks, everywhere. Men fired yellow smoke pistols as if deranged, which they were. The banners and smoke pistols were designed for the purpose of indicating the locations of friendly troops for the benefit of the heroic fly boys upstairs. The crunching thuds drew nearer and nearer, and with no let up. In a panic we dove for holes. I recall being on top of two GIs in a hole about six feet deep and maybe three feet wide. The man on the bottom kept counting the beads on his rosary and muttering something in Latin. I can feel the beating heart of the man next to me to this day.

Those 500-pounders were upon us. All three of us were lifted off the bottom of that hole as if we were in one lump. The screaming projectiles seemed to fall like rain. I felt a heavy, confining weight above me. I tried to move and couldn't budge. The kids below squirmed helplessly. I ordered them to try to remain still. An eerie silence prevailed. Fortunately, rescue crews and medics were already at work. After what seemed to be an eternity, I determined that the confining weight was being removed. I scrambled off those soldiers and out of the life-saving hole. Helping hands pulled them out.

A giant tree had been severed close to its base and toppled across the opening of that blessed hole in such a way that I was not hurt but pinned and protected by the kindly tree. The sturdy edges and sides of the foxhole had held and kept the weight of the obstacle off of me. It was only through the combined efforts of a tank dozer and a tank with a chain that they were able to free the soldiers and me. In retrospect, I suspect this incident may have inaugurated my continuous bout with claustrophobia. The problem exists to this day.

Fox Company had suffered six dead and a dozen wounded. Two or three men were never found. We assumed they were buried or blown to bits. We were told a long time afterward that the first wave of P-47s and a squadron of heavies had dropped their bomb loads on us before the air offensive could be terminated. Lieutenant General Leslie J. McNair, Commanding General, Army Ground Forces, was in our sector as an observer when the bombs hit. He was killed instantly. It was said that he was in the vicinity of the 30th Division command post when the tragedy happened. My dislike for fly boys was ripening. Old Hickory was hit again by American bombers on 26 July 1944. Not as badly as before, but other divisional units took a pasting.

Bombing attacks, whether friendly or enemy, knock out telephones, radios, and various other forms of communication. Chaos follows. No one controls anything. That's exactly what happened at the St.-Lô tragedy. The whole mess got out of hand early and then could not be controlled in time. GI doubts were justified. Our pre-bombing skepticism proved to be correct.

The 119th Regiment like other shocked components did not shove off as scheduled after the so-called saturation attack. Morale was low as a result of the bombing errors. When we finally moved, we ran into trouble immediately. Our tanks had problems, too. We also had the task of recovering two thousand yards of territory previously won the hard way. Ranking commanders, including Hobbs, asked that air support for ground forces be withheld for the time being.[29]

Realizing what had happened and having suffered little, the Germans proceeded to smash our positions with the most terrifying 88-mm artillery barrage we had yet experienced. It seemed to me that the whole world was coming to an end. A shaken Fox Company found itself pinned down in a small and confined hedged pasture. The artillery fire was most intense, and the company was taking a bloody beating with direct fire on our holes. The men who were miraculously still unhurt were inviting disaster by cowering in their holes, frozen with fear and hysteria. I realized that our casualties would continue to mount unless we got the hell out of that horrible place. In the confusion, I was unable to locate the captain. I guess I must have lost my sanity or something. At any rate, I crawled out of my hole and began to scream and holler at anyone who might by chance be able to hear me. I indicated that I was leaving that hellhole and to follow me as far away from that concentration of fire as we could get. The shame of withdrawal never dawned on me. I was trying hard to save some GI fannies, including mine. Listening to my bellowing pleas, the surviving men began to move out and we were able to find safer positions that were not in the fire patterns of the enemy. We also managed to reorganize our depleted ranks and get set for the impending attack. It wasn't long until we did continue the attack with modest success. To this day, I do not know what happened to Parlavecchia. He appeared as we moved forward. When things returned to a semblance of normalcy, my personal reaction was to almost faint from fear and exhaustion. I'll wonder about that episode forever. I still can't believe that was "Old Folks" Arn, but it was nevertheless.[30]

By 26 July 1944 Hebecrevon was in our hands. During the day, advancing up a hill with a soldier right behind me, I sensed an enemy slug whizzing right past my ear. That was nothing particularly new, but I knew at once it was from a sniper's rifle. Split seconds later and then the sickening "thwack" of a bullet hitting a human body. The lad's helmet hit my heels. He rolled lifeless back down that rise. The sniper had caught him right between and just above his eyes, for his helmet displayed a neat, round hole slightly above the front rim. That youngster never knew what hit him. Knowing that the sniper was really after me,

I crawled over to Sgt. William W. Pierce, who commanded one of the mortar sections of Fox Company in my weapons platoon. "Pierce, see that line of trees along the top of this hill?" "Yes, sir." "There are snipers in there. Set up and let 'em have it." The sergeant obeyed promptly. Later, we found several dead or wounded Germans with rifles among those trees.

Just then I saw Captain Parlavecchia propped up against the side of a farm building. I moved over to him. I could tell that he was seriously wounded, having been hit in both the shoulder and the chest. Aid men were doing their best. One lit a cigarette and jammed it into the captain's mouth. He smiled faintly, and then his head dropped forward. Captain Parlavecchia was dead.

Second Lieutenant Melvin Riesch was now the CO of Fox Company. Second Lieutenant Arn was the only other officer in the company. It would be necessary for me to work closely with Riesch. I was made executive officer (second in command) of the company a bit later. For the present, platoon sergeants would command the four platoons. Riesch was decisive and cool, assuming command quietly and efficiently. I was to learn much from this brave man.

By 27 July 1944 the situation eased somewhat, and we moved south along the west bank of the Vire, nearing our regimental objective: Tessy-sur-Vire. At this point, we ran out of luck and smack dab into elements of the famed 2nd Panzer Division, a veteran outfit of impressive reputation. On the 29th, the 2nd Battalion of the 119th, with all four companies committed, smashed into this formidable foe. It was bitter. Even the tanks were firing at point-blank range. The smoke was so thick we could scarcely see one another. For the first time, Fox Company's riflemen were using their weapons with effect. Slowly, with the aid of some excellent artillery support, we pushed back those crack German troops. We were inching toward Troisgots.

More violent activity followed on the 30th. I was trying to get a squad over a hedgerow. We had received many replacements, and this squad was particularly green and hesitant. As always, I resorted to bullying and threatening, and in order to be more effective, I stood up. I knew better, of course. An enemy antitank shell struck an American tank to my right. I have never known what really happened. I can only assume that a piece of shrapnel from the German shell struck my pistol belt with a glancing blow, severed it, and in the process dropped my pistol belt down around my feet. I was spun around by the force of the impact and hurled against the hedgerow. I grabbed my stomach and screamed wildly for a medic. One came.

"Lieutenant Arn, you'll have to get your hands off your gut so I can determine how hard you've been hit," he shouted. "If I pull my hands away, you stupid bastard, my guts will fall out." I was mentally upended, for sure. He prevailed, loosened my pants, and found I had a flesh wound of about three inches in length across my lower tummy, right to left and not deep either. It would be more of a contusion, a painful one, than anything else. That blessed pistol belt had undoubtedly saved my life.

Embarrassed, I ordered the medic to get on with more serious work in evidence all around us. He slapped on sulfa powder and a bandage and crawled away, muttering to himself. He would tell his grandchildren how inadequate American officers were during the war. I know, for I have listened for years to tales of officers' frailties and weaknesses from former enlisted men who delight in saying, "I was offered a chance to go to Officer Candidate School but I turned it down."[31]

I resolved not to say anything about the incident and went back to work. It was easy to find another pistol belt on the battlefield. I can assure you there was no chance or need to secure a signed requisition from the supply sergeant where we were. I caught up with our people.

That evening a runner from Riesch's command post found me. I was to report to the CO at once. "I have heard that you have been hit." Riesch never wasted words. "It isn't anything, Mel, really." "Drop your pants and let me be the judge." I was astounded to note that I was black and blue from the bottom of the rib cage to places halfway to my knees on both legs. Riesch ordered me back to the Battalion Aid Station (BAS) at once. The BAS medical people could find nothing of a serious nature. I was told it was a wound received in action, and I would be awarded a Purple Heart. I didn't argue, acknowledged the award, and mailed it home 3 August 1944.[32]

As a precautionary measure, I was taken back to the division's Field Hospital (FH). Doctors, nurses, aid men, stretcher bearers all performed among horribly mangled men quite beyond the call of duty. Miracles were accomplished. They lost many, but they saved more. It was gratifying to know that America's wounded were in the best of hands.[33]

Upon my return to Fox Company, Tessy-sur-Vire had been taken by elements of the 30th, 35th, and the famous 2nd Armored Division, nicknamed "Hell on Wheels." Avranches fell to other units on our right. A corridor had been opened and Patton's Third Army moved through, swung west toward Paris and south toward Rennes. Operation Cobra was over at great cost.[34]

A respite followed, and that was good for Old Hickory. The division had been in contact with the enemy for forty-nine consecutive days. The lull was not to last long. "This stationery was taken from a German soldier, who is now a prisoner of war. I am the oldest man in my company. I must hit the hay, I mean my foxhole. All is well." (5 August 1944)

It was quite obvious to those of us who saw a situation map now and then that to remain and survive in France, the Germans had to try and close up the so-called "Avranches Gap" through which Patton's forces were now pouring. The German high command made a decision with Hitler screaming at them. A counterattack was ordered. Although we did not know it at the time, four enemy divisions would participate in their plan. The German commander, Field Marshall Günther von Kluge, was reluctant, but his maniacal superior in Berlin would not be denied.[35]

Generally, the counteroffensive would head west along the Sée Valley. Highways on both sides of the Sée River would form the axis of the attack. The Sée emptied into the English Channel. Avranches was the ultimate objective for recapture. Another objective in the German thrust was a town called Mortain. A hill rose sharply at the eastern edge of the town, which became known as Hill 314. If it fell to enemy hands, they would have excellent observation to the west of the Sée Valley, a distinct military advantage. It was most important that Mortain be held.

On divisional order, the 2nd Battalion of the 119th Regiment proceeded by truck to an area near the town of Vire, about fifteen miles north of Mortain. Eventually, we were to become involved with the 117th and 120th in an attack eastward toward the Seine River and Paris. A change came in the orders for the division from First Army Headquarters. The 30th, *without* our 2nd Battalion, was to proceed to Mortain and relieve the 1st Division. Big Red One would go on about the business of extending the American lines to the east. All of this seemed within normal army routine. It now seems quite certain our 30th Division Headquarters, nor even higher echelons of command, had any idea as to what von Kluge was planning.

I cannot remember, at least at my level, any contemplation of trouble. The division's 120th Regiment moved into Mortain itself, and took up the same positions previously held by elements of the 1st Division, including Hill 314. The 117th occupied St.-Bartelémy north of Mortain. The 119th, minus my 2nd Battalion operating in division reserve, moved into a position northeast of Mortain near a place called Juvigny.

Early on 7 August 1944 von Kluge attacked Mortain from the west and north in considerable force. Old Hickory was totally surprised. German penetration was good, and matters looked bad. Although supposedly in reserve, the 119th, without our 2nd Battalion, was having plenty of trouble on the left flank. It was finally forced out of reserve status and became quickly and thoroughly involved in the now-famous Battle of Mortain.

The engagement lasted for six days, until 14 August 1944. It was the first serious counterattack to be launched by the Germans since D-Day. The 30th, accidentally or not anticipated, bore the brunt of the German effort. Hill 314 was completely surrounded by German forces. The 120th Regiment seemed doomed. The German effort was repelled, but only after a complicated, bloody, and furious engagement. The American air support had a definite influence on the final outcome.[36]

Most historians agree that the 30th Division "saved the break out" and ensured the liberation of France. But Robert L. Hewitt's standard history of "Old Hickory," *Work Horse of the Western Front: The Story of the 30th Infantry Division*, published in 1946, sees fit to leave the 2nd Battalion and Fox Company in the vicinity of Vire during the action in and around Mortain. One receives the impression that only the 1st and 3rd Battalions of the 119th were involved.[37]

I have some vivid memories of the period 6–13 August 1944. It is true that we were not with the other two battalions, but I have always had the impression that we were constantly in touch with Colonel Sutherland's 119th Headquarters. It was located just west of Mortain. I am certain that our battalion moved south along the Vire-Mortain Highway, and I know we were engaged with the enemy the entire time. I recall elements of the 4th Division being adjacent to us. We were pinned down for hours, on one occasion in tank crossfire in a hedgerow field as enemy and American tanks fired point-blank at each other. I remember I tried to pull one of our men out of one of our tanks, but he was dead and I dropped him back into the tank. I got out of there. The steady thud of shrapnel outside my hole created complete and engulfing fear in my heart. To be pinned like that in a foxhole is a terrifying experience. Militarily, one is quite useless.

About this time, Fox Company received some forty replacement recruits. We hastily tried to jam them under tanks or some other meager protection, but even so by nightfall we had lost nearly all of them. Apparently, someone back in the rear echelon assumed we were not heavily engaged. I abhorred the stupidity and senselessness of sending those kids into that horrible situation. I still do.[38]

I can even recall watching with satisfaction the brilliant colors of the parachutes as they dropped supplies on the beleaguered 2nd Battalion of the 120th on Hill 314. We had to be fairly close to the overall battle. So, in my opinion, the 2nd Battalion, 119th Regiment, was involved and helped to repel von Kluge's forces in the vicinity of Mortain.[39]

It was a desperate move by Hitler to try to break through to Avranches. Actually, there were no prepared defenses behind von Kluge's forces in France. The nearest defense line was far to the east, the "West Wall" or "Siegfried Line" along the German border, which had not been occupied for years. To fail now would mean to leave France to the Allied Forces.

Fail they did, with the 30th Division making a major contribution to that failure, and the Germans began an exodus from France. "Sensational developments are about to come forth. You'll read about it long before this letter reaches you. I have only the clothes on my back, but I do have some friendly lice in those clothes. So, I will not be lonesome. I'm fine. Our food consists of K-rations only." (14 August 1944)

For the remainder of August 1944, Old Hickory ranged more than 500 miles across France, Belgium, and the southern tip of Holland. We reached the West Wall of Germany in early September.[40]

During this push, we were given little time to catch our breath. Lieutenant Riesch informed us that the Germans were planning to abandon France. We would go after them tooth and nail. Riesch, by the way, loved to tell us how much he hated Germans. He had convinced me long ago. On 16 August 1944 we were loaded on trucks and taken to an area near Domfront without incident, as near as I can recall. Domfront was captured without too much difficulty. We found many of the German prisoners of war were hopelessly drunk.

We now proceeded east on foot. The French were wild with joy, with their good wine and fiery Calvados, gin or vodka's first cousin, a dry brandy actually made from apples, grown in better days for centuries in those now torn-up Normandy orchards, thrust at us. One had to sip it; too strong to gulp. I never saw Calvados mixed with anything. Neat and powerful. Dynamite. Flowers were strewn in the streets, on the carriers and tanks, and even wrapped around muddy and scarred helmets. Women would often try to get into the vehicles with us. It wasn't easy to maintain even a semblance of order, or to keep that long column moving to the more serious business still before us.

Pinched out by the British, we held up for new orders. A couple of days passed. Our advance "is not nearly as glorious as your newspaper and radio correspondents are describing it. Not by a damned sight. It is just not possible for me to write very often. I know you'll understand." (18 August 1944) We moved again on trucks on the 19th. Our objective was Dreux, about forty miles west of Paris. We talked about being in Paris in ten days.

Once again we were foot soldiers. Twenty to thirty long, exhausting, dreary miles per day. Stonewall Jackson's boys in the Shenandoah Valley in Virginia had nothing on us.[41] As executive officer of the company, it was my responsibility to move up and down that long line and keep the stragglers moving. Fox Company had two jeeps each, one of which hauled an ammunition carrier. Many times I would get to the line of march where those two vehicles were chugging along, only to find many of our tired GIs riding the jeeps and carriers. Off they had to come. I'm sure I didn't gain any brownie points with the men. I had to handle those kids in a brutal manner, for we had no idea when or where the enemy might pounce upon us. I accomplished my purpose.

In a briefing session, Riesch told us we would hit the Main Line of Resistance (MLR) of the Germans along the Avre River. Bridges were blown when we got there, but the resistance was spotty and weak. We crossed just west of Nonancourt. Dreux fell. On we went swinging northeast toward the Seine River, away from Paris too, damn it. On 25 August 1944 the city of Paris was taken by the 4th Division and the French, the latter through the courtesy of General Eisenhower. We crossed the Eure River with little or no resistance, taking some exhausted and dirty prisoners of war. We also eliminated timid roadblocks as we proceeded.

Meanwhile, we found out later, Patton's Third Army was enjoying the headlines in America's newspapers as it raced across France through the Normandy breach created by a valiant First Army, of which the 30th Division was an important part. Evreux was next to the north. The 119th Regiment found itself perched on the high ground south of the city. French resistance groups were now helping out in an effective way. I think, although I am not sure, we bypassed Evreux.

Elements of the 30th mopped up in Louviers within five miles of the Seine. The 79th Division was fighting hard to hold its bridgehead at Mantes-Gassicourt on the Seine. The high ridge on the north bank was giving the Germans a decided advantage. On 27 August 1944 Old Hickory came up to assist the 79th and to take over the eastern sector of the bridgehead. The 117th and 120th crossed the river. The 119th proceeded northeast along the river, but attracted heavy mortar and machine gun fire almost immediately. A three-day battle raged around the bridgehead with Fox Company right in the middle of things. I recall we had heavy losses that called for many personnel adjustments within the platoons. Frequently, a sergeant had to absorb considerable responsibilities. Had the enemy been stronger, we would have been held up much longer. As it was, we knew we had been confronted with a strong delaying action.[42]

Some of our prisoners of war came from the German Luftwaffe (Air Force), fighting as infantrymen. They told us that this was because the Luftwaffe had been practically annihilated.[43] At any rate, we finally broke out of the situation at the Seine, and continued our drive to the north and east. We took the town of Pontoise.

After getting out of the Seine Valley on a clear day, one of our sergeants borrowed my field glasses, climbed a lofty barn roof, and yelled down that he could see the Eiffel Tower in Paris, several miles upriver and southeast of our position. I never knew whether that lad was telling the truth or not, but it was as close as I would get to Paris for many weeks.

We boarded troop carriers with Fox Company's two jeeps sandwiched in between, and off we went in a northerly direction hell-bent for the Belgian border, more than a hundred miles away. At one spot an artillery forward observer and I, at his invitation and during a rest halt, cautiously approached a high ridge over looking the valley of the Oise River. We had perfect observation. Suddenly, a dozen or so American P-38s swooped in from the west and proceeded to strafe a long line of fleeing Germans on a highway stretching out before us. They had become so desperate for fuel that some of the heavy equipment was being pulled by horses. The .50 caliber slugs streaking from those relentless planes soon tore large holes in the concrete highway, as well as men and horses. It was really a rather sickening slaughter, and the fly boys had a ball. I was secretly grateful that the planes were American and not Luftwaffe, and that F Company was not strung along that fateful highway on that particular day.

Although we were moving surprisingly well, our supporting artillery would often set up behind us and would be prepared to fire in the event we ran into trouble. If not, they would move up as we moved up. On this day, after the P-38s had had their fun, my forward observer friend handed me powerful field glasses. He pointed. I picked up a lone German soldier creeping around a haystack. From his movements, it was obvious he was about to relieve himself. No more, no less. He unbuckled his belt and let his pants down. The forward observer, using his ever-present radio, gave a firing target, to my amazement, back to his battery. Soon I could hear the 105-mm shell swishing overhead. It landed beyond the stack. The forward observer radioed a correction while the unfortunate Kraut merely raised his head. The next round was short, but closer. The soldier executed a hurried conclusion to his elimination. Another correction. This time a direct hit on the haystack. The enemy GI and the stack were blown into the four corners of the compass. My faith in the division's 105-mm Cannon Company's accuracy was more than confirmed. The forward observer moved away with a swagger of confidence.

The Germans seemed to be in headlong flight. Our next divisional objective was the city of Cambrai, about thirty miles south of the Belgian border. On 1 September 1944 Old Hickory's dash began. On the division's left was the 2nd Armored Division. On the right was the 28th Infantry Division, known as the "Keystone Division" from Pennsylvania, later to receive heavy blows in the Battle of the Bulge.

No one told us there would be some strong points of enemy resistance. Leave it to the infantry to find them. According to our intelligence reports, the Germans had vanished into thin air. Nevertheless, the ever-cautious General Hobbs had created a very mobile and powerful task force under General Harrison, Hobbs' executive officer.

Our 119th Regiment was positioned right behind "Task Force Harrison," whose mission it was to clear the way for the division's long line of men, vehicles, etc. As usual, intelligence had muffed it. The task force became involved in small, close-in firefights. Mopping up each enemy unit, the task force kept moving north. The FFI (Free French Forces of the Interior) helped considerably along the flanks of our thrust by rounding up prisoners of war after the task force passed through. I imagine that some of that dirty work would have been the assignment of the 119th, but we didn't mind the FFI's enthusiasm one bit. That evening Task Force Harrison reached Péronne on the Somme River, a bit west of the famous World War I city of St.-Quentin.

The 30th Division had been fighting with the XIX Corps as a part of the First American Army under the command of Lieutenant General Courtney H. Hodges ever since the division landed in Normandy. Three Corps made up the First Army at this time: the XIX under Major General Charles H. Corlette, the VII under Major General J. Lawton Collins, and the V under Major General Leonard T. Gerow. Lieutenant General George S. Patton commanded the Third Army, which consisted of the VIII, XII, XV, and XX Corps. Patton's Third Army was advancing north also to the right flank of the First Army.

The task force neared Cambrai on 2 September 1944 but held up because of a diminishing supply of fuel. It waited and waited for replenishments that never came. The redoubtable Harrison ordered the task force forward anyway, with the remaining elements of the 30th Division now stretched out along the Cambrai-Paris Highway. During the early hours of the third, at a point just south of Cambrai, the task force ran into some serious opposition. The general's jeep was hit by some 20-mm fire just as he leaped into the road's ditch. Harrison was wounded slightly, and Colonel Sutherland, the 119th's CO, took command of the task force that swept on into Cambrai.

[Arn much admired] the courage and boldness of General Harrison, a 1917 West Point graduate, who became a lieutenant general during the Korean War and the chief negotiator at Panmunjom. [An incident that occurred in November 1944] illustrates Harrison's leadership qualities.

I can't remember the town to save me. It was in Germany. Fox Company was given the assignment to take this particular town. I was now in command. The town was occupied by veteran dug-in German infantry, and the artillery fire was really zeroed-in. I managed to maneuver my kids into the town, but the artillery was so intense I decided to pull the company back out to the high ground west of the place under cover of darkness. It must have been sunup. I was in my hole, studying my map, and ignoring the screams of battalion headquarters on my field phone and radio: "Are you moving?" "Are you moving?"

I was saying to myself, "There must be a way to take this damned town without sacrificing the whole company." A plan was beginning to dawn on me, but it would require air and artillery support. I was in communication with our artillery forward observer, but he was giving me some static: lack of battery fire in this particular area, etc. Battalion headquarters have been deaf, because they weren't sympathetic to what I was trying to do at all.

I was beginning to envision Arn going all the way back to battalion headquarters personally to secure the kind of support I knew I had to have. There was a commotion above and behind me. I peered out and in the early morning gloom. I was astounded to recognize General Harrison himself. He said in used-to-authority tones, "Are you the CO of this unit?" "Yes, sir. I am Lieutenant Edward Arn, sir." I was almost stuttering. "What's holding you up, Lieutenant?" I explained my situation. My previous occupation of the town had been too high in human lives. I had withdrawn my company in order to take a second look at the situation. With proper support, which I was having difficulty obtaining, I planned to enter the town as soon as feasible. "What do you want?" I could see his fine mind working fast. "An airstrike and a ten-minute artillery concentration before shove-off, sir." "Will that do it?" "I believe it will, sir."

He held out his hand, "Good work, Lieutenant. You'll get the help you need. Take that town." His jeep roared away. I did get the help of the type I needed, and that town was taken with a minimum of casualties, which was always important to me. Lieutenant General William K. Harrison was a great officer. We line companies needed more men like him.[44]

Back to the current situation. In order not to lose any of its momentum, "Task Force Sutherland" moved on through a crowded and littered Valenciennes, and during the late afternoon hours crossed into Maulde, Belgium. Arguably, the 30th Division (elements thereof) comprised the first American troops to enter Belgium, which had suffered under the German yoke for four years. By early evening, Old Hickory had forward units in Tournai, Belgium, northwest of Valenciennes.

As far as we dogfaces in Fox Company were concerned, the Battle of France was over. Now, all of this northward slant toward the Belgian border was not accomplished as easily as it is for me to write about it, nor as easily as it may sound to the reader. The 119th, as usual, managed to get into several engagements in the assembly area of Tournai, for we had moved too far, too fast, and we were so thin the enemy kept tormenting us as he withdrew. We would now have to wait for gasoline, ammunition, and food to catch up with us.

[During this rapid movement, a number of events affected Arn.] For example, intelligence reports would give us warnings of possible strong points up ahead. Frequently, we would de-truck and advance on foot in battle formation upon the indicated enemy concentrations. After we had left the Mortain area in mid-August 1944, Fox Company was moving with two platoons in front across an open wheat field. I didn't like the looks of things, but Riesch never seemed to be bothered by situations of this nature. The wheat was about two feet high and ready for harvest. I had become noted for my hunches. I just knew that the enemy was in position along the high ground just ahead of us. They were. Halfway across that field, they opened up on us with 20-mm guns and rifle fire. The company, to a man, was in the prone position in split seconds. I have every reason to believe that I was two feet down in the soft earth, beneath the wheat, in less than a minute. I could use that shiny trench shovel with a skill that could only emerge from sheer terror.

I raised my head carefully only to find our CO (Riesch) standing erect and studying the enemy positions with his field glasses. Since I was still the only other officer in the company (others had come and gone) and Riesch was drawing fire, I went into action. I bolted across the few feet that separated us, and put a tackle on him that would have pleased many a football coach. Down we went with enemy slugs whipping around us. We dug deep, both of us.

He didn't say much and seemed sort of subdued. The circumstances didn't allow for much communication, although I did get a plan across to him. Hurriedly, we sent a platoon crawling and crouching around to the flank of the enemy position, a sort of end-run maneuver, and succeeded in subduing a not-too-enthusiastic and worn-out squad of Hitler's best. That evening Riesch thanked me for what I had done. I think he finally realized that as a company commander, with replacement officers so scarce, he had been far too reckless. I had two purposes: to save him from injury or possible death, because I didn't want a rifle company, and to preserve my own fanny.

Another time, again on foot, we had moved to an open, woods-fringed pasture. The Germans detected our presence and opened fire from positions in the woods on the opposite side of the pasture. We responded, and things were hot and heavy for a few minutes with casualties unusually high for such a small exchange. The medics were busy. Foolishly, a few enemy fanatics attempted to charge at us across that bit of open field. Fox Company's riflemen didn't miss many. Survivors scrambled frantically back into the woods. It seemed to me and to those near me that we could hear them retreating pell-mell deep into the forest. It was a ruse, I thought. Anyway, we stood up and proceeded to administer aid to our wounded people. Some of the men even lit cigarettes. Then we heard a vehicle crashing through the trees. A carefully marked German ambulance emerged into the open.

"Hold your fire," Riesch barked. It was supposed to be an international rule of warfare never to fire upon a vehicle displaying the medical cross. Further, there were several German soldiers needing help in that little place. The ambulance roared to the center of the clearing, turned quickly, the rear double doors burst open and a machine gun opened fire from the interior of the vehicle, a neat, illegal, under-the-belt maneuver. We took more casualties before we could secure ample cover. One of our mortar sections set up, cleared the trees, a necessity for mortar fire else the lofting shells would burst down upon the firing crew, and planted several rounds right on the top of that ambulance within just a few ticks of the clock. The ambulance was demolished and so was the crew inside. I had a cautious attitude toward enemy ambulances after that horrible experience.

I also recollect that we had a brave medic in the company by the name of Rooney, if my memory serves me correctly. He was a skinny kid from somewhere in Dixieland. He had the usual slow moves and drawl, but was an incredibly courageous chap. He had performed all sorts of feats rescuing wounded men while under fire and dragging them to safety. I had become a great admirer of Rooney. I even envied him a bit and wished that I had his guts. He was so careless about his own well-being that I just knew we would lose him eventually.

One morning, in a situation long forgotten, we were subject to an intense artillery barrage. With my usual skill I dove into a nearby foxhole. Someone landed on top of me. It was Rooney. I made room for him. "Pretty fierce. Eh, Lieutenant?" he drooled at me through the grime and sweat. I took one look, and then I knew. "Rooney, let me have that canteen of yours." "Why?" he whined. "Hand it over. Now!" I unscrewed the cap, and I found Rooney's courage. It was in his canteen, in the form of alcohol from the Battalion Aid Station. Well, I couldn't requisition enough liquor for everybody in Fox Company even though our ranks were tragically depleted. Neither could I allow Rooney to continue his exhibition of false courage. I had him evacuated to the rear. Never saw him again. Ironically, we never had a medic of his quality again.[45]

In another instance in one of the towns, I've forgotten which one, the column's movement stopped longer than usual and we could hear the crowd roaring and hooting up ahead. Riesch ordered me to investigate. I found the reason for the hold up. Crouched forlornly against a huge cathedral's doors was a pretty teenaged girl as nude as the day she was born. The jeering crowd was pelting her head to feet with rotten eggs, overripe tomatoes, and most anything else the frenzied horde could lay its hands on. Her closely shaved head looked odd, and I remember asking myself if I had ever seen a shaven female head before. I had not. I could not let this go on even though I quickly realized that these outraged French people were venting their disgust and resentment on a person who had collaborated with the Germans during the occupation of France. I ordered the nearest soldiers to join me, although I had a feeling they were enjoying the spectacle. As soon as we gathered around her, the throwing stopped. A thoughtful soldier handed me a GI blanket. We wrapped her up in it, a bleeding, bruised, filthy girl. Two medics appeared with a stretcher, and she was removed to the nearest aid station. Then, I waited for the expected anger of the crowd. The GIs waited with me. We were too respected and admired at that time anyway for further demonstration. The crowd quickly lost interest, and the column began to move once more.[46]

I was later to learn that the Allied Forces spent considerable time and effort in the prevention of injury or even loss of life to collaborators before the due process of law could take charge. It was a serious problem for the Military Government (MG) people who would take charge of an area after the combat personnel moved on.

On another occasion, Sgt. Beatty and I were cowering in our holes, which we had dug behind a farmer's abandoned cultivating disc. Beatty told me during a lull he felt certain he would never make it back home. Now Beatty was one of perhaps only a few soldiers who joined Fox Company when it was formed back in the States to still be with us. He was an excellent soldier. I recall admonishing him, as enemy rounds kept pinging off the blades of that disc, for talking so negatively. I reminded him that when a combat soldier sounded off in such a manner, he usually got hit. He smiled rather sadly, lit a cigarette, rose slightly to look around, took his first puff, and then I heard that familiar thud of a bullet hitting the human body. Beatty simply sighed and sank back into his hole. He died instantly, proof that a fighting man who looks to the future convinced that he's not going to get through the mess can draw that fatal ending upon himself.[47]

[Arn also recalled] a genial chap named Lew Klewer, our 119th Regiment's Red Cross Field Director. I can see him now as he and his jeep driver would visit with us if the situation would so permit. He always had ample supplies of stationery, which were free, and usually he would disperse gum, candy, and cigarettes, all also free. More importantly, Klewer could be very helpful if a soldier had a problem of some sort back home. He would use the Red Cross facilities geared for such service. For example, I had not received any mail for weeks and I was concerned about my Dad's health. Klewer went into action, and soon handed me a Red Cross report from home. "Arn's father is recovering from his infected foot and is able to get about with a cane. Arn's divorce is completed; insurance beneficiaries have been changed as requested, and all money orders are coming through on schedule." I was relieved and impressed with the Red Cross's efficiency. Years later, while on a business trip to Toledo, I discovered that Klewer was the outdoors editor for the *Toledo Blade*. I had the privilege of thanking him once more. [48]

By early September, Old Hickory was solidly astride the Meuse River and the Albert Canal in the Liège, Belgium sector. "Somewhere in Belgium. We are moving fast. Lieutenant Malcolm Scott is our battalion S-2 (Intelligence) officer. He tells me that the *Cleveland Plain Dealer* has many stories in it about our division. The people of France and Belgium are delirious with joy as we liberate town after town. They swarm all over our vehicles. Dad, you guessed right on the number of my division. As you may have also guessed, we have advanced through several famous WWI battlefields to get where we are now. The women are most attractive but I have men's lives, weapons, and a war on my hands; later, maybe. I guess I'll be a bachelor forever. I want only to get back to my parents and my job. Things look good, but you get more news than I. We're trying to finish this thing up. I have been executive officer of the company for some time. Riesch has put me in for a first lieutenancy."[49] (5 September 1944)

The drive to liberate southern Holland was now underway. We wheeled east and north toward the ancient Dutch city of Maastricht. We reached Visé, Belgium, with little opposition. Maastricht and the Dutch border were only about three miles to the north. "I am writing with a German pen that I 'secured' from a German soldier I caught as he was climbing over a fence the other day. I am in a humble Belgian kitchen. They heat water for us and feed us boiled potatoes, onions, and garlic. Don't send me anything but letters. I'm not changed much physically, except I'm thinner. The Good Lord has been kind." (11 September 1944)

The 119th advanced north into Holland on 13 September 1944 with forward reconnaissance units in Maastricht. Fox Company was engaged in a sharp skirmish for Margraten, Holland, a small town just outside Maastricht. The resistance withdrew at nightfall, and, as usual, Riesch ordered me to secure the town. I recall placing two rifle platoons in defensive positions for the night. In doing so, I passed the body of a blonde, blue-eyed (still open) German officer. His well-made German boots were in excellent shape and about my size. I made a mental note that I would return for those boots as soon as I carried out Riesch's orders. I returned. His socks told me I was too late. My curiosity outweighed my disappointment. Someone in Fox Company had those damned boots. Maybe. Who? I never saw those boots again. A civilian? Perhaps.

The attack continued east. The 30th Division Headquarters was set up in Maastricht. The Wurm River, which forms the border between south Holland and Germany, was our objective. We could smell those Krauts and their homeland. The small town of Waubach nestled on the west bank of the Wurm. It lay directly before Fox Company in the 119th's sector. As darkness closed in, our forward platoon reached the outskirts of the battered town. Riesch ordered me to find a suitable company command post in the town, for he had reason to believe that we might be there for a while. Find one "with enough building left to provide cover from the weather," he grunted, and made preparations to wait for the results of good old Arn's reconnoitering.

"But lieutenant, it's almost dark now. The enemy, as far as we know, is all over this place. The town is thoroughly zeroed in by German artillery across the river and there is little actual protective cover anywhere," I complained. "You heard me, Arn, take some men and get moving. When you find a location send back a runner." When Riesch was in this mood, it was of little use to argue. I selected four or five well-armed men and entered the town. Inwardly, I reasoned that all of this could have been done in the morning when we could see better.

Cautiously and slowly, I moved forward. There was not a sign of life anywhere. We had to literally pick our way through the bomb-cratered streets, crumbled buildings, and torn-up sidewalks. Occasionally a German shell would crash among the buildings and in the streets. It suddenly dawned on me that we were receiving opposing fire for the first time from Germany itself, unless we would run into a rear action group of infantrymen in the town itself.

The men behind me agreed silently with me. "This was not the time for this sort of mission," they muttered into their fatigues. Groping in the darkness, I selected a street that seemed to slope downward, ever so slightly. I convinced myself that we would eventually end up on the banks of the Wurm with all of Germany on the other side. That damned river couldn't be more than a few hundred yards away. There was also the eerie reminder that perhaps only an hour or so ago, the whole town had been infested with rear-guard enemy troops fighting in such a way as to delay our forward movement to the river. They could still be hidden here in the shadows of those ruined buildings. And what about mines? God, never thought of that. I stumbled my way ahead, pausing now and then for familiar sounds that I really didn't want to hear. I could find nothing that would meet Riesch's terms for a command post. I was about to turn back and endure Riesch's ire.

Then an outline of a dwelling loomed high against the gray sky, maybe two stories high and worth investigating. I turned into a side entrance. It was a solid brick edifice. I noted a thin edge of light around the blacked-out basement windows. A stove pipe protruded through one of them. I smelled smoke. The poor beggars are actually living in their basement, I said to myself. I tried the side door. Locked. I ordered one of the men to join me. "Break the damned door down." Heavy GI boots complied. The door gave. I peered into the semi-darkness, and guessed from the worn furniture that this had been the family's dining room. To my immediate right was the cellar door. Again, a faint light glimmered around the door's entrance. It, too, was bolted.

"Open up," I shouted in English. What else? I certainly couldn't speak Dutch. Silence. I could hear my men breathing heavily behind me. Slowly, the lock turned and the door opened. A face peered out at me blinking in the glare of my flashlight. A plain, honest, fatigued, careworn face of a man. I shouted at him in a rather stupid way, and, shaking his head, he backed down the cellar passageway. I followed him, flashlight in one hand and my .45 cocked and ready in the other. Cowering over in the corner of that tiny basement were four people, the man who had been at the doorway, a woman about his age, a girl, and an old woman. They waited, frightened and breathing hard. I knew they had never seen American soldiers before. I managed a smile of friendship or some such. The younger of the adult females straightened up, and in horrible and fearful English asked, "American?" I nodded. The brave soul relaxed, jabbered away at her family, and Riesch had his damned command post.

After establishing security in defending foxholes around the command post, we placed the rest of the company in quarters, of a sort, in neighboring basements. Fox Company's command post was located in the home of the Dautzenberg family. Gerhardt was a coal miner. His wife's name was Johanna. His daughter was Bertien, or Bertha in English. She was about twelve. The older lady was Johanna's mother. I cannot recall her name. The family was actually living in that confining basement, cooking meals, sleeping, and praying for the Allies to come and liberate them. They were most grateful.

The house had been hit several times but not too seriously. Johanna showed Riesch and me a room on the second floor with two single wooden beds. The CO and I were welcome to sleep there. The Dautzenbergs had wisely, long since, chosen the basement. Riesch was pleased with Johanna's generosity. I wasn't. I didn't like sleeping on that second floor; too vulnerable even to stray shells. I sweated it out in the nights that followed, for I refused to show my intrepid CO my restless concern. Riesch slept like a baby. I preferred low, deep places.

Our Top Kick (First Sergeant), Thomas H. Kirkman of Miami, and little Bertien became the best of friends. As Top Kick, he had much to do, and Bertien would dart from building to building with him, much to my concern and that of her family. Waubach was subject every day to sporadic shell fire from the German batteries across the river. Casualties were relatively light because we, most of us, were hardened veterans by now and never took any measures to welcome injuries. Meanwhile, our own artillery would hammer away at the German positions. It must have been hell for the Dutch civilians in Waubach. I wondered how Americans in a similar plight would act as I watched the Dautzenbergs and others as they courageously proceeded with the business of staying alive.

"I am sitting in a Dutch family's sitting room. I must confess that I am in the midst of some of the most exciting adventures a man can go through. But there is more in store; that I know." (14 September 1944) "Yesterday, I took a sponge bath in a Dutch wash basin. Jerry, by the way, is far from licked at the moment. You'll see what I mean in a few days. Please don't send me food. It's moldy and stale when I receive it." (24 September 1944) "Still in the Dutch home. Rain of the drizzle type, mud, cold at night, but we are managing to keep dry." (26 September 1944)

The Allies were in a delaying action in the sectors south of Field Marshal Sir Bernard Montgomery's futile and disastrous attempt to shorten the war. The plan that Montgomery sold to Eisenhower was to combine the airborne forces of the Allies, and to drop them behind the German lines at Eindhoven, Nijmegen, and Arnhem, all in central and north Holland. The initial objective was to capture the crucial bridge across the Rhine River at Arnhem. Through that breach a vast army would drive on east to Berlin. The surprise factor would facilitate the whole offensive thrust. The plan became known as "Operation Market Garden."

Unfortunately, the American 101st, 82nd, the British 1st Airborne Divisions, and the 1st Polish Airborne Brigade landed in areas where German panzer divisions were engaged in rehabilitating and conducting field training for replacement troops. Immediate resistance developed. The Arnhem Bridge was never taken, although the British troops, suffering huge losses, fought valiantly for it. Total casualties, for the effort, exceeded those of D-Day. The abortive maneuver lasted from 14 September through 24 September 1944. It ended in a complete defeat for the Allies. Montgomery's star fell.[50]

At that time, I can't recall hearing anything that concerned Operation Market Garden. We knew we were being delayed, but we really didn't know why, not at our infantry rifle company level. So we went about the business of issuing new equipment, cleaning and replacing weapons, storing up fuel and food, and just generally preparing for the First Army's assault into the pillboxes of the Siegfried Line or West Wall, just across the Wurm River in Germany.

"Today, your son, Edward, became a first lieutenant and Melvin Riesch, our CO, became a captain. Nevertheless, we have much discomfort up ahead." (27 September 1944) I was putting it mildly, as it turned out.

On 2 October, we left our friends in Waubach to launch the renewed offensive against the Germans. Bertien cried as she bid Kirkman goodbye. Riesch merely nodded in a preoccupied way. I knew, however, that if I got through the war alive I would remain in touch with these brave, resourceful people for years to come. And I did.

A new chapter in the story of this horrible conflict was about to be written. My seat on the fifty-yard line would have the same occupant, but the Allied honeymoon was over. There would be no more dashing through towns on wheels to the joyous shouts of the people. We were once again about to engage in a fierce struggle against a still formidable and determined foe, fighting on his own soil at last and with his back to the wall.

5. A Fierce Struggle Renewed

2 October 1944–15 December 1944

In early October Allied forces readied for the invasion of Germany by thrusting into the Roer River area and beyond. Barring the way stood the tough Siegfried Line. After the Allies failed to flank this position in Operation Market Garden during September, the high command opted for a more direct attack at the Line's northern side at Aachen. Since Aachen also carried immense psychological importance, being the first German city the Allies targeted for capture, the Wehrmacht defended Aachen with fury. The 30th Division fought back with equal ferocity. Arn and Fox Company were in the midst of this bloody combat. They helped capture Aachen in nearly three weeks of bloody combat, completed the encirclement of the city, joined in breaching the Siegfried Line, and drove toward the Roer. Nothing came easily. The cost in men and equipment proved staggering. At Aachen alone, Old Hickory lost nearly three thousand men and Fox Company took 61.9 percent casualties, mostly among young and embittered replacements fresh from the Army Specialized Training Program. Allied commanders recognized the division needed time for repair and resupply. By the end of November, Fox Company took its turn, rotating to a quiet area in the rear for rest, rehabilitation, and the integration of still more fresh troops and materiel. No one among the Allies expected what would come next.

The September attempt to flank the Siegfried Line and seize Arnhem had failed. The defeat was regrettable, for the movement might have resulted in bringing the war to a conclusion much sooner than was now anticipated.[1] By midafternoon on the second of October 1944, Fox Company had reached the west bank of the Wurm River, which was surprisingly narrow but possessed of a swift current at the point of our attack. We had encountered no German soldiers on the Dutch side, but the mortar, machine gun, and cannon fire from the high ground and beyond in Germany were very effective. The 30th's combat engineers had constructed a Bailey Bridge at considerable cost over the Wurm. Against stubborn enemy resistance, most of the 119th's people were on German soil by midnight. A Second Lieutenant Baird had joined us in Waubach and he was now platoon leader of our Second Platoon. That unit was now the lead platoon in F Company's attack plan.[2]

Old Hickory planned to turn south after getting into the pillbox line, straddle it, and hook up with American troops hammering away at the edges of the ancient city of Aachen. It was a formidable but typical assignment for the division. To me, it meant that the division's eastern flank would be exposed to the enemy, which would invite counterattacks and constant harassment. Chancellor Hitler ordered his increasingly skeptical high command to hold Aachen at all costs. The battle there on the Wurm continued the next morning. Rimberg Castle, directly in front of Fox Company and others of the 119th's 2nd Battalion, was about 150 yards east of the river and would be the immediate objective.[3]

Captain Riesch and I were standing in a huge double doorway of a U-shaped barn on the Dutch side of the river, studying our map and trying to decide what to do next. We knew that the enemy was in that castle and in strength. We could even see an imposing Tiger Tank drawn up in front of the main entrance.[4] We were also aware that some of our people had reached a group of outlying buildings that, I later learned, comprised a combination of apartments and the castle gatekeeper's quarters. Just a few moments before, Riesch had motioned to me to crawl over to him on the enemy side of the barn's south wing of

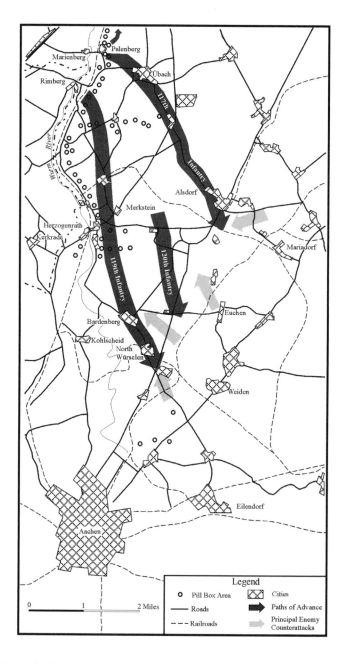

Map 3. Aachen and the attack on the Siegfried Line, 2 October 1944–16 October 1944. (Hewitt, pg. 92)

the U. He pointed to the heavily wooded high ground to the left of the castle. I noted a movement in the underbrush at the base of the trees.

Riesch was disdainful of the army's M-l Garand rifle. He always carried an old, well-oiled, and super clean Springfield, bolt-operated '03 rifle. The piece was even equipped with a special telescope sight mechanism. Riesch was an expert, an excellent shot. A German soldier was crouched in the coloring foliage. He had little idea that he was about to take leave of this mortal earth. The captain calmly balanced his '03 on the rusting spokes of a hay rake's wheels, took aim, and squeezed the trigger. I would guess his target was about two hundred yards away. The unfortunate Kraut never knew what hit him. His body tumbled into the river. With a grunt of satisfaction, Riesch turned back to me and our plans for the day. I made no comment.

Presently, an artillery shell hit the barn at the base of the U and perhaps fifty feet from where we were standing again in the doorway. It could have been a tiny piece of shrapnel or some sharp fragment from the barn itself. At any rate, the captain slumped against me without uttering a sound and, together, we dropped back inside the barn on the hay-covered floor. I yelled frantically for a medic. The din of battle was everywhere, and our medics were occupied elsewhere. No medic came.

I ripped at the captain's fatigues trying to find a point of entry. A small trickle of blood ran slowly from one corner of his mouth. I knew then where to look. I found a small opening in the left side of his chest. Whatever object had hit him had done so with tremendous velocity. Captain Melvin Riesch had succumbed instantly. [Arn cherished Riesch's memory. As he explained,] Mel was a dedicated soldier. He held the Bronze and Silver Stars at the time of his death. We would miss his cool leadership.

I laid him back on the hay and was wrapping him up in his tattered raincoat when 1st Sgt. Tom Kirkman dashed into the barn. He knelt down, took one look at the captain, and then at me. "Lieutenant Arn, you are now commander of this rifle company." Torn with shock and sadness, I felt like running which, by the way, was not an unusual feeling for me.

Somehow, I knew instinctively that "Top" expected a soldierly atti-

Captain Melvin L. Riesch, one-of-a-kind.

tude in a crisis such as this. So, feigning a calmness that was as unreal as hell, I yelled: "Yes, Top, and may I remind you that should anything happen to me (Lieutenant Baird had been seriously wounded that morning) and we do not receive any officer replacements, you are next in line to take command of Fox Company." He gulped and nodded his acknowledgment of that bothersome reality. It would be up to me to try to determine if I could pull on, let alone fit, Riesch's capable, courageous combat boots. For the rest of that memorable day, I was so busy my fear deserted me. Fox Company had a CO who was not too far away from his thirty-sixth birthday. The civilian in uniform had really come of age.

The 30th Division was now an element, along with the 2nd Armored and 29th Infantry Divisions of the XIX Corps, known as the Tomahawk Corps and commanded by Major General Raymond S. McClain. Major General Ernest N. Harmon was the leader of the 2nd Armored. Nicknamed "Hell on Wheels," Harmon's outfit had served admirably in North Africa and had arrived in Normandy on 14 June 1944 at Carentan. The 29th, under Major General Charles H. Gerhardt, had landed at Omaha Beach on D-Day. The division had captured St.-Lô, and played a major role in the campaign in Brittany and the surrender of Brest. The 30th was in good company.

The Siegfried Line or "West Wall," as the Germans called it, consisted of a fortified, defensive line of concrete pillboxes and emplacements extending from Kleve on the Dutch frontier in the north to Lorrach near Basle at the Swiss border. Built by the Germans to counter the French Maginot Line, the West Wall had no provision for open artillery earthworks. A pillbox was usually half underground, thirty feet by fifty feet in size, twenty feet to thirty feet in height. Overall, the walls and roofs were made of concrete, four feet to eight feet thick. The gun apertures, however, provided a limited field of fire, a fifty-degree arc at the maximum. The Germans had neglected the West Wall for years, thus helping the growth of Mother Nature's camouflage: grass, weeds, bushes, etc. that made the detection of the pillboxes difficult at times.

In the XIXth Corps area, the German engineers had constructed the Line in such a way that the Wurm River became an excellent natural obstacle to an attacking force. In other words, the pillbox layout tied in nicely with the river, its bends, and its banks. In and around Übach, the pillboxes were installed to a depth of two miles in staggered formation. The Wurm in our sector reached widths of about thirty feet. Long before, the Germans had established good observation of the river that made the combat engineers' job of constructing bridges across it very difficult.

There was plenty of high ground beyond most of the Wall, providing further opportunity for excellent defense. The Wall's original concept was to delay the enemy and then to hit him hard with counterattacks. The prepared fields of fire were excellent. Telephone wires, six feet under the ground, connected the pillboxes. Adding to the effective deception, the pillboxes were camouflaged as barns, houses, garages, even haystacks.

While the 30th was trying to reach Aachen to the south, the greater mission of the entire Tomahawk Corps was to rupture the Siegfried Line and continue east to the Rhine River in the Düsseldorf-Cologne area. The Palenberg-Rimberg sector was chosen as the point of the initial assault.

Captain Riesch had been thoroughly briefed during our two weeks' stay in Waubach on where particular pillboxes were supposedly located in our Fox Company's sector. I found excellent photo maps in his musette bag. He had made one unfortunate mistake. He had not briefed Executive Officer Arn as thoroughly as he should have. Thus, my new assignment became that much more difficult.

From the swishing sound of the stuff going out, I did know that we had been laying down a heavy artillery barrage from 26 September 1944 to 2 October 1944, the first day of the American effort. The XIXth Corps artillery had been concentrating on about forty-five pillboxes to our division's front. We were to find out in the days ahead that some of them had been damaged, and that German antiaircraft installations had been all but eliminated. In the initial assault, Fox Company was part of a two regiment thrust that found the 119th and the 117th abreast with the 120th in reserve.

Enemy "tree burst" shells hitting the tops of trees and detonating above ground didn't help to lessen the intensity of the situation. We soon discovered that their observation posts (OPs) were giving them excellent target pictures from the high ground behind Rimberg Castle. Other units of the 119th attacked Rimberg Castle from the north and south flanks. Fox Company attacked frontally, as near as I can recall.

It is with a still-nervous reaction that I remember the awful bedlam created by the noise and smoke when the fighting got underway from room-to-room within the castle itself. One of our men or perhaps someone from another outfit, I'm really not sure, developed a technique which was nicknamed "mouse-holing." Well-placed bazooka shells were fired to knock holes in the walls of the rooms, allowing men to slip through the openings without having to use the hallways. Enemy personnel would have those passages thoroughly covered at the ends in effective firing positions. It was mean and bloody, but the 119th Regiment, including Fox Company, cleared that castle after two days of close-in combat with a stubborn foe. The castle had four turrets, one at each corner of the brick, stone, and mortar building. I recall that one turret was completely destroyed. The whole building took a terrific beating, as one can imagine.[5]

A lull of several hours followed. That was just as well, for my boys from Fox Company had found the family wine cellar and "school was out." Personally, I was filled to the brim, not with wine, but with apprehension over the responsibilities that were now mine. Much as I wanted to join the men, it would not have been militarily wise.

While I waited to be called back to battalion headquarters for the next attack order, I decided to explore Rimberg Castle. I found the family portrait room. The walls were lined with priceless paintings. The room had another occupant. One of my own GIs, name long forgotten, had slipped into the room and was cutting one of the portraits out of its frame with his trench knife. Paint burst in all directions as he hacked away, totally unaware that I was watching. I stood there in disgust without speaking for the moment. Once the painting was out of the frame, my energetic lad rolled it up, as I winced, and tucked the ruined masterpiece into his field jacket.

He turned and walked straight into me. A more surprised GI has never been seen on the entire Western Front. "What in the hell do you intend to do with that, Soldier, now that you have it, and particularly where you're going in the near future?" "Well, sir, it's an excellent souvenir and probably worth a lot of money. I'd like to send it home eventually." I snorted, "Get out of here and back to your platoon. Now!" I suspect the rear echelon troops thoroughly destroyed or at least confiscated those paintings, but we front-line Joes had little accommodation for bulky souvenirs.

A day or so later, in drenching rain, we continued the attack east, using a small, private gravel road behind Rimberg Castle to guide us to the high ground and further penetration into Germany. I was not surprised to note shortly, as I trudged along, many bright paint colors gushing down that hill in the water-filled ditch beside the road. A few feet further and there was the abandoned painting, tossed aside by my thoughtless soldier, slowly losing its life and value in the relentless downpour. It's not an earthshaking story, but I've often wondered what an invading army could and would do to this country.[6]

Breaking out of the Rimberg Castle area, the 119th Regiment turned and moved in a southerly direction toward an important objective: Aachen. The 120th and 117th Regiments flanked us, one on the right and one on the left, and created three regiments in the attack comprising twelve companies. To make our assignment even more difficult, we frequently found ourselves in wooded areas. The thick forests concealed village after village until we were almost in them, single-street hamlets, effectively defended. To add to our woes, the Germans often counterattacked with surprising vigor and strength. By 5 October 1944 the 2nd Battalion had taken a score of stubborn pillboxes. It was a new kind of warfare for us, but we were learning fast. During the afternoon of the next day, Fox Company had succeeded in taking three pillboxes, in a vast open field about a mile or two north of Merkstein and the same distance east of the Dutch border.[7]

A dense forest lay beyond this field. I nursed one of my hunches that the Germans were in there in strength, for we had driven plenty before us in the day's fighting. I suspected infantry, foot people. I contacted battalion headquarters, and expressed my reservations about advancing any further before night fall or even remaining where I was. "You will occupy those pillboxes! Now! Stay there come what may." "But, sir, I'd prefer to pull back to a better defensive position. We're in an extended location, too close to those woods to our front. Anything could emerge from them at any time. We've occupied the three pillboxes, but I just don't like the situation at all. I'm not in contact with any of our own people on my flanks either. It's not a good situation at all, sir." I was trying to reason with the colonel. "You have your orders, Lieutenant." "Yes, sir."

A good soldier obeys orders. I had placed a platoon in the pillbox nearest the woods, although I had done so with misgivings. I ordered another to remain in a box about three hundred yards to the right rear of the forward pillbox. In order to keep an eye on things, I occupied the third pillbox with people from the Third Platoon and a mortar from the weapons platoon. This pillbox was perhaps three hundred or four hundred yards to the rear of the forward positions. We kept in touch with one another by walkie-talkie (WT).

I didn't like the situation one bit, and I chewed gum furiously. I do not smoke. Never have. People kept me supplied with chewing gum. When I chewed, my men knew that we were either headed for trouble or already in it. An occasional enemy mortar shell would land in among those pillboxes. We called such situations a "lull" in military parlance. Darkness fell. I ordered personnel posted as security outside in the German-made trenches, which were dug in a circle around each pillbox.

Dawn brought the rattle of small arms and the crash of heavier stuff as we exchanged fire with the enemy. Shouting similar orders to the forward platoons, I ordered everybody in our pillbox outside and in firing positions. I picked up my field glasses. My heart sank. An imposing line of gray uniforms was emerging out of those dangerous woods and moving directly toward our forward pillboxes. My people were firing desperately and from the number of Germans going down, accurately. But they were greatly outnumbered, and I had little or nothing to send forward to help. Helplessly, I watched my kids finally give up.

I have never been so damned frustrated in all my life. Holding their hands above their heads, as the morning sun slanted through those pesky trees, over seventy of my Fox Company people were routed out of those two fatal pillboxes. Using them as shields and preventing me from any return fire, the Germans guided them into the woods. My lads disappeared.[8]

I had ordered the remnants I had with me not to fire and I also instructed the artillery forward observer to so order his battery far to the rear. Reorganizing, the Germans now made for our woeful, isolated position. I now asked the forward observer for all he could get. He went into action. My men out in the trenches were firing steadily. T/Sgt.

William Pierce of the weapons platoon was with me. "Pierce, get that mortar up on top of this pillbox and zero in." "It has no base plate, sir." I will never know why the base plate was missing, and I was in no position to send out a search party. "Fire without it, Pierce, unless you want to join our buddies, and damned soon." Using a pair of German gloves someone had tossed to him, Pierce put shell after shell into those oncoming ranks with telling effect. In a sitting position, he would judge the needed range by moving the angle of the mortar barrel back and forth between his legs while another soldier dropped the shells into the barrel. I have no idea where the sight mechanism was, and neither did Pierce. He didn't need it or the base plate. Now and then he would have to yank the barrel out of the pillbox's earthen-covered roof, as it would bury itself a bit with each fired round. Suddenly, the enemy dragged one of our captured machine guns up on top of one of the lost pillboxes. It was quickly turned in our direction. "Knock it out, Pierce." Within three rounds, Pierce put the weapon and its gunners out of action. It was an incredible performance.

Meanwhile, I had reached battalion radio and I asked for reinforcements and an air strike. I never did receive the requested reinforcements, but within a matter of minutes three P-38s were zooming in very low and strafing the pillbox areas as well as the woods beyond. I prayed that they would not hit our captured people. We found out later that they didn't, for they had been evacuated by truck.

My riflemen were superb. Not a single man had been ineffective. What with division artillery, the air strike, Pierce's mortar, and my intrepid Joes, the shattered gray line faltered and broke up. German GIs fled helter-skelter back into the woods. We had halted the counterattack, but I had only twenty-three men left of all the front-line elements of Fox Company.[9]

I was to discover that the pillboxes, all three, which we had taken and occupied the afternoon before, were in the most forward positions of any in the entire 2nd Battalion sector. All the other rifle companies were to our rear, at considerable distances, on our right and left flanks. My company and I had actually been out on a limb. The enemy was probably, although I'll never know as their attack came frontally only, positioned along both of my flanks when the fighting started on 6 October 1944. Battalion was aware of my precarious situation and yet had ordered me to hold my position. A selfish and stupid battalion CO had taken advantage of my men and me. He was Lieutenant Colonel William Cox, who was soon removed from command and transferred to regimental headquarters.

Major Hal McCown of Ruston, Louisiana, was selected to succeed Cox. McCown was a professional soldier: thin-faced, slight build, hard-bitten, extremely military, a no-nonsense graduate of the Virginia Military Institute. The major had the habit of volunteering the 2nd Battalion for any hazardous undertaking that might be available. One couldn't love the man, but he did have everyone's serious respect.[10]

I'll never forget the nervous exhaustion which permeated my entire being after that harrowing experience. What would we have done, our depleted handful, had the Germans not given up and retreated? Did I keep my cool? Were my men brave because I was a good example to them, or were they thinking of only their own survival?[11] And then I realized I had been so busy keeping what I had in the fight, I had never entertained any thought of giving up that damned pillbox. Later on, I found an article by an unknown writer, probably from World War I, who said it all well: "MUDDY, BLOODY MEN OF THE LINE. Until a man has done a doggie job, he simply doesn't know the score; he doesn't know how danger punishes the nervous system. . . . He doesn't know how much guts it takes to move forward a yard, a foot, or even an inch, or to hold a precious place against all odds. Until he has lived in the blood and the mud, he can't realize what an ALL-TIME MIRACLE A DOUGHBOY REALLY IS."

T/Sgt. Fred Unger was the forward observer with me on 6 and 7 October 1944. He was ultimately awarded the Distinguished Service Cross (DSC), the Silver Star, and the Bronze Star, as well as the Purple Heart with Cluster (meaning two Purple Hearts) and the French Croix de Guerre. A highly decorated soldier who once refused a furlough home, he explained "I'm adjusted to combat now. I don't want to readjust after a furlough. When I go home, I want to go home and stay." He lived through it all, and did go home to stay. He once said to me, "I like to work with you, sir, you get things done." I didn't deserve that, but I loved having an incredible guy like Unger say it.

"I am now a company commander for reasons I'll try to explain later. Right now, we're reorganizing, so to speak." (9 October 1944) I recollect that we did spend the next two or three days reorganizing the four platoons of Fox Company. I had to request replacements in a hurry, and I promoted people as if promotions were going out of style. Two new platoons were created and two were replenished. Fortunately, they also sent me some ASTPs (Army Specialized Training Program). These ASTPs came from various colleges and universities with some exposure to the Reserve Officer Training Corps program. They had dropped out of school for a variety of reasons, taken some specialized training courses, refreshers in a sense, in various military centers before being shipped overseas as above-average replacements. They were usually NCOs. ASTPs were, as a rule, competent people, and I promoted them quickly. I needed their leadership in the situations now confronting the company.

The Siegfried Line assault continued. The 119th Regiment moved slowly south toward Aachen, pillbox by pillbox, village by village, with the Germans resisting every inch of the way. We used all sorts of techniques against these obstinate obstacles. Bangalore torpedoes to blow communication wires; flame throwers to "cook 'em alive," as one of our men put it, by aiming them directly into the apertures; bazookas, our effective antitank weapon, also got into the act.

Most all of the apertures faced in one direction: west. We learned early to maneuver men behind the pillboxes and attack from the rear against the rear entrances. If we hit 'em often enough with enough firepower, the Krauts would come out with their hands over their heads, dazed and incoherent with blood running from their ears and mouths. I always thought it was concussion, but I really didn't know or care. Just so they came out, helpless. Or we found them inside, wounded or dead.

We discovered that the artillery 105s or even 155s and the tanks' 75s had little effect except to blow away the growing, green camouflage, thus revealing the pillboxes. These heavy shells were valuable in destroying the superfluous or fake camouflage such as haystacks, barns, etc. Otherwise, the thick concrete resisted most of the heavy stuff. On the other hand, these heavier blows would often drive the enemy outside. My kids would finish them off with small arms, mortars, and automatic weapons as the harassed opposition would dive for the entrenched positions surrounding the pillboxes. I never developed any faith in the Air Force's attempts by bombing to reduce the pillboxes. The planes could stay back in their warm, comfortable quarters in England, or wherever, as far as I was concerned.[12]

I had a tough, heartless codger with me. This man was one of the best in the handling of a Browning Automatic Rifle (BAR) I had ever known. The BAR would frequently jam. His never did. He could furnish the ultimate in effective firepower whenever needed. But somewhere this man's respect for human life dissolved. As I noted, one of our favorite tricks was to concentrate artillery and tank fire on the pillboxes so relentlessly, the personnel within would finally rush out and into the trenches to escape the earsplitting din inside. From carefully chosen spots, I was to discover, my BAR expert would mow these helpless, unarmed people down with his deadly skill. Most of the time all these hapless Krauts were trying to do was to surrender. I had to have him evacuated eventually.

Another gruesome modus operandi developed at this time. With infantry troops providing covering fire, tank dozers were used to cover up apertures, vent holes, and exits with tons of good old Mother Earth, sealing the pillboxes completely and cutting off all air. The effects inside would be left to the burial units which followed the combat troopers.

As we advanced, the engineers would follow and blow up all of the pillboxes that had not been destroyed previously. The concrete, triangular "saw teeth" (tank obstacles) never did hold up our tanks. Luckily for us, the Germans had not yet completed this particular phase of the obstacle network when our assault began.

By 10 October 1944 it was becoming increasingly clear that Old Hickory had ruptured the supposedly impregnable Siegfried Line. Now the Battle of Aachen was underway, with the division advancing from the north while the 1st and 9th Divisions hammered away from the south. We struggled for the next ten miles, the worst kind of combat, digging in, pulling back, moving forward, taking casualties that made my heart sick, and clashing in villages, street by street.

I was down in a cluttered basement, heavens knows where, studying my map and trying desperately to determine what to do next, when 1st Sgt. Kirkman slithered abruptly down the stairs. At this particular moment, heavy fire was coming in on this little village from almost all directions. It seemed like in fact all hell was breaking loose. Top blinked at me and then cleared his throat, hesitating. "Good God, Top, what in the hell is on your mind?" "Well, sir, I was just wondering, now please don't misunderstand, but well, when was the last time the captain has had his ashes hauled (vernacular for sexual intercourse)?" I must have dropped my map and my flashlight, for I couldn't believe my ears. Here was F Company in about as serious a situation as it could get into, and my valued first sergeant is inquiring about my sex life. Well, I said to myself, there is no question about it. I am losing the best first sergeant on the Western Front. He has really had it. The man is suffering from acute combat fatigue. "Top, are you really serious?" I didn't know what else to say. "Well, yes, sir," he sincerely and emphatically answered.

I tried again, "I don't know what you're talking about. Why in the world, in the situation we're in, are you concerned about my private sex life?" "Well, sir, I'm not. I only thought you might personally need a little relaxation. It seems to me that you've been a bit uptight lately (the most glaring understatement of the entire war), and we've been under fire for some time now." Again, the hesitancy, "You see there's this German girl in a basement about five houses back down the street and she's puttin' out to anybody who has a candy bar or some chewing gum, and I thought . . . Well, I could clear the place out for the lieutenant; place a guard at the upper doorway, and . . ." "That's about enough, sergeant," I said with firmness that was purely anything but bona fide, "and I mean it. I have no time at all for such entertainment right now. I am surprised, as close to me as you are, that you don't sense my responsibility to you and to the company. What kind of a CO would I be to participate in such a foolish prank as you're suggesting. Now, you get your ass out of here. Get back there and straighten the situation out. We need firepower, not sexual satisfaction."[13]

With a tolerant look in his eyes, he shook his head and scrambled up the stairs. When he had disappeared, I propped myself up in a corner of that basement and I began to laugh for the first time in weeks. I laughed until I cried. I've always been grateful to Kirkman for providing me with that opportunity to relax. I didn't do it his way, but I did relax, a commanding officer's way, all alone, through the bizarre humor in the incident.

I did take my mission seriously and it preyed on my mind a great deal. I even slipped into a moment or two where I thought myself unworthy of the responsibility so quickly thrust upon me. Maybe I should eliminate myself, since the Krauts were having difficulty accomplishing the task. Maybe a replacement officer would do a better job. I am being honest when I say this thought of personal removal obsessed me. I recall being crouched in a foxhole by myself with a field phone beside me. Artillery shells were pounding the area around me; shrapnel was whirring and swishing right above my head. Dear God. I must get out of here and run—run—run, somewhere, but away from here. I stuck my head just a wee bit out of the hole.

A recent rain had established a large mud puddle just outside the hole. One half of a C-Ration can with razor sharp edges was floating around in the water. Edges up. Hey, what if I can scramble out of here, slip in the mud, and fall in such a way that my wrist would be exposed to the can's cutting potential? The resulting laceration would at least get me back to the aid station and maybe further back with a "million dollar wound." That's it. I was about to put my witless plan into effect when my field phone rang demandingly. Someone was in trouble, and I was needed. The C-ration can became only a memory of what might have happened. I merged into reality.[14]

Old Hickory's objective was an east-west line on the map drawn through Würselen, a suburb of Aachen. It was to be another week before we reached this area. The Wurm River, still with us as we moved south and on our right flank, ran through Herzogenrath. The entire 119th Regiment got involved with this place at one time or another. I had never seen so many treacherous booby traps and land mines. In some cases the Germans had these explosives cleverly concealed, but in others we found mines laid right out on the cobblestone streets. It was slow going. We finally reached Bardenberg, south of Herzogenrath. We found more trouble. The enemy mounted a strong offensive and a major battle developed. At this point, I recall, the Germans introduced what came to be known as "personnel bombs." I'm not sure just what they were, but I did know they could be terrifying in effect. Fired from artillery cannon, the shell would burst above ground, releasing a large number of small individual "bombs" that flew off in every conceivable direction before bursting. They were particularly deadly in among the houses and along the streets of villages and towns.[15]

I remember establishing a command post in a small frame home somewhere. The upper part of the home was taking a heavy pounding from tank fire coming from two different directions. Forward Observer Unger and I raced up the steps from the basement, and, using field glasses, we looked for muzzle bursts among the ruins around us. We were able to pinpoint those damned tanks. Unger radioed positions back to the batteries. Within ten minutes, the tanks were out of commission.

The going got so tough that the whole 119th Regiment was pulled out of Bardenberg while our artillery blasted the town all night long. The fury of the counterattack was much greater at this place and time because the Krauts knew that if the Americans ever hooked up in or near Aachen, the position of the German troops surrounded in Aachen would be untenable and complete surrender would be the final answer.

Some elements of the 119th Regiment got back into Bardenberg. Some reached an area north of Würselen. I remember being in Kohlscheid for a short time. This town was just west of Würselen. It became a center of activity for the 30th Division later on, and a rest area, too. At any rate, it must have been around 16 October 1944 or a little later, when we did get into Würselen. I received orders to form a patrol and send it down through the valley to the immediate south of our Fox Company positions. The mission? To look for American GIs from the "Big Red One" Division and form a hook-up to close the Aachen Gap.

From my command post in the cellar of a unit that was a part of what was once a handsome and modern housing development, I sent out a patrol under the leadership of S/Sgt. Frank Karwel. The patrol included a Corporal Holt, Pfc. Ray Messner, Pfc. Kurry, Pvt. Evan Whitis, Pfc. Jack Krashin (bazooka man), and Pfc. Edward Krauss. Two of these people returned late that evening (16 October 1944) with a shoulder patch from the 1st Division. Karwel's patrol had made actual physical contact with men from K Company, 3rd Battalion, 18th Infantry Regiment, 1st Division. These troops had cautiously approached each other, identified themselves, and then shook hands, a sign that they had accomplished their mission. Karwel had been killed. Krashin was wounded and did not return. My two stalwarts also had information as to where the American positions were around Aachen, how far, etc. Aachen, the first large city in Germany to be taken, was now surrounded by American troops.[16]

My little Fox Company had achieved a mission of historical importance, the closing of the "Aachen Gap." I adjusted our own positions without opposition to the south. I radioed battalion and the good news flashed to regiment, division, corps, First Army Headquarters, and then to the civilian wire services. I still have that 1st Division patch among my souvenirs.[17]

At about this time in Würselen, I had two sentries posted at the head of the stairs leading down to my cellar command post. Some faded, chewed-up laundry was still hanging on a clothes line just outside the upper door. It was a clear, moonlit night. First Sgt. Kirkman and I were trying to get some needed rest when two M-1s roared at the top of the stairs. "We've had it, sir. That's an enemy patrol just as sure as hell." Top began to collect company papers and records for the purpose of burning them, as he had been trained to do in like circumstances long ago. They were not to be confiscated by the enemy at any cost. I drew my pistol and began to creep cautiously up those stairs, expecting anything.

My two sentries lay prone on the hallway floor, peering anxiously out into the moonlight through the smoke of their own rifles. "What's up?" I whispered. "Enemy movement out there, sir, and we took no chances." I waited, hearing nothing but the wind. I crawled through the doorway. Not a sign of the enemy anywhere. I proceeded to investigate further, and then I realized what had happened. My men had mistaken the shadows and the movement of the woebegone laundry on the line and in the moonlight for enemy personnel, and had opened fire. They were a couple of sheepish-looking soldiers when I returned from my look-around. I didn't scold. No one was more relieved than Kirkman who, fortunately, had not applied the match to our company records. "This is a 'Heine' typewriter and not worth a damn. History is in the making again where I am. And, as always, I am right in the middle of it." (24 October 1944) "Once again, I am Executive Officer of the Company. They sent us a new CO, Captain "Cotton" Kirklin from Odessa, Texas. I got my first pass to 'Gay Paree' the other day. What a town. Seventy-two hours, and what a relief to get away."[18] (27 October 1944)

The passes to Paris were based on the amount of time a soldier had been in contact with the enemy. In the entire battalion, only two or three officers had been on-line longer than I. I was an easy and grateful selection. I now proceeded to make a mistake, a small one to be sure, which I have always regretted. I had no money and I knew I would need some in Paris. Several weeks back, I had relieved a German officer of his Luger pistol: 1918 model, blue steel, hand-tooled. It was a veritable beauty, and I took pride in its possession. There was an officer in E Company who was rather dippy over items of this nature. I asked him what he would give me for the pistol. He offered $250. Flabbergasted, I accepted and then spent the whole amount in Paris within seventy hours. I came back to Fox Company exhausted and broke, but in a better frame of mind than when I left. To this day, I can still envision that lovely Luger.[19]

Captain Kirklin was a small, nervous man with sort of reddish-blonde hair. He talked and smoked almost incessantly. His Texas twang seemed to emphasize his deep pride in all that was Texan. Kirklin had been wounded in Normandy while commanding another rifle company in the 119th Regiment. Recovering from wounds, he had been sent back into action and assigned to Fox Company, for said company was in the

command of only a first lieutenant by the name of Arn. Kirklin outranked me, and, under the rules, was entitled to the command.

I hated to give it all up, for I was beginning to know, if at all possible,
what to do and what not to do with men's lives. I soon discovered, however, that the newcomer would not make a single move without con-
sulting first with me. I could sense that 1st Sgt. Kirkman was quite
aware of the situation, but like the regular army soldier he was, he made
no comment whatsoever.

"Took another shower yesterday. Every day of this current breathing
spell seems to bring me closer to respectability." (2 November 1944)
"This day, Armistice Day, means little to us although our radio tells us
that Franklin D. Roosevelt has been elected again. I would imagine,
more importantly to us, that several hundred thousand old doughboys
back home must have been truly happy twenty-six years ago today. No
one can appreciate more than I, how they felt. Well, they had their final
day, and we will also. But when? The first snow came yesterday. We
now have gloves, four-buckle arctics, and long overcoats. I had mine
shortened by a Kraut tailor. I can move faster with instant speed when
the occasion demands." (11 November 1944)

"I can't understand what keeps Hitler going. He has to be a maniac."
(15 November 1944) My observations about Hitler at the time were actually made from ignorance and were simply my own opinions. I have
now read much about him, and I know that he *was* a maniac. Isn't it
strange how invariably demented leaders will change the course of history? While those around him were even planning his assassination
and made the attempt once, he managed to survive and to continue his
diabolical influence over his able commanders. He was obsessed with
the idea that Germany could and would survive and rule the world.
Could that be why Studs Terkel refers to World War II as "The Good
War?" But an American GI in a front-line infantry rifle company in Europe in November 1944 knew little or nothing about what was taking
place in Berlin. To us, this war seemed as if it would go on forever.[20]

During this period, the 30th Infantry Division, still a unit in the
XIXth Corps, was taken out of the First Army and placed in the Ninth
Army under the command of Lieutenant General William Hood Simp-

son, a tall, lean, immaculate, tough soldier. Soon, we were told, we would move out of the area north of Aachen, swing east, and continue the attack to the Rhine River. The target date would be the latter part of November. Würselen, where F Company and the balance of the 119th Regiment continued to be harassed at night by tanks and in the daytime by mortars and artillery, would be the pivot for our movement forward.

Somehow, I cannot recall how or why, Fox Company found itself in the town of Setterich, too far from Würselen. We had little difficulty, as I recall, in getting there. The town was almost completely destroyed. I remember that we had difficulty finding sufficient cover among the ruins and out of the weather for the company's personnel. The men were used to the situation. We had settled in fairly well by the early morning hours of 16 November 1944, waiting and gathering a little shut-eye. The waiting period was to be somewhat brief.

Battalion headquarters was some distance behind us in a large three-story brick home which had most of the first two floors intact. Not long after we had established communications with battalion headquarters, the field phone rang and Captain Kirklin was ordered back to the battalion command post. I knew instinctively that he would receive an attack order. So I told Kirkman to prepare the company for a quick move out. All equipment was to be double-checked, K rations issued, and every man's ammunition supply brought up to the maximum. I was moving by muscular reaction, and Top knew it. He went about his duties with unusual vigor.

Out of the morning mist a battalion runner picked his way through the rubble and scrambled into our company command post. "Lieutenant Arn, the CO wants you back at the battalion command post on the double, sir." "But Captain Kirklin is back there now." "Yes, sir, but the CO wants you!" Back I went, perplexed and concerned up to the second floor, pausing on the stairway landing a moment to discover why I had been called back. Captain Kirklin was there on a stretcher, wrapped in a blanket and shaking like a leaf. His teeth were chattering and his eyes were darting back and forth like a haunted and caged animal. Captain Kirklin's combat days were over. He had had it. Period. A disgusted battalion CO officer barked at me, "I want you to take command of F Company immediately, Lieutenant." "Yes, sir." I felt sorry for Kirklin, but not for long. I proceeded to get too busy to feel sorry for anyone, unless it was for myself.[21]

I took the attack order, questioned it here and there as had been my custom when in command of the company in the past, and I was astounded to discover a smile on the CO's face. "Well, gentlemen," he said addressing the COs of Easy, George, and Howe companies as well as his battalion staff officers, "It's good to have Old Man Arn back with us once again. We'll make fewer mistakes here in battalion." I didn't detect any sarcasm, so I didn't mind. I knew he respected me and my cautious attitude.

In another day or two, the 117th Regiment occupied Mariadorf. The 120th was in Euchen, and the 119th was in trouble, all sorts of trouble: crack Panzer troops, deadly mortar fire, and so on. We didn't advance very far at all out of Setterich. At times we were so close to the enemy our artillery couldn't help. The uproar and the smoke mingled in strange ways. The stretcher-bearers worked overtime.

I kept sending out combat patrols, as I did not want to commit the entire company. The small units were forced to return to position. It was an exasperating situation. On my flanks, the other companies in the battalion were not doing well either. Bothersome mine fields were everywhere. Then, all of a sudden, apparently realizing that their flanking units were slowly giving way to the Americans, the stubborn people directly in front of F Company began to withdraw slowly to the east.

With the 117th and the 120th Regiments continuing to push forward, the 119th took Weiden. By 21 November 1944 we were halfway to the Roer River in Germany. The weather was becoming increasingly wintry every day. Life out in it under fire was filled with additional misery. I shall not attempt to describe the conditions, for no one would believe me. We captured Aldenhoven and Pattern.

In the latter town a haunting tragedy took place. I had set up the company command post in the basement of a residence. For precautionary reasons, I always had a sentry posted just inside for his own protection on the entrance above the cellar stairway. Kirkman always took care of this detail. The sentries were on this particular duty in shifts. Now and then when I couldn't sleep, I would climb the stairs and keep the guard company, chatting in low tones and at the same time keeping a sharp lookout for possible enemy patrols. I had just returned downstairs to my filthy blanket when an M-1 exploded up above. I dashed upstairs to find a dying American soldier on the floor of the hallway. His relief was staring down at him in a horrified way. He had just shot one of his best friends. The medics came quickly, but the lad had died.

It was difficult to get any sense out of the now hysterical soldier. As near as I could ascertain, the relieving GI was not sure where the command post doorway was located. Dawn was just arriving and the shadows were long and dark, making it difficult to see. Mistaking a movement in the doorway, the confused and nervous soldier had simply fired point-blank. Names have long since been forgotten, so it really doesn't matter anymore. I turned the dead soldier in on the Morning Report (MR) as "killed in action" (KIA), and released the grief-stricken man to the Battalion Aid Station. He never returned. I hope the Good Lord will forgive me for falsifying the official records.

In the drive to the Roer River, further action occurred at Merzenhausen, Germany, another one of those one-street towns. Fox Company was held up by a huge German tank firing 88-mm shells flat trajectory right down this single street. We were really stalled, for it was impossible to move anyone down that rubble-strewn avenue without heavy losses. In addition to the problem furnished by the pesky tank, enemy observation on the elevations beyond the town brought almost instant artillery fire every time I tried to move people along the rear of the houses through the backyards.

I had an excellent bazooka man, S/Sgt. William Brazeau of Chicago. We were being supplied about this time with superb aerial photos of towns, highways, etc. On my photo map, and judging from the muzzle blast, I had a pretty good idea of where that irksome tank might be located. I could judge from the sound also. Close by the supposed location of the tank was what appeared to be a reasonably whole church and steeple. My plan was to get Brazeau and his bazooka into that church and up into its steepled higher regions. I reasoned that from a superior height he might be able to place a round or two into the turret opening of that tank. Of course, the turret would have to be open for the bazooka shells to be effective. Plans such as this depend on circumstances being just right in order to succeed.

I sent for Brazeau. We discussed my plan and studied the photo map carefully. Once again, and all too often, I was asking an American youngster to risk his life. Simply nodding his head, he understood what I had in mind. This tall, dark-haired, quiet, city chap disappeared into the ruins equipped with his bazooka, some shells, and a walkie-talkie. I waited and agonized. The tank kept blazing away. In about an hour, I'll really never know how long it was, his voice—and he was breathing hard—came to me over my walkie-talkie. He whispered hoarsely, "I'm at the church, sir." "Good. Is there any superstructure left?" "Yes, sir, and I can get up one more story. I can just make out a window at that level too. The tank is only about twenty-five yards away from me. They're loading and firing about every five minutes. There are about a dozen soldiers around the tank. They seem to be relaxed." His voice clicked off.

"Good luck, Brazeau. Take care." Then, I prayed silently as I always did in similar situations. It must have been a few minutes later; to me it was an eternity. I heard Brazeau's bazooka explode, and then silence. The 88s ceased pounding down that street. Brazeau had not only knocked out the tank, he had done away with the crew inside. The tank caught fire and proceeded to erupt inside like a popcorn popper. The infantry people outside took off at once, probably thinking the Americans were in the immediate vicinity in considerable strength. I ordered Fox Company people to move down that street at once from doorway to doorway. We secured the town, and I put Brazeau in for a well-deserved Silver Star which he eventually received.[22]

By the end of the month, the entire 119th Regiment was pulled out of line and sent back to Kohlscheid for showers, new clothing, and replacements. Kohlscheid was in pretty good shape and provided some warm buildings for Fox Company's weary people. Some American outfits had already reached the Roer River, about eight miles to the east.

But the Roer was not the Rhine, and our top brass was disappointed. Lieutenant Arn was glad to be back in Kohlscheid and so were the men. "I am once again the company commander. I am in a new Army. Subtract two numbers from the date of the month my birthday falls on and you will have the number of the Army. [Ninth Army]. Thanksgiving Day was spent in foxholes. Most of these towns are in shambles." (30 November 1944) "Like a bolt out of the blue this morning, I was called back to Division and our commanding general pinned a Silver Star on my chest. Our division commander, General Hobbs (I am now allowed to tell you) was very complimentary, but, boy, was I nervous. Would rather have been back in the pillbox the citation tells about. How Jerry keeps on in spite of the awful beating he is taking is way beyond all of us." (2 December 1944)

The award of my Silver Star covered the pillbox incident of 6 and 7 October 1944. On that morning of 2 December 1944, fifteen or twenty officers and enlisted men, as well as I, were assembled in a pasture outside Herzogenrath waiting for General Hobbs. Suddenly, his command car roared up. Leaping out, à la General Patton, he ran into the field on the double. A staff officer had placed a rather flimsy table in front of our small formation. The various awards were placed upon it.

Mistaking the table for some sort of speaking platform, I guess, and trying to be impressive, the good general leaped up on the table. The table collapsed immediately and the general went sprawling. So did his helmet, the awards, and, I am sure, his pride. A muffled snicker or two could be heard from the ranks. The general made a quick recovery, and we were properly recognized. After all we had been through for several months, the incident added fuel to the conversation of miserable human beings for days afterward. Personally, I have often wondered what happened to the officer or NCO who produced that weak little table. At any rate, the lucky civilian-soldier, not a hero by any stretch of anyone's imagination, now held a Purple Heart and a Silver Star. I would have given them both to the Salvation Army for a ticket to East Cleveland.

The Roer River in Germany was controlled by huge dams at its headwaters. The Ninth Army now discovered that the river was a formidable obstacle to the advance to the Rhine. Nevertheless, we trucked to positions with little or no resistance along the Roer in the vicinity of Jülich. As I recall, decimated units of the much-mauled 29th Division took up a several mile front to the left of our division.

"I am amazed that you are able to follow me so closely. You evidently know more about where I have been than I do. The weather is awful, wet, snowy, and cold." (3 December 1944) The Roer was overflowing in many places because of the heavy rains. Even we lowly rifle company commanders had been advised that the Germans could blow those dams at any time. Such action would cause major flooding everywhere in the valley and would hamper our advance if, in fact, we could advance at all. We were supposed to stay in position here for about two weeks, so they told us, while plans were formulated by the brass for the assault across the Roer.[23]

Surprisingly, Fox Company was ordered back to Kerkrade, Holland, for a three-day rest in the buildings of what I thought was a Dutch university or some such.[24] Greeting us were clean beds with sheets, hot showers, and, above all, hot food. Even new fatigues graced our tired bodies. It was absolute heaven. The men relaxed and I proceeded to eliminate all discipline, temporarily. "It's like a dream or a fairy tale," remarked one grateful GI. The German gal broadcasting from Berlin known as "Axis Sally" proceeded to announce that the 30th Division had been annihilated in the Siegfried Line.[25]

During that rest period, John Mecklin, a reporter from the *Chicago Sun*, interviewed me about the October "pillbox counteroffensive" incident. He believed it was most worthy of a story, and I assume that regimental headquarters agreed. Further, I had entered the service from Evanston, Illinois, a suburb of Chicago. I described for him how the Krauts had used our own captured men as shields from our fire. To be sure, I gave Pierce and the men the full credit due them. Mecklin quoted me correctly throughout the news release. The story made the front page of the *Sun*. The clipping sent to me by one of my Chicago friends is still in one of my scrapbooks.[26]

"I wore my green blouse (jacket) for the first time since I left the States last evening. I loved to wear it in that long ago time. Still do. Had a date with an American Red Cross girl. My enterprising kids have managed to hook up some electricity from somewhere and we have lights. We had been relying on candles and flashlights. It is snowing." (10 December 1944)

The breather at Kerkrade provided time for letter writing. I censored letters until my eyes got tired. I remember one letter which one of my GIs had written to his mother, something like this: "If my hand writing is shaky it is because I am crouched in a foxhole under a tremendous artillery salvo. I may not finish this, for I may not live much longer. Please always remember that I love you very much."

We were completely out of danger when he wrote the letter. Kerkrade was many miles behind the front lines. I called the soldier to my quarters. He couldn't explain why he had written in that foreboding way. I ordered him to tear the letter up and write another one, which would tell his people how much we were enjoying the rest. His next version I okayed.[27]

One of my men came to me with a real problem. He let me read a poorly written letter from a small town in Louisiana. It seemed, according to the mother, that the lad's wife was being unfaithful to him, and the mother thought it necessary to let my soldier know of the wife's errant ways. She was the talk of the town. It was a bitter condemnation. I asked him what he proposed to do. He said that his wife was the beneficiary on his $10,000 GI insurance policy. He wanted that changed, and he wished to start proceedings for a divorce. His sincerity impressed me.

I decided that we needed to consult with Colonel Patterson, the 30th Division's Adjutant. I ordered my jeep, and we drove to division headquarters in Herzogenrath. The colonel was sympathetic and had the GI sign the necessary change of beneficiary forms. My soldier also gave the colonel the name and address of one of his hometown attorneys. Patterson indicated that he would see what could be done about a divorce, in absentia. It wouldn't be easy. Some time later, during the Battle of the Bulge, the young man was a KIA on Kirkman's Morning Report. Many times since I have speculated as to whether that woman from Louisiana collected the ten grand, and if she was really unfaithful?

Our sojourn in paradise was limited, and we moved back to our defensive positions on the Roer in Germany. Nothing much was happening. Only occasional artillery barrages from long range would pound away, usually when they guessed our troops might be eating. Incidentally, our adroit Mess Sgt., Riley Jones, had managed to bring F Company's kitchen and crew up to the position, and we were getting hot food now and then.

One afternoon soon after we had returned to the line, two Air Force sergeants reported to me to my complete astonishment. I stared at them. "And may I ask what in the all billy hell are you two doing here?" The two young men explained: The high and mighties had decided that certain Air Force personnel should be exposed to the operations of a front-line infantry outfit carrying on in its "native habitat," so to speak. They were to go back and tell their own people what it was like down on Mother Earth and under fire.[28]

I apologized to them by saying, "You won't experience much up here because we're in a rather quiet spot, and only occasionally will the enemy 'throw' anything at us. We have outposts between here and the river and they exchange sporadic fire with positions of a similar nature across the river. And that's about it." They didn't seem to be too disappointed. So, I decided to start showing them around the command post that I had established in the cellar of a nearby farmhouse.

I explained how we kept in touch with our three forward rifle platoons by walkie-talkie, and, if the situation permitted, by field phones that required the laying of wire vulnerable to bursting shells, etc. I talked with them about the organization of a full-strength rifle company, how we deployed our fourth or weapons platoon, and so on. It was really becoming quite comfortable down there in that cellar. I love to talk and they were listening to me when all of a sudden German artillery shells began to pound our positions. For the next ten minutes or so, we were literally saturated with shell after shell after shell. Debris and dust trickled down through the floor above. Smoking hot shell fragments whistled down through the stair opening resulting from some direct hits on the building we were in. The noise was of the usual intensity, but must have sounded like the end of the world to the two sergeants.

I recollect that Riley's company kitchen equipment was almost destroyed, and the medics were busy with some casualties. Real pandemonium. And then: silence. I looked around for my fly boy friends. They were both huddled over in a corner, out of their wits with fright. If they are alive today, they must still talk about the prevaricating GI company commander who led them to believe they were in a "relatively quiet sector." I sent them back, much to their apparent relief, leaving me with apprehension as to when the "wheels" would create their next silly idea.

"As I write, I have been thinking. I have never seen a reporter or a photographer for that matter on the front lines. They linger around the rest camps, hospitals, and various headquarters units. You'd be surprised how much I welcome a delousing station."[29] (14 December 1944) I had developed scabies from dirt, sweat, etc. The tiny mites had lived with me for some time. I had tried to get rid of them, but, gosh, did I itch at times. These mites—some referred to them as lice—would create welts which would turn to sores as I would scratch and scratch. The itching would come and go, but I don't remember the irritation being absent for any great length of time. After the war, medics subjected me to the "seventy-two hour treatment." First a shower, a lengthy one and as hot as I could possibly stand it. Next, a good scrubbing with a strong GI soap and a stiff GI brush. It hurt, but I was pretty desperate. Then they applied a thick coating of sulphur salve all over my body. I was ordered to put on GI long john underwear immediately. The weather was quite warm, too. I was then told that I must keep the underwear on for three days without taking a shower. Boy, did I sweat and was I uncomfortable. At the end of the time period, I spent a solid hour in the shower getting rid of the damned sulphur salve. The treatment worked and the scabies and I parted company forever.[30]

"Nothing much going on. Guess you'd call this a holding action. We are waiting for attack orders." (15 December 1944) I didn't know, but I was about to become involved in another chapter in the world's military history.

6. A Maniacal Vision Expires

16 December 1944–29 January 1945

Overly confident Allied troops found that the Wehrmacht's fighting capacity had not crumbled. Chancellor Adolf Hitler gambled on a counteroffensive punch through the Ardennes in Belgium to gain the initiative, split the Allies, and cut their supply lines by capturing the port of Antwerp. Although Field Marshals Gerd von Rundstedt and Walter Model warned Hitler that his plan was risky, the chancellor believed surprise would give the Wehrmacht the winning edge. Adding to this secrecy, the heavy forests, rugged terrain, and wintery weather in the Ardennes provided excellent cover for the enemy buildup of troops and materiel.

Germans targeted five unsuspecting American divisions— the 4th, 28th, 99th, 106th, and the 9th Armored, with their support groups—strung along a thin eighty-mile front, for their breakthrough. Even worse for the Americans, most of these men were either exhausted, busy integrating new units after the brutal Siegfried Line Campaign, or untested such as those in Major General Troy H. Middleton's VIII Corps, including the 106th Division, which had no combat experience and had been on-line for merely four days. By nightfall on 16 December 1944 American forces found themselves under heavy assault by an enemy of considerable but indeterminate strength. The Ardennes Campaign and the Battle of the Bulge had begun.

Like other American units, the 125 or so men in Fox Company up north by the west bank of the Roer River near Jülich were taken by surprise. For the next month, their only reality was survival or death.

In the middle of the afternoon on 16 December 1944 I was ordered to report to the 2nd Battalion Command Post where Lieutenant Colonel McCown, with eyes shining, announced that the "entire 30th Division" was moving south by truck. "Have your company ready and on a certain road by nightfall and wait for appropriate vehicles. The 119th Regiment will be in the lead trucks of the division and the 2nd Battalion will lead the Regiment," he barked with a grim smile. "There is to be a complete and necessary blackout. We will be back here in ten days. Put signs up in all your company areas, 'RESERVED for'. . . ." There was no further explanation at all. We were now picking up rumors, however, that "thousands of enemy paratroopers" had landed behind our lines down in Belgium. That was all.[1]

What followed, initially, was a ludicrous nightmare, never to be forgotten. I recall loading Fox Company personnel into five or six one and a half ton troop carriers driven by black quartermaster people. I crawled into the cab with the lead vehicle driver. He could tell me nothing. His orders were simple: never to lose contact, in the pitch-black night without headlights, with the vehicle just ahead. I had one of my Arn hunches that we were to help some people in trouble down south, but it was only a hunch. Apprehension was increasing, as always, within my being.[2]

The whole move to our de-trucking point, which proved to be near Aywaille, Belgium, couldn't have been more than a hundred miles. Nevertheless, it took all night. The roads were clogged with fleeing civilians, military vehicles, and turn-tail (we found out later) GIs of all ranks and types, heading away from Belgium or wherever, just trying to get out, apparently, from whatever was happening. It was a real mess and those truck drivers on that particular memorable night deserved awards of some sort.[3]

"Axis Sally" from Berlin announced on my truck's radio, "the fanatical 30th Division, Roosevelt's SS troops, is going to try to rescue the American First Army." How she knew that our division was involved was quite beyond me, and still is.[4]

We would hold up for minutes on end. Without the use of headlights, the chaos was simply augmented. It was truly a never-to-be-forgotten night. My frayed nerves were screaming. Eventually as dawn was breaking, stiff, cold Fox Company stalwarts climbed out of the trucks. I would be dishonest if I indicated that I knew where we were, for I didn't. I simply formed a "a column of ducks" (staggered double single files), and took off down a road. My compass indicated that we were proceeding south. To me, that was as good a direction as any.[5]

I was absolutely astounded at the disgraceful picture now presenting itself. Spa, Belgium, the famous resort town and First Army Headquarters, was to the east. Officers and enlisted men of all ranks were getting out of there and moving west in any manner possible. I even saw some hanging desperately from overloaded vehicles. Utter panic and disorder reigned. "We're getting the hell out of here as fast as we can," seemed to be the prevailing attitude. Disgust mingled with my increasing confusion.

Quite by accident as we were moving through the area of First Army Headquarters, I noticed a familiar figure up ahead. It turned out to be, to my absolute amazement, Lieutenant Mat Beck, my former "hutmate" during the sojourn at Fort McClellan. He was filthy and his eyes were glazed. Beck was in a complete state of shock. He had no idea where he was or how he got there. He just wandered aimlessly. It was quite obvious that he didn't recognize me. His speech was rambling and incoherent. I suspected that he might have been a platoon leader with either the 422nd or the 423rd of the 106th. Calling on one of our own company medics, I ordered him to take the lieutenant back to the nearest medical aid station for processing to the rear. I never saw or heard of Beck again.

Amazed at the brass's show of cowardice, my kids plodded on following me down that unknown highway in the direction, supposedly, of the enemy. First Lieutenant Arn wasn't sharing his concern with anybody. Outwardly, he attempted to show an assured confidence, but at the same time he fervently hoped that someone would come along soon and inform him as to what he was supposed to do and when and where. The road took a southwesterly direction.

During that morning, and I have no idea how far we had moved down that highway, McCown's jeep roared to a screeching stop. How

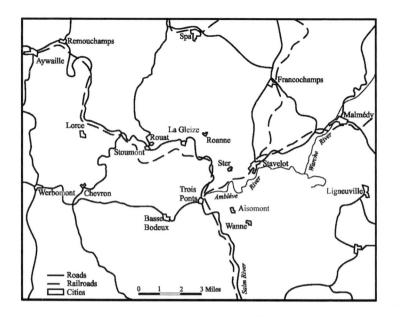

Map 4. The Ardennes: Aywaille to Malmédy. (Hewitt, pgs. 180–81)

he knew where to find me, I'll never know. I was relieved when I saw him. Signaling the company to halt, I double-timed to the colonel, who had already spread his map across the hood of his jeep in his usual flamboyant manner and had placed his finger on a spot on the map.

As near as I can recall, the colonel said, "Arn, here is where you are." He indicated that we were south of the Amblève River and were moving toward a place called Werbomont on the Liège-Bastogne Highway. "I want F Company in Vielsalm with the place secured by nightfall," his crisp, military voice was crackling. I glanced at the map, located Vielsalm, then spoke straight back in a pretty good military voice of my own. "Sir, that's a good distance from here. What does S-2 (Intelligence) say about enemy dispositions?" "Not much." Evasively and then more firmly McCown said, "There is evidence that a counteroffensive is underway of considerable strength and we must contain it. Fast! Now! Move!" And his jeep scurried away, knifing through the weary columns of my Fox Company people. I decided right then and there to follow those orders in my own way, with as little foolhardiness as was humanly possible. I was always aware that McCown never cared for an argument.

The colonel had given me a beat-up map of sorts, thank goodness. I located a town called Chevron about eight miles east of Werbomont. If we were lucky, I hoped to reach Chevron by nightfall, for I had already decided the colonel's objective of taking Vielsalm was completely out of the question. I had no idea what friendly elements might be on either of my flanks, if any at all. I noted that the road we were on followed a small river or creek called Grandmont Rivulet, at a lower level and to our right flank. Wooded hillside sloped down to the edge of the road on our left and to the tiny stream's banks on the other side. It was a damned scary situation, and I had foreboding thoughts as to what might be in store for Fox Company.

I placed a small squad of men from S/Sgt. Ken Austin's Third Platoon out ahead of our column by several hundred yards.[6] We relayed to the squad leader by walkie-talkie. The idea was to expose only a few men when a contact with the Krauts would materialize. The whereabouts of the enemy were completely unknown to me, or, apparently, to anyone else. I took up a position in the middle of the column, which was far from a battle formation, where I would be able to make the necessary decisions sooner than if I were walking along at the head of the entire unit and the enemy hit suddenly. Nothing happened in Werbomont. Neither did we find any Americans there. I felt very lonely, if that's the word for it. Lonely in the military sense.[7]

We learned later that the German unit we were to contend with was part of SS Lieutenant Colonel Joachim Peiper's 1st SS Panzer Division of Colonel General Joseph "Sepp" Dietrich's 6th SS Panzer Army. Most of the 12th SS Panzer Division had become involved with the 2nd and 99th American Divisions. Dietrich turned to Peiper to carry on the counteroffensive in our sector. He was a natural choice to lead the spearhead assault. His record was one of ruthless action on the Eastern Front. Kampfgruppe Peiper [consisted of between 19,000 to 22,000 officers and men, six panzer-grenadier battalions armed with machines guns, and 250 tanks of varying firepower. This battle group also contained a number of artillery batteries with weaponry that included 20-mm and 37-mm antiaircraft guns, antitank guns, 88-mm guns, 105-mm light field howitzers, and 150-mm heavy howitzers, some towed, others self-propelled. Rates of fire for these artillery pieces ran from two rounds per minute to four to six. The 30th Division had approximately 13,500 officers and men, with four field artillery battalions, three with 105-mm howitzers, one with 155-mm howitzers. Further backing came from three attached units, the 743rd Tank Battalion, the 823rd Tank Destroyer Battalion, and the 541st AAA Battalion].[8]

Peiper was ordered to penetrate down the Amblève River valley through Trois Ponts and on to Werbomont. He intended to cross the Meuse River at Huy. His strict orders were to keep moving regardless of events on his flanks. He was also to create complete chaos in the Allied rear areas if at all possible.

Turning the southern flank of the 99th, he pushed west. Alone now, it became apparent that a shortage of fuel would be disastrous. He moved north to an American fuel dump at Büllingen. Here he helped himself to 50,000 gallons, and moved on down to the Ligneuville Highway. He then sent Major Jupp Diefenthal (Panzer Grenadiers) along that road to Baugnez while he approached Ligneuville from the south.[9]

It was at Baugnez that Diefenthal ordered the massacre of some 120 American soldiers in the 285th Field Artillery Observation Battalion. Eighty-five died in the open field just outside Baugnez. This proved to be not the only Peiper atrocity. Prisoners were shot later at Ligneuville and Stavelot. At 1700 hours on 17 December 1944 Peiper left Ligneuville for the important bridge at Stavelot. The road was a poor one, and Peiper said later it was a "road for bicycles." But on 18 December 1944 he took Stavelot.

By now, General Hodges, commanding the American First Army, was able to deploy the 30th Infantry Division into the fracas at the "North Shoulder" of the Bulge, as it was to be called. If Peiper were to take Werbomont to get to the Meuse River, he would need to cross the Salm River where it joined with the Amblève at Trois Ponts. However, the 51st Engineer Battalion stopped him at Trois Ponts by destroying the bridges over the Salm and the Amblève. Peiper then swerved north to La Gleize. At this point, when the 30th Division rushed into the general area, its objective was to block any enemy movement beyond or west of Lienne Creek. I am now as certain as I will ever be that my little old F Company was *the* forward element of the 30th Division.

At our forward element, a radio message from battalion headquarters assured me that Werbomont would be occupied by Americans soon, and to "get the hell moving." Without really knowing it, although it is now to me clearly evident, Fox Company was way out on a limb and ahead of all other people in the 2nd Battalion. The 3rd Battalion was supposed to be in Stoumont about four miles northeast on the north bank of the Amblève, but no one really knew.

About this time, 2nd Battalion Headquarters indicated that German tanks were near Stoumont, but there was no knowledge in what strength. Our forward squad made a directional change. It had reached a point where the main road and the Grandmont Rivulet turned south. The squad leader stayed on the main road. Had he taken a secondary road, due east, we would have reached Chevron in short order. I have no quarrel at all with that squad leader. I would have followed the main road also, but his decision added an interesting and challenging chapter to the history of Fox Company.

Operating on Arn's schedule and without incident, Austin's Third Platoon reached one or two buildings on the western edge of what proved to be a wide spot in the road called Neufmoulin, where the Grandmont Rivulet joined Lienne Creek. Nighttime was upon us. I was still back down the road in the middle of our formation. There were two or three sharp curves in the road between me and Neufmoulin. I had no way of viewing the little place in the gloom of the night.

By runner, I ordered Austin to set up a roadblock for the night. I also ordered the machine gun section of the weapons platoon to move forward under Austin's control. Austin's bazooka man was there, too. My valiant and able Third Platoon leader was to let me know when I could move the rest of the company into Neufmoulin. I was not about to place all of my people into a narrow situation without knowing more about conditions. I awaited Austin's advice. With men relaxed all along that

First Lieutenant Kenneth F. Austin.

highway, I strained my ears for enemy movement in the woods above and below the road on our flanks. Battalion headquarters was continually screaming over the Signal Corps Radio (SCR) to keep moving. I could easily have wrung some rear-echelon necks, given some time that I didn't have. I would do this my way. My radioman, Sgt. Alex Harvey, grinned as always at my stubborn maneuvering with battalion.

It was now extremely dark. One could scarcely see beyond his nose. I could hear that small stream gurgling down below. Where was the enemy? Did they have infantry in those thick woods? On a hunch, I requested a tank destroyer (TD) from battalion headquarters, which assured that one was on the way. What disposal should I make of my men still on the road in front of and behind me? Why doesn't Austin get on the stick?

Abruptly, he was on the walkie-talkie. "Jesus Christ, Lieutenant, there are tanks or something, I think, moving toward us from the east. They're firing wildly and point-blank." I could hear them, too. "What should I do?" "Do you think they have any idea you are where you are?" "No, sir, I think they're just coming on in the dark and firing away." "Good. Don't expose your position. Stay under cover. Hold your fire. I have requested a tank destroyer and battalion assures me it's on the way. If the Krauts come on through maybe we can get a crack at their lead vehicle. Meanwhile, Ken, I'll order Beaudoin's platoon up on the high ground above this rat hole, and see what he can do from there in the way of support or a flanking movement." This was the same Ray Beaudoin who as a Pfc. had brought me forward to Fox Company five months before in Normandy, and who was now a battlefield-promoted second lieutenant in command of the company's Second Platoon.

I sent Ray and his men on their way. Thank God they knew how to move at night, having done so many times. We could now hear the mumble and clank of the German vehicles. Another sound was more welcome from our rear. It was an American tank destroyer. I stepped up on the highway, and managed to halt it. I gave the commander the situation as I estimated it to be. The first of two or three curves in the highway was just ahead of where I had established the company command post by the side of the road.

"Take a position on this side of the first curve," I yelled above the noise. "Shut your motor off. When the lead vehicle, whatever it may be, that we're letting come on through our forward position, rounds that curve let him have it." Quite often these armored vehicle commanders could be extremely arbitrary, but this one nodded and moved on. I was indeed relieved, because I had not developed too much faith in tank destroyers. They had a tendency to hold back and be a bit timid without "doggies" out in front of them. They were also more vulnerable to enemy fire than conventional tanks, which might explain their attitude in part.

This tank destroyer pulled ahead of me a few yards, nestled into the side of the road and up against the rising ground, silenced the motor, and waited. I notified Austin of what was going on. From the sound, a German vehicle lumbered around that curve. At least I guessed it had, and then I knew it had, for the tank destroyer's muzzle blast was terrific and nearly blinded me as I tumbled part way down the slope on my side of the road and almost into the river. It proved to be a German half-track, and the tank destroyer's shell had destroyed it completely, thus blocking the road perfectly. I couldn't have asked for anything more efficient. I could have kissed that tank destroyer commander, which I am sure he wouldn't have appreciated at all.

Within seconds, I heard a blast from one of the company's bazookas in Neufmoulin and then another. I discovered later that one of Austin's bazooka men, Pfc. Mason Armstrong, had worked his way from the wooded high ground north of town into the second story of a residence, and had fired down on two German half-tracks, knocking out both. Several weeks later, I put Armstrong in for the Distinguished Service Cross (DSC), the nation's second highest award, for this particular action. He got it, too.[10]

Austin's men now came alive, and Beaudoin's people could be heard from above and on the left flank. I decided quickly that this was probably an advance enemy reconnaissance unit, for according to Austin the three destroyed vehicles were half-tracks and not heavy tanks. What remained of the enemy effort could now be heard withdrawing to the east on the other side of the Lienne, evidently assuming that they had bumped into a position of some strength. I ordered Austin and Beaudoin to establish a strong roadblock at the eastern edge of Neufmoulin beyond the little creek's road bridge. At dawn, both of these capable officers reported back to me that the block was established.

Then something else of considerable note happened that I shall never forget. Just as I was preparing to go into Neufmoulin with the remainder of Fox Company, I heard a jeep coming down the highway behind me. I nearly fell down into the Grandmont Rivulet when it pulled up, and a tall, lean paratroop officer with two stars on his helmet leaped out. "Who's in command here?" "I am, sir, Lieutenant Arn, F Company, 119th Regiment, 30th Division, at your service." I was flabbergasted and showed it. Front-line GIs seldom, if ever, saw a ranking officer of that level.

"I'm *Jim Gavin of the 82nd Airborne Division.*" He waved away my salute, which I brought up from about thirty feet under that road, with a grin. "Looks to me, Lieutenant, as if you've had quite a night of it."

"Yes, sir, we have, but my men have secured Neufmoulin and we are about to complete its occupation. We have also set up a roadblock." "Good. You'll be pleased to know that my people will be relieving you here and moving through your positions. We're on the ground now in this emergency. I'll go on up ahead and have a look around if that's alright with you, Lieutenant?" "Yes, sir," I responded with wide-eyed admiration. Major General James Gavin, CO of the entire and famous 82nd Airborne Division, out ahead of the whole division with a jeep and a driver! I was dumbfounded, and so were my men with me. I learned later that Gavin was actually acting CO of the XVIII Airborne Corps, which included both the 82nd and 101st Airborne Divisions.

I still recall with amusement Austin's voice on the walkie-talkie. I hadn't contacted him as yet. "Sir, I wish to suggest that you have me relieved. I'm going nuts. There's a two-star American general coming into town in a jeep. I can't believe it. Do you think I've had it?" "No, Ken, you're okay. That's Major General Gavin, CO of the 82nd Airborne Division. He's way out ahead of his people who are moving through us some time today on foot. They will continue the attack. Give him the VIP treatment, although he strikes me as the kind of a guy who doesn't desire that sort of attention at all." "Yes, sir," Austin replied incredulously.[11]

All of this happened on 17–18 December 1944. I still recall the incident with great pride. Our little rifle company had actually halted, temporarily at least, the westward push of a forward spearhead of Lieutenant Colonel Joachim Peiper's 1st SS Panzer Regiment of the 1st SS Panzer Division, dubbed by the Germans "Combat Group Peiper." We had accounted for about twenty-four dead enemies and had evacuated about a dozen wounded. There were three knocked-out Kraut vehicles. Our own casualties were light. No one had been killed, and I think that we had some five or six wounded. My men had performed in a military manner.[12]

But on 19 December 1944 I was still a good distance from Vielsalm. Somehow, I didn't much care. McCown continued to be unhappy, but I sensed that he was as confused as many others in the battalion. No one from battalion had ever mentioned the 82nd Airborne to me. It seemed to me that even Gavin was feeling his way. I knew one thing for certain. I had suffered few casualties so far, and I, with no other option, had also been feeling my way.

Through all the uncertainty, the various units of the 30th Division had created a series of blocking actions over a wide front stretching some seventy miles in the rough triangle consisting of Stavelot-Stoumont-Trois Ponts, along with elements of the 82nd Airborne in and around everywhere. These tough paratroop youngsters were having a ball as infantry soldiers, and I suppose trying to forget and perhaps make up for the sad fiasco in North Holland (Operation Market Garden). They didn't seem to have much discipline or organization, for every now and then one or two paratroopers would hook on with Fox Company, stay a day or two, and then move on. I used them.[13]

I was becoming conscious of the fact that, generally, the 30th Division's mission was to contain the counteroffensive from Malmédy west through Stoumont, an area that became known as the "North Shoulder" of the Bulge. The Amblève River would help a lot as a natural obstacle for the Germans. However, Liège, supposedly one of the enemy's main objectives, was only about twenty kilometers northwest of Stoumont. So, once again, Old Hickory had taken on a major assignment and was providing some serious resistance to the enemy. The 120th Regiment was trying to break through to Malmédy, and the 117th was in and around Malmédy and Stavelot. Suddenly further west, the 119th's 3rd Battalion lost Stoumont. The 1st and 2nd Battalions were ordered to retake the town.

For reasons unknown to me to this day, the 119th's 2nd Battalion, minus Fox Company, had been held in reserve to the north, near Remouchamps, about six miles from Stoumont. The 1st Battalion had been detrucked in an assembly area northwest of Stoumont. Some hours after Fox Company, all alone, had shoved off and passed through Werbomont, the remainder of the 2nd Battalion was ordered to Werbomont. What unit had the 2nd Battalion been using in the forefront of the effort to repel the enemy? Fox Company. Thank God for General Gavin. And all that pressure on me, too. Vielsalm. My fanny.

Out of all of this mess it was now determined that the general objective of the 119th Regiment was to secure the Amblève River line from Stoumont through to La Gleize. The 82nd Airborne units were ordered to consolidate the area around Trois Ponts to the south on the Salm River. Yielding to overwhelming odds, as I understand the situation, the 119th's 3rd Battalion had to withdraw from Stoumont, passing back through Colonel Robert Herlong's 1st Battalion. The enemy's fanatical surge continued, and forced Herlong back to Stoumont Station where his battalion made a staunch stand. On the 20th, the 3rd Battalion attacked and finally achieved a position about 500 yards west of Stoumont near St. Édouard's Préventorium. This sanitarium, which had sheltered children along with nuns, priests, and elderly civilians, overlooked Stoumont and was somewhat isolated from the town.[14]

I remember sitting inside a horribly mangled Belgian home in a woods near Stoumont, trying to collect my thoughts and relax just a wee bit. Enter the indomitable 1st Sgt. Kirkman, carrying the scrawniest looking dead rooster one could imagine. "Sir, I'd like to share this with you." Too tired to care, I nodded. I never knew how that incredible soldier ever managed these miracles—I suppose over a makeshift fire somewhere—but in a few minutes later I had fried chicken. I didn't even notice the pin feathers. It tasted great and raised my spirits. Top was thoughtful, brave, and resourceful. It was just a privilege to have him around.

Contrary to some of the movies about the Battle of the Bulge, the ever-present wet snow was often waist-deep. We suffered almost as many casualties from trench foot as from enemy firepower. Trench foot is a disease peculiar to soldiers fighting in winter conditions. A combination of dirt, sweat, water-soaked shoes, wet socks, and cold weather resulted in the creation of blisters, deep sores, and, finally, infection in the feet. Unless treated promptly and professionally, it could result in amputation. Many men had to be evacuated because of the problem. One of our men, who had been sent back because of trench foot, returned fully recovered to tell us of seeing an oil drum full of amputated feet in a military hospital in Liège.[15]

I developed a solution to the problem in Fox Company. I had several pairs of socks issued to each of our people. I still don't know how

1st Sergeant Thomas H. Kirkman.

our enterprising supply sergeant discovered an ample supply. I then put out an order that wherever the situation warranted, each soldier was to remove his wet socks, put on a dry pair, and then place his wet socks inside his fatigues and against his warm, bare skin. Body heat would dry the socks and they could be used again, not clean, but at least dry. This system helped a great deal in Fox Company.

We used prisoners of war in many ways to secure information about the enemy. One night during a furious snowstorm, I was huddled down in a spacious, German-made foxhole somewhere around Stoumont, I think. The hole was big enough and long enough that, if I were of a mind to, I could lie down in it and stretch out. This home away from home even had a log-enforced roof on it. All of a sudden, I heard a noise at the hole's opening. A pair of snowy, wet hobnailed boots, obviously German, poked down through the aperture. Out came my .45. A scared Kraut followed the boots. He was unarmed, cold, lost, and frightened out of his wits. I covered him with my pistol by flashlight, and walkie-talkied to one of the platoons. I asked for a soldier on the double. Soon an NCO scrambled down into the dimly lit hole. His look of amazement was quite wide as he took in my companion. "Sgt., take this prisoner back to battalion headquarters for interrogation. If you'll glance at this map with me for a moment, I'll show you where headquarters is located." My sergeant was unhappy: take a German prisoner all the way back to battalion headquarters, during a middle-of-the-night snowstorm? The CO must be losing his marbles. But he nudged the miserable German out of the hole, and they disappeared into the raging night. In his mental condition, I knew the German would be easy meat for the intelligence experts at headquarters.

Before dawn, my radioman advised me that I was wanted back at the battalion headquarters for the day's attack order. I floundered through the deep, drifted snow. A familiar mound appeared in the snow just ahead of me. Suspicious, I kicked the snow aside. The forlorn prisoner of war stared up at me. I checked him quickly and found a neat, round hole in the middle of his back. My sergeant had never completed his mission. Under the trying circumstances we were in, I decided not to make an issue of the matter. If he's still alive, only that sergeant and I know what happened that long-ago night deep in the snow-clad Ardennes.[16]

Shortly later, S-2 (Battalion Intelligence) informed the four company COs that Peiper's Command Group was concentrated east of Stoumont in the La Gleize area. Apparently he was trying to reopen his rearward line of communication and supply through Stavelot. Although we were not aware of it at the time, Peiper's supply of gasoline was running low.[17]

McCown's 2nd Battalion, now including Fox Company, had moved to the vicinity of Targnon, just west of Herlong's 1st Battalion's position near Stoumont. The nearby St. Édouard's Préventorium was to become the focal point of a ferocious nighttime mechanized battle. Herlong's people had taken some buildings around the place and the beleaguered infantry of A, B, C, and D Companies were the occupants. In the early evening of 20 December 1944 the Germans sent a blistering tank attack against the few American soldiers trying to hold the huge building. American armor was brought up when the infantry had to

withdraw and the resulting inferno was memorable. The civilian occupants huddled in abject terror in the basement of the sanatorium. The
situation was very grave and costly.[18]

I was ordered to Herlong's battalion command post, even though
my company was a part of the 2nd Battalion. McCown offered F Company's services to see what could be done to help. On a hunch, I took
only a runner with me. I'll never forget the distraught condition of
Herlong and his staff officers. His command post was in a large barn,
as I recall, behind St. Édouard's. The point-blank tank fire had converted the whole hill into a blazing and exploding conflagration. Parts
of the sanatorium caught fire, shells detonating all over the place, and
the command post was wallowing in complete confusion. The orange
flames of the tanks' guns and the screams of the terrified people huddled in St. Édouard's basement completed the chaotic picture. Herlong's infantry were taking a horrible beating. Herlong managed to
scream at me to commit my kids into that holocaust. He and I argued
most of the night, and I took one hell of a verbal going-over. Nevertheless, I never ordered one Fox Company rifleman into that bloody
mess. It would have been stupid to do so and would have accomplished nothing.

The 119th Regiment's *Combat History* indicates that "F Company,
from the 2nd Battalion was alerted and moved up into the 1st Battalion's positions as a safeguard against a possible breakthrough."[19] Yes,
that's what they wanted me to do, but I never moved a man during that
horrible night. Only myself and my runner. At daylight, we sneaked
back to my own command post outside Targnon. A great many men in
two of the 1st Battalion's rifle companies became casualties along with
several valuable platoon leaders. General Harrison later agreed that infantry would not have turned the tide. It was a mechanized tank battle,
and men suffered brutally.

As I recall, and I could be wrong, the action lasted the better part of
three days with the Germans finally winning possession of the harried
sanatorium temporarily, and Herlong's people eventually pushed into
the woods north of Stoumont. Later, the Germans withdrew. I cannot
recall determining whether McCown ever knew that I refused to com-

mit my unit. Herlong never brought the matter up either. Incident closed.[20]

Most of 21 December 1944 was spent making plans for a regimental attack on Stoumont by encirclement. On the morning of the 22nd, the 119th got underway. Our 2nd Battalion's assignment was a cross-country one: to develop a swinging action that would chop the Stoumont-La Gleize highway and block it. The snow-covered hillsides, thick growth of evergreens, and underbrush made it tough going. Heavy resistance and serious casualties caused regimental headquarters to order the weakened 1st and 3rd Battalions to hold up. The 2nd, however, reached its objective and established the important roadblock.

Fox Company dug in. I had all three rifle platoons in a defensive perimeter on high ground at the northeastern edge of Stoumont. I would send reconnaissance patrols out now and then to ascertain, if possible, enemy dispositions, their location, and strength. I knew enough to persuade myself to do nothing unless an attack were ordered, one that I expected momentarily.

It was the afternoon of 22 December 1944. I recall tramping around in the snow in Fox Company's area checking our positions with the platoon leaders. Suddenly McCown appeared out of nowhere, accompanied by a radio operator, or some such, and a runner. "What's out ahead here, Arn?" "Well, sir, my reconnaissance patrol probes have led me to feel certain that there are enemy positions in some strength on the other side of the highway and on the high ground beyond over through those trees." "Do you intend to do something about them, Arn?" "Not at the moment, sir. We'll determine our next move when we receive the attack order. On the other hand if the enemy should make a move, I'm ready for him." "You're too damned cautious, Arn. I'll see what's down there, and make some decisions if you aren't willing to."

Whereupon he and his two companions scrambled down the hillside in the snow and disappeared in the laden trees. I had a gut feeling that McCown expected me to alert a squad and follow him. I alerted no one. I remained at McCown's point of departure, worried and anxious. In a few minutes we heard a Kraut "burp gun," an American .45 and an M-1 rifle, and then silence. Ordering a couple of men to follow me, we flopped down that snowy incline expecting the worst: a wounded and perhaps dead battalion commander. There were many tracks in the snow among the trees, but no blood and no bodies either. Our CO and his men had evidently been captured by the enemy. I didn't delay. I crawled back up that irritating hillside and notified battalion headquarters just what had happened.[21]

Reports differ as to what transpired during McCown's captivity. His own version indicates that he and his two soldiers "were moving away from the front lines where I [McCown] had inspected the front line positions of my battalion." No mention of Fox Company or Arn, or any of the elements of my version of what happened. McCown further states that he was "captured by a German patrol that had us covered from all sides in a trap."[22]

It is my understanding that several days later about 150 Americans were liberated by our advancing people from the basement of a large building in La Gleize. I also now know that McCown conducted himself with great bravery during his captivity, demanding food for the men with him, etc. But he was not among the liberated Americans.

In his report, McCown describes his incarceration as one in which he gathered much information from his captors, information that he later turned over to the proper American authorities. He even tells about a session of many hours with Lieutenant Colonel Peiper on "the defense of Nazism and why Germany was fighting." The retreating Germans took him along, according to his report, on foot. In due course, he made his escape during a German-American firefight and reached the lines of the 82nd Airborne Division. McCown never brought the subject up during the remainder of our relationship.[23]

23 December 1945 was cold and snow was falling. Our 2nd Battalion was inactive while the process of change of command took place. Weather of this type meant that no help at all could be expected from the fly boys. I recall that the infantryman's version of the famous Air Corps song was, "Nothing will stop the Army Air Corps, except the weather." So be it.

Other elements of the 119th Regiment did retake Stoumont on the 23rd and 24th to find it empty of enemy. The Germans had withdrawn toward the east, but not far. The fighting continued. La Gleize came into the picture. Moving on La Gleize from the north, Fox Company fought well and often in small fire fights of the delaying nature in which the Germans were quite adept. We continued the attack on Christmas Day. Meanwhile, the colorful and adored fly boys did manage to get into the air in time to bomb the hell out of the 120th people in Malmédy, instead of the proper objective, La Gleize. The 120th lost over forty personnel during the inexcusable error. The toll among civilians was also high.[24]

Rumor had it that we would have turkey and all the trimmings on Christmas Day. As it turned out, there was no time or place for such conventional customs. We did get good hot turkey about ten days later. After the fall of La Gleize the entire pocket was cleared out, and the 30th Division was given credit for having routed Peiper's famed combat team.[25]

On Christmas Eve, one of my best sergeants, Guy Bates of Philadelphia, was evacuated to the rear. An artillery shell had landed in among the men of his squad, killing and wounding several. The shock of it all was too much for Bates, who had been through many ordeals. He crawled into my command post. I took one look, and ordered him evacuated immediately. He eventually recovered fully, but his fighting days were over.

Bates had earned the Silver Star several weeks before in a hair-raising way. A Yale University student before signing up, Bates spoke good German. We had some SS troopers holed up in a town whose name has long since left me. They were refusing to surrender even though they didn't have a chance in the world of surviving their situation. Bates offered to try to talk them into surrender. With considerable misgivings, I agreed to let him try. Exposing himself to possible German fire if they wished to open up, he walked out of the buildings we were in toward the enemy locations some distance away. He yelled in German the hopelessness of their situation. Listening carefully, assured that they would not be fired upon, the Germans decided to give up and came out of their building with their hands over their heads. Bates led them back to us. On my recommendation, Bates was awarded the Silver Star, this nation's third highest decoration. He deserved it.

All three regiments of the 30th Division advanced to the north bank of the Amblève River on 26 December 1944, with units of the enemy fleeing to the southeast. The 1st Panzer Division had now lost two-thirds of its equipment and one-third of its men, and Old Hickory had successfully blocked the enemy's costly effort on the North Shoulder to open up a quick route to Liège. We learned that Peiper's combat team had been so thoroughly mauled it would never operate again as a division.[26]

Gathering his remnants, the wily German leader shifted his forces into the area of Bastogne, twenty-seven miles south of Stavelot. The Germans managed to circle that city, but the Americans never surrendered. In fact, the American resistance to the counteroffensive was beginning to become just short of magnificent.[27]

The 2nd Battalion of the 119th Regiment was moved into reserve near Ster, Belgium, southeast of Spa. "We have had many uncertain days. I am somewhere in Belgium. Things have happened that could alter the length of the war, not the final outcome. Until yesterday, we had little time to think. We have been back in it again for better than ten days. We had been between Jülich and Linnich on the Roer River in Germany. Obviously, we aren't there now. We are called 'Roosevelt's SS troops' by the German broadcasters. We are really respected." (26 December 1944)

Somewhere about this time, I read and kept an American writer's war dispatch: "The 30th Division took their places among the crooked contours of the Belgian hillside in an hour of utmost urgency. Von Rundstedt's lighting rapier became a blunt and rusty sword." Wes Gallagher, a top-flight war correspondent for the Associated Press, added: "The 30th Division, one of the very best in this bloody business, has clashed 'head on' with Hitler's 1st SS Panzer Division and ripped it to pieces." Since we were once again attached to General Courtney Hodges' First Army during the Battle of the Bulge, it was gratifying that General Hodges wrote General Hobbs: "The 30th Division is doing a most spectacular job."[28]

Less successful was the Lion Head Division, the 106th, my former outfit back in the States. In late November 1944, the 106th shipped overseas as a combat division, but filled with replacements from other training units to bring it up to full strength. By a strange trick of fate, this inexperienced division had been brought up in relief of other units and placed on-line where the main thrust of the counteroffensive struck on 16 December 1944. I heard later, perhaps not wholly accurately, that the 106th did not have even its artillery batteries in place and there was other evidence of almost total unpreparedness.

In two days, the German forces put out of action the 422nd and 423rd Regiments with all supporting elements, including their artillery. Their lack of combat experience was indeed a crippling handicap. How did the German High Command know that this green group of people had moved into that particular sector? Some 300 soldiers were left from both regiments, and they were wandering around bewildered and shaken. The 106th soon counted over 7,000 missing in action (MIAs), 416 killed in action (KIAs), and 1,246 wounded in action (WIAs). These initials were used on all line outfits' Morning Reports, including Fox Company's. The weary remnants joined the surviving Regiment, the 424th, and continued in action around St. Vith, Belgium.[29]

The Battle of the Bulge continued. "Somewhere in Belgium. I can only tell you how much I miss you both. This area was a lovely part of Europe at one time. It will be again some day. The situation here looks encouraging." (27 December 1944) "Our warm clothes help a lot. It is 20 degrees above zero. We are still arguing with Jerry. One of the privates in our company is a lad named Bennett.[30] Everybody calls him 'Benny.' He has attached himself to me and has been looking after me. He feels that I don't give enough thought to myself and my own personal needs. He has been a great help in many small, needed ways. One of my company runners is Pfc. Lazarus Montalvo, a young Latin-American chap from California. 'Monty' also follows me everywhere, into a great many places where I am sure he doesn't want to be. When I need him to carry messages, I need him right NOW. He knows that. He's a good one, an artist of considerable ability." (29 December 1944)

At this point, the 119th Regiment held a defensive line along the Amblève River and our sector was quiet. I sensed deep down that big plans were being formulated by the brass. I knew that the Allies would

Malmédy, Belgium, December 1944.

change to the offensive from containing and defensive military tactics. The objective: to drive the enemy out of the Ardennes, straighten out the "bulge" created by the German counteroffensive, and continue the original movement toward Berlin and a cessation of the war in Europe. Studying a map, I concluded that the 30th Division's objective would be St. Vith and vicinity.[31]

The heavy snow continued to annoy us. At times we would be so wet, miserable, and cold, it seemed as if there were no hope and the world was coming to an end. And we would be pleased to end with it. It wasn't exactly a Sunday school picnic to be pathetic physically and frightened mentally. We noted that the Germans wore white camouflage capes designed specifically for operating in winter conditions. We had to resort to our inimitable GI ingenuity and make crude facsimiles out of whatever we could apprehend from the Belgian natives: curtains, tablecloths, sheets, pillowcases, and the like. Even some of our equipment was painted white.

"New Year's Eve and the only thing we're celebrating is the fact that we're alive. 'Benny' brought into this deserted Belgian farmhouse just now (I have no idea where the family went) a stolen coal-oil lamp. I don't know where he obtained it, nor do I ask any stupid questions. 'Moonlight requisition', 'Benny' calls it. Don't worry too much about the news. We're going to change our ways soon and get things under better control.

"My Executive Officer is First Lieutenant Bob Henglein of New York City. Has a baby at home he has never seen. He holds two Purple Hearts and the Distinguished Service Cross. 1944, a rugged year for all of us. As a company commander, I have done my best to accomplish as much as possible with minimal losses. As 1945 comes in, let's keep the Faith, continue our prayers, and maybe somewhere through these over-hanging 'clouds of war' a sudden 'light of peace' will shine." (31 December 1944)

"I have received a clipping from a friend taken from the *Chicago Sun*. I enclose it. Please paste it in the scrapbook, Dad. I promoted three sergeants to second lieutenant today. We call them 'battlefield promotions' because they have shown the ability to lead men under most demanding circumstances.[32] Christmas turkey came through today. Mess Sgt. Riley Jones deserves a lot of credit. It was delicious. I am sending 1st Sgt. Tom Kirkman home on a ninety-day furlough. He deserves it. He and I work together well. He's regular army and has a whole military career ahead of him. He wants to come back to Fox Company though, no matter where we are. Officers are generally the last to get leaves, so don't build up any false hopes." (1 January 1945)

Our sector remained quiet for several days in the new year of 1945. "I am closing in on my 36th birthday. When I have time to think of other matters than this damned war, I realize that I have no prospects of a family of my own at all. That worries me." (4 January 1945) On 5 January 1945 the 2nd Battalion pulled back to the vicinity of Bernister-Metz-Burnenville, Belgium for a rest. "Things are going well and are quiet where we are. But you know by now what that could mean." I should reprimand myself for writing that last sentence. It was the type of message I had criticized my men for. I wasn't practicing what I was preaching. Later in the day: "I was called back to regimental headquar-

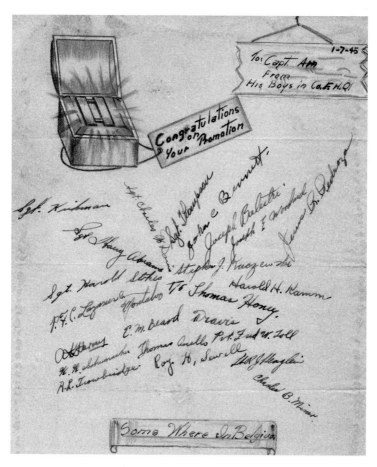

Congratulations from the boys in Company F Headquarters: I was pleased and proud.

ters this afternoon. Colonel Sutherland pinned captain's bars on me. So, I guess it's Captain Eddie Arn now. I hope and pray that someday I can tell you both personally how I feel tonight." (7 January 1945)

"Lieutenant Victor Simone of New York City returned today from a thirty-day furlough. He looks fine." (9 January 1945) Simone, also the possessor of a battlefield promotion, insisted on returning to Fox Company. "My 36th birthday, Monty Montalvo presented me with a sketch of myself and a card signed by many of the men of Fox Company. I am pleased." (11 January 1945)

The respite was over on 12 January 1945. We moved into Malmédy, Belgium, prepared to continue the attack toward St. Vith on the northern flank of the Bulge. The following day, a report in the *Stars and Stripes* noted that: "More than a hundred frozen, bullet-shattered bodies of Americans, captured and then slaughtered, were located in a field one mile south of Malmédy. A patrol of the 119th Regiment found the bodies."[33]

I saw the frozen bodies stacked in small buildings as we passed through Malmédy, proceeding in a southeasterly direction. I can recall staring at the rows of shoes. These were the men who had been captured by the Krauts and then unarmed and with unresisting hands over their heads, had been gunned down in a brutal display of German animalism. The "Malmédy Massacre" the writers called it. A real atrocity.[34]

Malmédy had been also bombed by our own planes in December. The city's water mains had burst and then frozen. It was a weird-looking place in that strange winter background. I am unable to recall all of the particulars, but the bombing experience in Malmédy reminded me of another time when our own Air Force dimwits bombed the hell out of us somewhere in Belgium. I can't remember the location now to save me. It was a bright day: blue skies, sunshine. We heard the planes behind us, then we could see the bombs falling and hear their scream—our own bombs, incredibly. We headed for the nearest cellars. That horrible screaming sound and the "crr-r-rump" of those 500-pounders had become too damned familiar. Our July experience came back to us, in spades.[35]

Strange things happen in towns and cities when they are being bombed. Strong air currents develop from the tremendous concussions and force of the heavy missiles. For example, I have seen furniture fly out of windows perhaps several hundred feet from the point of impact. I can smile now as I recall a ranking officer, almost purple with rage, pointing up at his jeep, which was resting precariously on the roof's edge of his headquarters, two stories above the street. The updrafts created by the bombs had placed it there.

Street scene, La Gleize, Belgium, January 1945.

Military records show that the 30th Division was bombed thirteen times during its adventures in Europe by the Army Air Force. Ironically, those daring fly boys probably reported back to base the following: "Mission Accomplished." Whereupon they would indulge in "hot chocolate and clean sheets."

Inept coordination of air power and infantry soured my attitude toward such pilots. This friendly fire bombing recalled an incident that had happened during my October pass to Paris. I walked into a café, and noticed a fly boy: white cravat, crushed cap and all standing at the bar. I went up to him. "Are you in the Eighth Air Force, Lieutenant?" "Yes, I am." He replied politely. "Were you on the bombing mission at St.-Lô last July?" "Yes, I was." "Would you mind stepping outside, friend?" "Not at all." He could see that I meant business. "Thank you."

He was much younger, but I was in battlefield condition and really angry. I have no idea what would have happened. Fortunately, others intervened and the fly boy and I ended up buying each other several drinks. It was, in a way, an education for both of us. I recall that he asked a million questions about "front-line doughs" and our modus operandi. He never did, as near as I can recall, explain how our Air Force made all those bombing blunders. I suppose it's just as well.

On 13 January 1945 the 2nd Battalion went into action south of Malmédy. T/Sgt. Hobdy Hayles from Mobile, Alabama, distinguished himself in a skirmish with the enemy. A Fox Company stalwart, he often showed leadership of the highest order. Leading his platoon, he managed to take some prisoners and helped us reach the high ground around Bellevaux. I put him in for an award, forgotten which one, but he got it.[36]

That afternoon, I became a part of an incident that probably should not even be mentioned, a sorry outgrowth of combat and men who couldn't take it. An "SIW" on a Morning Report indicated "self-inflicted wound." At this particular time, I had my field glasses sweeping the slope of a snow-clad hillside to just generally determine the state of things. I noticed a GI figure against the snowy background, climbing a farm fence. The soldier paused at the top of the fence, and then I detected a puff of smoke. The GI fell back in the snow. Damn, thought I, another casualty. I managed to get to the fallen person somehow and in a relatively short space of time. He was groveling around in the snow and holding his foot. Blood was pouring through his fingers, and his pistol was just a foot or two away from him. It was one of my platoon lieutenants. The shoe was blown away and there were powder marks around the wound. The nearest shell crater was perhaps fifty yards away. It was obvious. My young officer had taken his own pistol and had almost blown his foot off. His tortured eyes searched mine. I called for a medic. I said something to the effect of, "Get the lieutenant out of here fast, before I finish the job." I was incensed and disgusted. What an example to his men. I ordered the first sergeant to turn his name in as an SIW on the Morning Report.

Two GIs volunteered as witnesses and their names were turned in with my report. The lieutenant had only been with us a few days, but I needed commissioned platoon leaders. He just couldn't take it, I guess. I cannot remember his name, and it's just as well. I am also not aware of the Army's procedures in cases of this type. I never heard any more about it. However, the episode did help me to recall my struggle with my own pistol and the C-Ration can. If only that lieutenant had become as busy as I. Or, did he really want to be busy? Maybe I lacked a special kind of nerve to carry on my own shameful temptations to a conclusion.[37]

We took Bellevaux the next day against only half-hearted opposition. On 15 January 1945 the whole regiment moved south toward Francheville below the Amblève. About this time, we ran into a clever enemy withdrawal tactic. They would place belts of explosives around tree trunks where they lined the highways on both sides. When the explosives were detonated, the trees would fall across the roads in a criss-cross fashion, completely blocking any of our vehicles, including tanks. The fallen trees reminded me of giant matchsticks. The foot soldiers took to the fields and woods in pursuit of an enemy now in headlong flight. The blockade of trees was called an "abatis."[38]

The snow turned to rain and the rain to sleet. The sorry GI raincoats we wore stiffened and became coated with ice. We were all wretched. Words fail me. On 22 January 1945 we ran into some stiff resistance, near Kappelle. The enemy was dug in on the ridge south of the town. Battalion headquarters, for reasons unknown to me, had sent me a replacement by the name of Pvt. Anthony Pistilli. I've forgotten where he came from, but his record indicated that he was a real "foul ball."

I gathered that no company commander wanted him. Needing people, I decided to have a talk with the young man. We spoke in private. I laid down the law. I told him that Fox Company had real pride and that we had no room for anybody but honest-to-God soldiers. During the session with this woebegone character, I discovered something: this guy had been kicked around so much he had lost faith in himself and had discovered some sort of release in goofing off. Maybe a worthwhile assignment with some responsibility would bring him back.

On a hunch, and after discussing Pistilli with one of my platoon leaders, he was placed in an outpost for the night. We carefully explained to him just how much his buddies in Fox Company depended on people remaining alert in outposts to warn and to prevent, if possible, enemy patrol infiltrations, etc. The Germans were desperate and we could expect most anything at night, notably in the way of rash and often dire moves on their part.

During the night I heard a firefight of some magnitude on the company's flank. It died down. The platoon leader didn't yell for help. So, I continued my always-restless sleep. The next morning the platoon leader reported Pistilli as KIA. I investigated by checking the outpost myself. My yardbird had really come into his own. He was lying half out of his hole and had been hit several times. Finally, his M-1 had been silenced forever, but not until he had taken seven enemy with him only about fifteen yards from his hole. As near as I could determine, the whole combat patrol had either been wiped out or driven away. I secured the Bronze Star for Pistilli, awarded posthumously. Strange things happen to men when the chips are down. "God gives some the courage to defy even death," says the 119th *Combat History*.[39]

We moved on that morning. At Hinderhausen, three miles from St. Vith, we took many prisoners. Out on a highway, I heard a commotion coming toward me. Around a curve stumbled a formation of about twenty to twenty-five German prisoners of war, hands clasped above their heads and dressed only in their boots and their underwear shorts. Shivering and wretched they came on, goaded by three or four of my own people. I bellowed at them. The whole lugubrious aggregation came to a ragged halt. I picked out one of my own NCOs. "What in the Hinges of Hades are you trying to do, Sgt.?" "Well, sir, we just decided to have a little fun. So, we ordered them to strip." One of my seasoned and experienced NCOs, too. "Well, you get 'em back down that road. Get 'em dressed somehow and I want you back here in ten minutes. That's an order. I'll be waiting. Move!"

Back they came. This time with the prisoners of war dressed once again, but stripped of anything of value. I was used to that. It was always regarded as a front-line Joe's combat privilege. The rear echelon yardbirds would take the stuff anyway. I ordered my people to get those particular prisoners back to the rear compounds, fast. It's perhaps a trivial incident and maybe it was "fun." But it provides an inkling of the peculiar thinking of men who have been on-line perhaps a bit too long.

On 24 January 1945 tanks of the 7th Armored Division entered St.

Vith, from which they had been driven out in December. Old Hickory continued the drive forcing the Krauts to withdraw several miles south and east of the city and toward the German border. Then came the good news. The 30th Division was ordered to withdraw to an assembly area around Vielsalm, about fifteen miles west of St. Vith.[40]

"I am in a sort of second class Belgian chateau. We are catching our breath and thawing out. Have been living intermittently in raw winter weather, snow, ice, sleet, the whole bit. I could never begin to describe destruction I have seen since last July. I can only say it has been hard work being a rifle company commander. By the way, we'll be back in the Ninth Army soon." (27 January 1945)

"We are very proud of the role our rifle company played in this last fracas. As they say 'the situation is well in hand'. A bulging line has been straightened out. I am convinced that I am serving in one of the most famous infantry divisions in the history of warfare." (29 January 1945)

The famous Battle of the Bulge was over. From my fifty-yard line seat, I once again expressed my hatred of the insane Adolf Hitler. I had not the faintest idea, though, that he was about to give up. And he didn't, not for another bitter three months.

7. A Termination Is Culminated

2 February 1945–8 May 1945

After the successful conclusion of the Ardennes Campaign, the Allies set plans in motion to cross the Roer River and then the Rhine into the German heartland. Delayed by nationalistic jealousies, the need to restock manpower and stores, and bickering among their leading generals, the Allies put off a full assault until 24 February 1945. Arn and Fox Company, part of the Ninth Army, used this time to good advantage. They spent weeks integrating replacements, restocking supplies, and learning new methods for river crossing. Before the main attack began, Arn's luck ran out. While driving in a jeep to check his position, an enemy shell exploded near him. Wounded and angry at himself for taking a foolhardy risk, Arn left Fox Company for an evacuation hospital in Belgium and then for more specialized physical therapy in Paris. While he convalesced, Old Hickory accomplished the move across the Roer. Rotated off-line, the division went into reserve for more training and rehabilitation before spearheading the Rhine River breakthrough in Operation Flashpoint. Arn itched to return. After an absence of almost two months, he rejoined his command in time for the climactic battles that ended the war with Germany.

During the first few days of February 1945, rumors flew all over the place. We could move in several directions. One rumor was silly enough to indicate that we might even be going back home. We did in a way, but not in the direction of the United States. On 2 February 1945 we were trucked to an assembly area in Kohlscheid, Germany, and from there right back to our old positions on the Roer River. Even our reservation sign for Fox Company was still there. This amused me a bit in a way. Who would ever even want our position?

The eastern offensive into the Rhineland had indeed been delayed. We concentrated immediately on preparations for the crossing of the Roer River to our immediate front. We filled our depleted ranks with replacements, refurbished equipment, and acquired ammunition and fuel.

A new type of training was upon us. The 119th began river-crossing instruction around 9 February 1945. Training and more training followed. Often it meant that platoons would be withdrawn and sent to the rear for boat and pontoon crossing of rivers long since in the Allies' hands. The use of rubber boats were part of this river-crossing training. Due to the severity of the training, recuperation was the order of the day during the idle periods. I sent back units of Fox Company to the Inden River, Inden, Germany to participate in an intensive program. I was always grateful that the Krauts were content to harass us with sporadic, long-range artillery fire rather than actually launch an attack during this training period. But, on the other hand, the Roer River was as formidable to them as it was to us.

"My goodness! This would have been my tenth wedding anniversary and I could care less. We often take over as living quarters partially destroyed buildings and patch 'em up with canvas, old pup tents (who needs pup tents over here?), etc. In the open we use and live in foxholes. There is no protection to a pup tent. One has to burrow into the ground like a mole to stay alive. We also try to make sure we are as much protected from rain and snow as is possible. The ingenuity of the American soldier will remain in my memory forever." (3 February 1945)

"'Top Kick' Kirkman is still on leave in Florida. Meanwhile, another fine lad, 1st Sgt. Charlie Davis from McAlester, Oklahoma has taken Kirkman's place." (4 February 1945) "Christmas was bad but things got some better after that. No, I was unaware that a lot of our boys were marrying these European women. Must be happening in the rear areas. Certainly none of my 'doughs' are. We don't have time

1st Sergeant Charles H. Davis.

to think about that sort of thing up here. By the way, we have received strict orders to have nothing to do with German civilians of either sex."[1] (6 February 1945)

"We have much yet to do although Hitler is now sending old men and young boys against us. He's scraping the bottom of the barrel. What keeps him going? You should hear what I am hearing, 'way off' in the distance. Will you forgive me when I say that I am weary and sick of all of this?"[2] (8 February 1945)

Then the rains came. As we knew they would someday, the Germans blew the control sluices on one of the dams at the Roer's headwaters, and the lowlands beyond the banks of the Roer were filling with knee-deep water. The incessant rain didn't help. The attack shove-off was delayed.

I found out that the 8th (Golden Arrow) Division was somewhere near us, but I was not able to locate Lieutenant Harry Pender, my nephew. I also spent many hours with aerial photo maps. First Lieutenant (later Captain) Robert Henglein, my executive officer, joined me in those studies. We were informed that Cologne and the rich Ruhr sector would be the general objective of the Ninth Army. "Axis Sally" broadcast from Berlin that the 30th Division had returned from the Ardennes and was on-line for the Roer assault. I was always amazed at the enemy's knowledge of our exact locations.

We then practiced the crossings at night and that wasn't a pleasant experience at all. The Roer began to drop from flood stage on 14 February 1945 and the 30th Division was ready. Each man knew his specific assignment in each boat. Fox Company, to a man, understood all about the individual buildings in the town across the river in our particular assault sector. The aerial photos had been most helpful. Knowing our plans and sensing our build-up, the enemy stepped up the intensity of their artillery fire. Often it would be a pretty serious going over. Our own stuff was constantly harassing the enemy, and that activity sometimes accounted for some the Germans' silence or slowed action. Combat soldiers had to always be concerned about friendly fire. We restricted vehicle road traffic, and the division sector was covered with a smoke screen every morning, often several miles deep.[3]

Then I proceeded to make another foolhardy mistake. On 18 February 1945 I became apprehensive about the position of one of our platoons on our left flank. It seemed to me that they were taking an unusual amount of artillery fire. Even though I was getting no desperate messages, neither did I check for same. I decided to reconnoiter the platoon's area by jeep along a road that had been subjected to intermittent artillery fire from the enemy for some time. All vehicles making the run through necessity, not foolishness such as mine, had been harassed when scooting across an open stretch of this particular road. Somehow, the Krauts had good observation of that road. My perplexed and concerned driver and I took off with the motor wide open.

It was a mistake in judgment on my part. I'll never really know what happened. I guess my luck had finally run out. There came a deafening

Author (left) and Captain Robert J. Henglein.

noise and blinding flash. The driver and Captain Arn were launched into the air like tenpins. I came down on all fours in the middle of the road. The jeep bounced over into a roadside ditch. The driver, unhurt, thank God, was already scrambling up the road bank where he had been blown and looking for me. At first, I couldn't move. I knew that my right knee had taken the most punishment as I landed in the road. It seemed dead and numb. My neck hurt and my back, never strong anyway, pained seriously clear down into my groin. My driver got me on my feet and dragged me back down that damned highway.

Fortunately, we hadn't progressed too far from the main company area. A company medic examined the knee. He indicated that there was evidence of shrapnel or some substance from the road itself buried in the knee just to the left of the kneecap. The point of impact was bleeding, but not badly. However, the whole kneecap area was swelling rapidly and my whole body ached. The force of the blow from the fall was very evident, a major contusion if nothing else.

I was so disgusted with myself that I brought up every cuss word I could think of, and I had a choice selection. I had the medic clean the injury and slap some sulfa powder on it. At the time the knee was bandaged only. I indicated to Henglein that there would be no report to battalion headquarters, and also that I was NOT going to the rear for further attention. I planned to suffer for my stupidity.

Henglein seemed relieved, but I had a feeling he knew more about my condition than I did. Although he respected me and my judgment, I am certain now that he wondered why in the world I had not sent someone to check that platoon instead of going myself. He may have even decided that he detected a bit of combat fatigue in Fox Company's "Old Man." He might just have been right.

The next morning, I couldn't move my leg or bend the knee and the pain was intense. In fact, my whole body ached. I could feel something hard buried near the knee cap. Gosh, did it hurt! By nightfall, I was in such pain that I had a medic give me a shot. I was also becoming increasingly immobile. That was not good, for I expected the river-crossing attack order momentarily. In despair mixed with self-contempt, I called for Henglein and ordered him to take over, as I was going back to the Battalion Aid Station. I would be back, I informed everybody, in an hour or so.

I never saw Henglein or Fox Company until several weeks later. At the Battalion Aid Station, the medics made a hasty examination, and I was soon in an ambulance headed for the evacuation hospital which I have always thought was in Liège. "I am in the hospital. Not serious. My right knee is giving me the most trouble. I expect to be 100 percent in no time at all. Perhaps I'll be able to write more, for awhile at least." (22 February 1945) Again, I thought I wrote that letter from the 108th Evacuation Hospital in Liège. Friends in Belgium, whom I have made in recent years, tell me that there never was an evacuation hospital in Liège, or at least they've never uncovered it in their research. So where was I?[4]

The Roer River crossing took place on 24 February 1945, my Mother's sixty-fourth birthday, without Captain Arn. Incidentally, Henglein thanked me later for keeping him fully aware of what Fox Company was expected to do in the assault.[5]

A decision was made to ship me to Paris for further examination and possible therapy. On the trip, a bizarre incident occurred. The narrow, noisy hospital trains were lined with stretcher racks, three high on each side of a middle aisle. They tucked my stretcher into a floor level rack. The train pulled out in the dead of night bound for Paris. The ancient French railroad cars on those worn, bumpy, often hastily-repaired tracks made a clang and a clatter that constantly annoyed our tired, nervous American nurses and those patients that were conscious.

Many of the men in the car with me were seriously injured, and they kept the nurses busy up and down that aisle all night long. So I lay there, listening to the moans and groans that could often be heard above the train noise. I thought about my kids and what might happen to them in the next few days. I vowed that I would pray for them at every opportunity.

The car was lighted by kerosene lanterns. I idly checked my stretcher tag for lack of something better to do and to take my mind off the pesky pain in my knee. It wasn't my name on the tag at all! I had another name. I had lost a leg, and I was destined for England. What the hell? I glanced across the aisle. Ingeniously, the nurses had elevated the soldier's leg, what was left of it, into the air with a series of canvas straps attached to the rack above. It was, well, sort of in traction for want of a better description. But there was no leg below where the knee used to be. The lad's stump was thickly wrapped in heavy bandages. Not a new sight for me, but usually without the bandages.

He was completely unconscious. I reached across the aisle and checked his stretcher tag. His name was Captain E. Arn, O-1320396, and he had a major contusion of the right knee with evidence of possible shrapnel penetration and other body injuries. I lay there for an eternity in that jolting hospital car actually debating, I am ashamed to say, about what I should do. Hell, in the confusion in Paris, with the hordes of injured people they would be processing, I could be in a plane, across the Channel and bedded down in a quiet English hospital before anyone would discover the mistake. It would take weeks and weeks to get back on the line, and by that time maybe Hitler would have given up.

I muttered to myself, "Yeah, and this poor bastard, for the same stupid reasons, might be side-tracked in Paris for a long time before he would get the attention he so richly deserves. Maybe even long enough to die." I knew he needed expert care and attention. So did I, I found out later. But in no way was I as seriously hurt as he. Minutes passed while I had the shameful guts to argue with myself. I recalled other similar hysterical debates: that day in the hedgerows; the endless, hellish artillery concentration and my .45 at my head; the Siegfried C-Ration can floated by once again in that unforgettable mud puddle. Abruptly, I came to a decision. Calling a nurse, I showed her the mistake in the stretcher tags. As she changed them, she looked at me with a strange, inquiring look in her fatigue-rimmed eyes. "Thank you, captain." "You're welcome, sweetheart."

At the station in Paris, I watched them bundle my one-legged companion into an ambulance bound for an airstrip. I can't remember his name, and he never knew mine either, for he never regained consciousness while in my presence. Confession is good for the soul, they say, and there it is.

I was in the 40th General Hospital, a maternity hospital before the war. I was to be subjected to considerable therapy, but, fortunately, no surgery. The army surgeons had removed some foreign objects, either shrapnel or road debris, from the knee injury. However, the old knee was stiff as a board. I could not bend it at all.

"I am in Paris and coming along fine. Saw Mickey Rooney and his USO show this evening. There are movies every night if we are able and wish to go." (25 February 1945) "I have been transferred to another medical center in a suburban area of Paris. It is a former Jesuit monastery. There is a high brick wall around the lovely grounds outside. In this ward we swap yarns with one another. Evidently, an infantry rifle company commander who has been through what I have been through, according to the odds, is not supposed to have lasted as long as I did. I now wonder what I have neglected. Was I too cautious?"[6] (2 March 1945)

"My knee needed more sophisticated treatment than they were capable of giving at the other place. I am a special patient of a female therapist. She is a captain also, and gives me orders as if I were the last man in the third squad. I am performing all sorts of odd exercises." (8 March 1945) I remember that the captain produced a dish full of marbles. She would spread a towel on the floor, spill the marbles on it, and place the empty dish beside the towel. Using the toes of my right foot, I had to pick up each marble and place it in the dish. There were at least fifty marbles in the exercise. It was painful at first, because she insisted that I sit down to perform the exercise. The plate or dish could not be moved out of position. Eventually, I was forced to bend the knee, which was the whole idea of the exercise. Twice a day and an hour at a time. I had to do many other strange things with the wary eyes of that captain always upon me. The darned leg and knee began to respond.

"The medical people tell me that I suffered a terrible blow to my right knee. There was a danger of a blood clot at first, but none ever appeared. The treatments are to prevent a blood clot, as well as to restore the normal function of the knee once again without resorting to surgery. I understand the Germans used this place as a hospital during their occupation of Paris." (11 March 1945)

[Meanwhile, the Allies had launched the offensive into Germany.]

At 0245 on 23 February 1945 Old Hickory began the assault across the Roer River following a tremendous artillery barrage along the division's entire twenty-five mile front. Germans were seen scrambling for basements and holes. The 2nd Battalion crossed that afternoon after the 1st and 3rd Battalions. Selgersdorf, the 119th Regiment's immediate objective, fell before dawn with little resistance to the 1st Battalion. The prisoners taken were in a dazed condition from the brutal bombardment. By midnight of the 24th, Daubenrath, Hambach, and Niederzier had fallen to the eager beavers of the 119th. On the same day when the 117th Regiment took Steinstrass five miles east of Jülich, Old Hickory's units were the most advanced of the entire XIXth Corps. Königshoven, to the northeast, fell on the 28th of February. The German commander there stated after his capture that the 119th's action was the best example of infantry tactics he had ever seen in seventeen years of service.

The division now met only haphazard defenses in small towns. The main thrust was north toward Düsseldorf and the Ruhr Valley. On 6 March, Old Hickory rotated off-line, and moved back to Holland. The 119th Regiment occupied an assembly area near Susteren. Rehabilitation, rest, and further training were in order. My people were in no more danger, I found out later, than their restless captain. The Roer River campaign was over as far as the Ninth Army was concerned.[7]

In our former haunts in Holland, old friendships with the Dutch were renewed amid many ceremonies of gratitude and recognition. Passes to England or France were plentiful. Fox Company spent seventeen days, 6 March through 23 March 1945, in training and completely out of danger. This information came to me later, but I would have been very pleased had I known. However, another assignment was just around the corner. The Ninth Army was selected to spearhead the assault crossing of the Rhine River with Old Hickory to be the initial division in the action.

Back in Paris the Old Man, as I recall, was responding well to the treatments. Yet I was unable to get any of the doctors to sign an order of release. So I looked around for some diverting adventures. Nobody had any money in these hospitals. How could one acquire money as one became more and more ambulatory to get out of the place and see

Paris right there under my nose? I had met a Captain Maxwell of the 3rd Infantry Division who had taken a large chunk of shrapnel in his shoulder and back. I learned that he was my kind of a guy. I liked him, and it was mutual.

So in due time, I asked him if he were aware of the desperate shortage of soap in Europe. Yes, he was aware of that problem. I then presented a scheme to obtain some spending money. We would collect soap secretly, used soap of course, in the hospital washrooms. Then, somehow, when we had collected a good supply, we would get to the outer walls of the hospital and see what our precious product might demand in the current market. At first, Maxwell was reluctant. This guy had been a soldier for some time and he had met some real dandies. This Arn might be another of those loony-birds. I compromised. If he would help me collect the soap, I would take it from there.[8]

During the next day or so, wandering innocently around the vast hospital, he and I collected huge numbers of used bars of soap. We thrust the soap quickly into the generous pockets of our bathrobes and then secreted the loot under my mattress, in an old pillowcase, which we hoped the staff people wouldn't miss. Thoroughly intrigued by the scheme by now, Maxwell decided to continue his participation and join my sales staff.

One morning after breakfast, we sneaked out of the hospital (fortunately the weather was favorable), clad only in our pajamas and robes, and carried an ample supply of soap in all four pockets of our two robes into the surrounding garden. Luckily, we ran into a French gardener. Using my GI and high school French, I got him to understand what we wanted to do. He grinned and disappeared. In a moment or two, he was back with an ancient stepladder. Propping it against the brick wall, he motioned for us to climb. Because of my game knee, I hesitated, but only for a little bit. Laboriously and carefully, I reached the top of the wall. It was about a foot thick and provided ample room for comfortable sitting. I gestured to Maxwell to join me. He did.

A well-used sidewalk and road was right beneath us. We waited. Soon a civilian appeared. I motioned to him, and he approached us slowly and cautiously, looking up at us with an incredulous expression on his face, for we must have seemed like a couple of Martians. I selected a particularly large and inviting bar of soap out of my pocket. He stared at me and then the soap. I jabbered away, as if I were born in France, trying to convey to him that the soap was available to him and his friends, for a price.

He thought a moment, and then, strangely, ran away and around the nearest corner. "Well, that's it, Arn," groaned a disappointed Maxwell. "He didn't get the pitch at all. It's just another damned fool idea." "No, my friend," said I not too confidently. "He'll be back. He probably didn't have any money. You'll see." We waited. Minutes passed. I was about to give up when around that same corner came our Frenchman with a sizeable group of people. The word got around to the point where I was afraid the crowd would attract the hospital authorities, but the wall was high and there was plenty of thick brush and trees between the wall and the hospital building. Furthermore, security at the hospital was somewhat lax. Instinct told me that the market would stand a price of five francs per bar, regardless of size. Ten cents in U.S. money. No problem. The market was there, and the price was right. Within a half hour or so, we were sold out.

I made our newfound customers to understand that we would be back the next morning. I also warned them that if they made too much noise, the GI salesmen would no longer be available and neither would the soap. Our spree went on for three mornings. Maxwell and I soon had enough money to enjoy, within reason, an eight-hour pass in Paris. That precious gardener never said a word. Bless him! I slipped him four or five pieces of soap. He was most grateful. I charged it off as a sales expense.

"I secured an eight-hour pass yesterday to Paris. Captain Maxwell and I saw much of this 'Open City,' practically untouched by war. The Arc de Triomphe, Champs Elysées, Notre Dame Cathedral, Napoleon's Tomb, and a host of other places."[9] (15 March 1945)

Although I didn't describe or indicate such activities to my parents, my wounded friend and I also wandered through some of the nightlife of "Gay Paree." For example, there was the Bel Tabarin where the chorus line of I-don't-know-how-many lovely ladies appeared topless, an expression that would become popular in America a bit later, but which was quite familiar to the Parisians in the mid-forties. Prices were beginning to soar, and good champagne cost about seven hundred francs, or fourteen dollars a bottle. I thanked the Good Lord that the used soap business had been exceptional.

We also had our first glimpse of Pigalle or "Pig Alley," as the GIs referred to it. In this area the "femmes de la rue" (prostitutes) swarmed and their charms were available at rather reasonable prices. Maxwell and I had other problems, lodged in the rather generous quantities of cognac, champagne, and even beer which we had consumed during the course of our eight hours. We were apparently making up for lost time.

Needless to say, we had considerable difficulty locating the metro station where we were to catch the train that would take us back to the hospital before the expiration of our passes. Stumbling about, Maxwell fell and opened the wound in his shoulder. Noting that he was beginning to bleed, I managed to signal a passing MP jeep. These guys were wonderful. As soon as they ascertained our problem, and learned that we were Purple Heart combat Joes, they became our buddies. First, they took us to the nearest Military Aid Station and had Maxwell's wound dressed. Then they whisked us out to the hospital only minutes before our passes would have expired. It was quite an experience. I never could dislike MPs after that. My wild trip to Paris' sights and scenes had not done my game knee any good at all and I was set back some. The staff people involved were quite disgusted.[10]

By the way, earlier in the evening at the Olympic Theater, we heard the Glenn Miller band with Johnny Desmond singing and Ray McKinley on the drums. Miller's plane had disappeared in the English Channel several weeks before, and neither he nor the plane were ever found. McKinley led the band. I loved the whole concert and so did the capacity crowd.

"My captain from basic training at Camp Croft was admitted here yesterday. He's still a captain. He didn't recognize me but I knew him. 'You've come a long way in a short time, Arn,' said he. 'I had some good training under some able people, captain, and I've been more than lucky also.'" (17 March 1945) My badly wounded former CO flashed me a grateful smile.

"The 119th Regiment made the Rhine River crossing at 0200 hours at Büderich, Germany. Casualties were light. I sure wish I had been with the company. I have to be absolutely nuts, for I miss those guys of mine. Incidentally, I have become acquainted with one of the regimental COs of the 106th Division, my old outfit in the States. His room is across the hall. The colonel is in serious condition but he will recover. He is pleased to know that one of the 106th's former officers is alive and recuperating. We have exchanged many a story."[11] (24 March 1945)

I think the colonel's name was Perkins, but I am not sure. An attractive, long-legged French girl would come and visit with him everyday. I never knew how he got to know her. She was living in Paris when the Germans arrived in 1940. When the city was retaken by the Allies, she was wounded during the course of the liberation. "Show the captain where you were hit," ordered the colonel one day when both the girl and I were visiting in his room. Unabashed, which was not too unusual in Europe, she pulled up her skirt and displayed a nasty scar high on her thigh. Inwardly, I enjoyed looking at her shapely legs, but openly expressed my admiration for her courage. I wonder how American women would react in the middle of an intense battle in the heart of one of our great cities? I haven't the faintest idea.[12]

"I consider myself fit for return to active duty. However, the medical authorities here are taking their time. I could be lost also somewhere in military red tape. I know there is much going on where F Company is right now. I have had no mail now for over a month, but that is understandable." (26 March 1945) "I miss my gang deeply. I'm 100 percent now, and cooling my heels. The 30th Division seems to be in the middle of everything as always." (27 March 1945)

"Went to the Casino de Paris last evening. My French continues to improve. These French natives sure love fun and excitement. I am impatiently waiting for shipping orders. The 30th is in the Ninth Army and the 21st Army Group under Field Marshal Montgomery." (2 April 1945) "Received a cluster to my Purple Heart today, this one for injuries received 18 February 1945. That means two Purple Hearts. Had a good physical. Passed okay. I'm overweight, up to 178 pounds." (3 April 1945) "Somewhere in France and on my way back to destiny."[13] (4 April 1945)

Men in mess line.

[By the time Arn received clearance to rejoin Fox Company], Old Hickory had played a key role in the Ninth Army's assault across the Rhine. In the 30th's sector, the Rhine was about one thousand feet wide, but it was deep and the current was swift. The obstacle presented some problems to the five-mile front assigned to our division, extending from where the Lippe River entered into the Rhine on the north to Mehrum on the southern flank.

Old Hickory went from Echt, Holland, to an area close to the Rhine. All three of the 30th's regiments were to attack abreast. The 119th Regiment moved up on the night of the 19th, and bivouacked in the woods near Issum. The 2nd Battalion led the crossing and when across was to seize and hold a bridgehead. The battalion took only forty minutes to get across at 0200 on 24 March 1945. Apparently, it was a tactical surprise. The enemy didn't even seem to be ready for the assault. By the 25th, the 119th had advanced three miles beyond the river. On the 26th, they were in Gahlen, ten miles east of the Rhine, where house-to-house street fighting developed against a fanatical enemy. By the 28th, Gahlen was in American hands.

The brass by now was doing everything possible to keep casualties and battle fatigue to a minimum, particularly since the Allies outnum-

Bivouac, kitchen of F Company.

bered the enemy who were becoming increasingly demoralized and exhausted. Why waste people unnecessarily? After only four days of fighting, a drop in the bucket by the standards of just a few weeks ago, the 30th Division was pulled out of line, and the 8th Armored Division passed on through to continue the move toward Berlin.

As the spring days of April 1945 arrived, the 30th Division moved back into action, with the 119th Regiment being credited with having taken over fifteen thousand prisoners of war since the hectic days in Normandy. The Ninth Army was really rolling, ever eastward. Germany was on its deathbed, everywhere. Bielefeld, Detmold, and Hamelin (of "Pied Piper" fame) on the Weser River fell. Brunswick was next, and General Hobbs asked the German commander to surrender unconditionally. He refused. On 6 April 1945 Brunswick succumbed with only token resistance. The division then learned that its next objective was to reach the Elbe River in the vicinity of Magdeburg.[14]

"Somewhere in Holland. My outfit is moving fast. Hard to keep close behind. I'll never forget those sheets, mattresses, and toilets in that hospital. I have heard that the 30th Division may be ordered to the

Tent city.

China/Burma/India Theater (CBI) after this European struggle is over and invade Japan."[15] (7 April 1945)

"I am back in Germany, and Roosevelt is dead. 'Now he belongs to the ages,' as they once said of Abraham Lincoln.[16] I crossed the Rhine by truck at Wesel, coming up from Roermund, Holland, Hamm, then Münster. The Rhine was 'just another river crossing,' a British soldier told me. Ran into one of my old NCOs from the Ft. McClellan days at Roermund. He had been hit, recovered, and was returning to his old outfit. He wanted me to have him transferred to Fox Company. I told him I'd try.[17] The Air Force has done a devastating job, in evidence everywhere. In Hamelin, on the Weser, the roads were choked with Czechs, Germans, Poles, Russians, Jews, and French from everywhere. They call them 'slave laborers' or 'displaced persons' (DPs). There is hate on some German faces, but I could care less. I carry a pistol wherever I go, loaded. I am in an old twelfth century castle. It is filled with historical things. Wonder how long those historical things will be here? Trucks roar through the village on the road below the castle in a steady stream eastward. Surely, the Germans must now be convinced they are not the 'Super Race' Hitler told them they were." (13 April 1945)

Word came to the place where I was hanging my helmet, most likely in the Hanover-Brunswick area, that the American singer, Dinah Shore, was in the neighborhood. Would any of us care to visit with her? I was the first one in the vehicle. We rode forward to a designated spot, a wooded place, in a hard rain, a good April shower. Getting out of the vehicle, we were led to a sort of clearing in the woods. There, surrounded by an enthusiastic bunch of GIs, was Dinah. She was standing on the tailgate of a troop carrier, drenched to the skin with the rain pouring down over her hair and face. This wonderful gal was doing her best, which was especially good, to entertain. The soldiers would pop song titles at her and she tackled them all. "If I don't know the words, do you mind if I just hum the tunes?" she queried with water streaming down her face. She never faltered, nor did she once complain about anything. We stood there enthralled. The men with rifles carried them over their shoulders with butts up, thus preventing the rain from entering the barrels. Dinah had been singing for sometime when we got there, and she performed for at least another half-hour. When she finally decided to leave, she gave us a little talk about how grateful she was to be there, and she thanked us all from the folks back home for the great job we were doing. Then that carrier rumbled off down the road. I shall never forget Dinah Shore as she was that particular wet afternoon. The unabashed trooper of 1945. A soldier's woman.[18]

I reached Fox Company, at last, on 15 April 1945, after nearly two months' absence. I like to remember that the men seemed glad to see me. Benny, my good friend, was extremely happy. I am fairly certain that Bob Henglein perhaps greeted my return with the same inner feelings that I had when Captain Kirklin came up and took over several months before. However, I had been the CO of Fox Company longer than anyone else, during its tour of duty in Europe and during its most trying times. I had earned and deserved my return to the responsibility involved, no matter how hazardous it might continue to be.

It was gratifying to discover that Henglein had performed well. I was shocked beyond belief when I received the news that my brave and

First Lieutenant Ray O. Beaudoin, platoon leader extraordinary and Congressional Medal of Honor winner, and author (right).

valiant Ray Beaudoin had been killed in action back in the vicinity of Hamelin. Ray held the Purple Heart, the Bronze Star, and the Silver Star. He died a first lieutenant. I immediately inaugurated the process for gathering full details for the action in which his death resulted. I found out that he and his Second Platoon were in the attack toward Hamelin across some open terrain. The platoon had been pinned down by intense enemy fire. He proceeded to wipe out a three-man sniper nest, all alone, and continued to advance against a machine gun emplacement. In the process of wiping out the latter, he was killed. His individual heroism allowed his Second Platoon to advance to the outskirts of Hamelin.

I determined to put Ray in for the Congressional Medal of Honor. After the shooting war was over, I conducted the research necessary with the assistance of Bob L'Herreux, one of our brilliant and well-educated enlisted men in the company, and submitted the story to the proper authorities for consideration. Many months later, his parents notified me that this nation's highest honor had been awarded to Ray, posthumously, in Holyoke, Massachusetts. Over a thousand people came to Holyoke's War Memorial Building for the ceremony conducted by Lieutenant General Oscar W. Griswold of Washington, D.C. The famous medal's ribbon was placed around William Beaudoin's neck. He was Ray's father.

Ray was first buried in the American National Cemetery in Margraten, Holland. Here, the Dautzenberg family of Waubach, Holland, took loving care of his grave. His family, sometime later, had Ray's body brought back to the States and he is now buried in a cemetery near Holyoke, Massachusetts. I visited his grave with members of his family in 1975. During the Korean War, a troopship named the "Raymond Beaudoin" carried men to the Korean Theater of War. He was a lad of excellent character and an intrepid soldier. I will respect his memory forever.[19]

Sgt. Kirkman had returned from leave, and I was able to retain 1st Sgt. Davis. Fox Company was now blessed with the two finest Top Kicks in the entire Ninth Army. They shared duties graciously and efficiently. After clearing through Lieutenant Colonel McCown, who greeted me as warmly as he was capable of greeting anyone, I located Fox Company dug in somewhat east of Magdeburg on the River Elbe.

We moved on through a series of relatively light firefights that were usually sustained by diehard SS troopers still armed and unquestionably dangerous. Less fanatical Germans were surrendering in wholesale numbers. Often, a whole battalion would be lined up at the side of a road with their officers at stiff attention extending their pistols butt forward in surrender. Magdeburg was just sixty miles west of Potsdam; suburban Berlin. We dreamed of entering that city soon. The strategy for the taking of Magdeburg required Fox Company to move back to the west bank of the Elbe River in order to coordinate with the 117th and the 120th Regiments in the effort to subdue the huge city.

On 18 and 19 April 1945 Old Hickory took Magdeburg, with all three regiments involved in the action. The Air Force had bombed the city into a gigantic pile of rubble. Once again, however, the fanatics held out. Flame-throwing tanks were used to drive out Hitler Youth snipers. But here again hordes of less enthusiastic Germans surrendered without firing a shot.

Schönebeck, up river to the south and about ten miles from Magdeburg, became the objective of the 119th's 2nd Battalion. I recall proceeding cautiously, on a long-forgotten mission, down one of the streets of Schönebeck. Suddenly, a rifle cracked and a slug chipped the brick wall just above my helmet. A Browning Automatic Rifle spoke insistently right behind me. The rain of bullets seemed to pull the sniper right out of a high window several yards ahead. The riddled body proved to be that of a teenage girl. "She was trying hard to get you, captain," shrugged my blessed BAR man somewhat indifferently. "Thanks, soldier," and I moved on. It had been that close many times before, but I didn't like to remember them.

The preliminary bombing attack of the Air Force had also played havoc with Schönebeck. Miserable, frightened, hungry civilians crawled out of their basements crying "Hitler! Kaput!" or "Hitler! Nix gut!" It was ironic, for I knew that the German people had, outwardly at any rate, "bought" Adolf Hitler for over twelve years and they followed him like robots. What a price they had paid for their misguided belief in him. Nevertheless, one more vast heap of rubble was in the hands of Old Hickory.

"Somewhere east of the Rhine. Pfc. Monty Montalvo has found a cute Pekingese dog. A company mascot, if you please. When one yells, 'Heil! Hitler!,' the little fellow gets up on his hind legs and raises his right forepaw. Many of the Kraut civilians are scared of us. They take one look and then dive back into their cellar hovels. They have been told by Hitler's propaganda machine that we Americans will loot, rape, and destroy. Not all of us intend to do that. Thousands of American GIs feed these 'unfortunate German kids' out of their own rations. During the past in precarious situations, I have seen them share their chocolate rations with youngsters one moment and open fire on Kraut soldiers the next. I have a German radio in my jeep. Things have been a lot worse than they are right now."[20] (21 April 1945)

The 2nd Battalion was now occupying all of Schönebeck-on-the-Elbe. In Fox Company's occupational zone, I stationed a full platoon and dug into the Elbe River bank, watching carefully for any movement on the other side. I rotated the rifle platoons for this assignment. The rest of the company was quartered in buildings, of a sort, keeping dry and eating Sgt. Jones' hot chow once again. Alex Harvey, our communication sergeant from Minneapolis, was a professional photographer in civilian life. He had discovered an abandoned photographer's studio. Several of the men "requisitioned" cameras and huge supplies of film. Fox Company was well photographed, and Harvey developed all film in the vanished photographer's dark room. Alex was in seventh heaven.

"When the shooting war is over, we will do occupational work until the Military Government (MG) people come in and take over. Since we are getting little or no enemy fire now, we are performing some of the Military Government's functions." (29 April 1945) "The war in Europe must be almost over. We're still on the Elbe River." (4 May 1945)

I had organized a Fox Company Command Post in what had been a nice brick stucco home near the river. It was fairly intact and unoccupied. One night in the middle of a good rest, I was roused out of my bedroll by the sentry at the door. It must have been about 0200 in the morning. He had two dripping wet people with him, a uniformed Luftwaffe pilot with an empty sleeve dangling at his side and a forlorn German female. They were both in their late twenties. Much earlier, I had found all sorts of GIs in Fox Company who could speak whatever language was needed at the moment. One of my people who could speak German was called to the command post. We pieced their story together.

He had worked in Berlin before and during the war. After his injury, he had been stationed in Berlin on special assignments. They had met and married. Stalin's oncoming animals frightened them both. The woman related stories of rape and pillage at the hands of the "Russkys," which we found almost unbelievable. Later, facts drifted through to confirm her stories and those of many others. Knowing their cause was about lost, they had managed to get through the Russian lines now encircling Berlin and stumbled west. The ex-pilot reported that there were roving, disorganized bands of Germans between the Elbe River and the Russian lines still fighting fanatically against Russian troops. He had the impression the Russians were moving west to meet the Allied forces at the Elbe. This proved to be true, eventually. These two wet and exhausted people had decided that the Americans might be a little less barbaric than they had been led to believe. They couldn't possibly be as inhuman as the Russians. They would try to seek refuge behind the American lines, and were finally picked up by my river bank kids after they had swum the Elbe. I sent both of them to battalion headquarters for further interrogation and disposal.[21]

During this period, I recall my men bringing in another young German girl. She had a bright, blue-eyed, blonde boy in her arms of perhaps one or two years of age. She had violated the civilian curfew established by the Allies and had been picked up. Questioning revealed that she had been one of thousands of carefully selected young girls who had been whisked out of their homes and taken to isolated places. Here, they were mated, or bred, whichever expression you prefer, to equally well-screened young males for the creation of the "Master Race," as defined by Hitler. His purpose, in conjunction with his attempt to exterminate the Jewish race, was to create a super race of Germans, who would rule the world in the not-too-distant future.

The young lady wore with pride a handsome medal on a chain around her neck. I asked to examine it. She complied. The inscription made clear that she had produced a child for Hitler. The Nazi government had recognized her patriotism and devotion to the cause by presenting her with this medal. I was given the impression that when Hitler was at the zenith of his popularity, such women had acquired status and social distinction. I was not about to predict what would happen to her in a defeated Germany from now on, and I didn't bother to even care. We warned her about the curfew and sent her on her way.[22]

Then came a real shocker. I was called back to the battalion headquarters. "Captain Arn," barked McCown. "We're not at all certain of the enemy strength across the river, nor do we have any idea where the Russians are at this moment. Our instructions are to hold here and wait for them. I want you, personally, to take some men, cross the river, and come back with whatever information you can uncover."

I was astonished. I could have fallen over dead. I wanted to. "Sir, the war is almost over. We have every reason to believe there are Germans over there, although we haven't seen or heard of any for some time." In desperation, I added, "Why must we run the risk of more casualties?" "Arn, some of our people in tanks crossed over on a bridge built by the engineers, down river, several days ago. They hadn't advanced ten miles toward Berlin when division ordered them to pull back to this side of the Elbe and wait for the Russians. Evidently, our leaders have decided that there is no particular advantage to the Allies to be involved with the fall of Berlin. The Russians are there in force, and will take the city soon. Nevertheless, I think it's most important for us to know what's going on across the river in our own battalion sector." Still looking dumbfounded that out of a whole battalion of men and officers he would pick me, I glared at him and said simply: "Yes, sir." And left.[23]

I proceeded to handpick a squad of my very best and most experienced men. I ordered them armed to the teeth with everything from hand grenades to Thompson sub-machine guns, bazooka, BARs, the works. One of my sergeants commandeered an old flat-bottomed river boat. We climbed in and made for the opposite shore, not knowing what to expect or where it would come from. I can barely recollect some sort of village, hamlet, group of buildings, or what-have-you opposite Schönebeck. In my exasperation, I had failed to ask whether there would be any support from battalion on the west bank. Unusual for me, but it will give you some idea of how upset I was over this whole damned-fool project.

Having long since qualified for membership in the "Nervous in the

Service Club," I expected all sorts of trouble. I was convinced that McCown was having his own mental problems from months of combat duty and was still trying to "play war" to the ultimate end. We reached the far bank of the Elbe without incident. Dispersing the squad over a reasonable wide expanse, we made for the buildings. Nothing. Ruins. Dead cattle. No Krauts. Not even dead ones, and probably more important to me, no Russians. Should I return or should I explore further for Russians?

Suddenly, I was becoming interested in the mission, returning to the old groove, so to speak. I would go on and radioed battalion to that effect. What the hell; maybe we'd reach Berlin. Organizing the squad into a column of staggered ducks, with wide intervals between people, we moved east using the one road available away from the river. My map indicated that there was a town about five or six miles further east. Nothing. I sent two scouts way out ahead; still no problems. No signs of life, either. We trudged on. I am sure that my men must have thought I left my good sense back in the hospital.

I have no idea as to how far we had progressed when we heard music, even singing, shouting. But we still had no evidence of guards, outposts, roadblocks, or any kind of security. We entered a small hamlet without challenge of any type. Unless I was completely out of my mind, there were Russians all over the place, having a ball and for the most part intoxicated.

Halting the squad, I called Pfc. Igor Karpenko forward. Thank God I'd had the foresight to select him to come with me. Igor was from Baltimore and of White Russian ancestry. He spoke Russian fluently. Motioning to the men to stay where they were, Karpenko and I grabbed the first "Ivan" we came to. Blinking his bloodshot eyes, the guy's mouth fell open. He was looking at the first Americans he had ever seen. He just stood there. Igor began to jabber away at him asking for his CO, headquarters, and so forth. Now, the stupefied Russky was really perplexed. An American soldier speaking Russian? Motioning to us to follow, we moved down the street.

A building was indicated to us as our destination. We entered, and found nothing but chaos. Drunken pandemonium. "King Vodka" had taken charge. A real orgy was underway, including German women and what passed for Russian females. The latter were truly ugly. Only vodka, in large quantities, could help to make them the least bit presentable.

There was a tipsy curiosity in evidence very quickly, but not for long. The bleary-eyed Russians had other things than matters military on their sotted minds. I had orders to carry out, and I was exasperated. I turned to Karpenko for help out of the dilemma. He finally discovered the ranking officer in charge. When, through Karpenko, I was able to penetrate his drunken incredulity, he arranged to use a Mercedes Benz, over which he had assumed ownership, to get us back to the river, as he had recovered enough to comprehend my mission. It would be necessary for my men to follow on foot. Putting a sergeant in charge, I ordered him to return as quickly as possible.

We reached the river, turning down many offers out of the Russian's jug. Igor and I managed, somehow, to get the weaving, loaded Russian into the river boat together with two or three of his staff. McCown was waiting for us. He also had an interpreter. I didn't say anything, and neither did McCown. I left him with the problem.

Igor and I returned to the other shore, and waited for our squad. We all returned to Fox Company's area. I never heard anything more about the caper. As they say, "I had seen my duty and I done it." To this day, I think it was a stupid, play-soldier, potentially dangerous undertaking.[24]

"Nobody is supposed to have anything to do with German civilians. My big-hearted GIs want to be friendly, especially with the kids. I suppose the situation will get worse. We are living in what we call 'luxury.' There is an air of suspense everywhere. We are dealing mostly with civilian problems right now." (6 May 1945)

At 0900, 7 May 1945 battalion headquarters issued copies of a telegram, issued under General Eisenhower's authority, to the four company commanders, which announced the unconditional surrender of all German land, sea, and air forces in Europe. Tuesday, 8 May 1945, would be V-E DAY, Victory in Europe henceforth and forevermore. Grand Admiral Karl Dönitz, successor to the late Adolf Hitler, had ordered the surrender.[25]

The author at his desk
on V-E Day.

I can easily recall now the emotion that welled up into my breast. In
the privacy of my quarters, after the battalion runner had left, I cried
like a baby. Recovering finally, I thanked God for the ending of a horrible chapter in American history.

I called my four platoon leaders to the command post. I read Ike's
wire to them. Only silence greeted me for a second or two, a poignant
second. The emotions involved were just too much for them. Silently,
they turned from me and made their way back to their various platoon
areas to give the news to the waiting GIs.

I sat down that evening and wrote to my Mother and Dad: "Tonight,
I should be gloriously elated. Perhaps I should be doing something
which would indicate that I know this ghastly nightmare is over. But,
Mother and Dad, I look about me and there is no elation. These men
have really won this war in Europe and yet they show no signs of that
touching fact. We have news that Times Square in New York City is

teeming with humanity, delirious people almost mad with joy. Here, we can only remember the men who are not here with us tonight: the heat and the dust of St.-Lô; the cracking limbs and falling leaves above me as I crouch behind those wretched hedgerows; the ominous, stubborn pillboxes of the Siegfried Line; the cold unhappiness and black shell holes against the unfeeling snow of the "Bulge." These are only a few of the reasons why we are silent tonight. I swear I will never gloat over the laurels of victory. In this hour I humbly thank God for my life and for both of you."

8. We Long for Home

10 May 1945–28 July 1945

Assigned to occupation duty in west-central Germany, Arn participated in the preliminary stages of the far-reaching postwar decisions that the victors made about establishing order, disarming the enemy, administering humanitarian relief, securing economic recovery, and restoring civilian rule. Yet Arn knew that with the war only half over, the Army would redeploy men and equipment from the European Theater of Operations for the proposed invasion of the Japanese home islands. He further shared the feeling typical of many battle-weary and homesick troops who believed they deserved the right to be discharged. This attitude posed a dilemma for the Department of War. Losing such seasoned front-line troops might prolong the war, but keeping them in service might also hinder their morale. As a solution, the Army adopted a redeployment and discharge program based on a complex set of points soldiers had earned during active service. The highest point men would either be reassigned to stateside duty or be discharged. Although Arn had enough points, he felt torn by his loyalty to his comrades in Fox Company and his human desire to resume his life. Making a painful decision, he chose to become a citizen without a uniform.

Somewhere in the heart of rural Germany. This is my first letter since peace is absolutely certain. We have moved to a small German town deep in farm territory untouched by

Arn's headquarters, Ausleben, Germany. Note his Jeep and civilian car parked out front.

war, physically anyway. I have taken over a large chateau, and have four German women as house servants under the direction of Pfc. Bennett. I am known as the 'Commandant' throughout the village. My men have located an ice cream plant and the man who owns it. With the help of Sgt. Jones, we will have ice cream soon. Free. A bakery has been discovered by my ingenious people. Our Fox Company baker will operate it under the close supervision of Sgt. Jones. I feel like a political power backed up by military might. I am almost feared wherever I go. The Germans are used to this. They expect arrogance. If I am stern, I do try to give attention to their needs. In turn, I demand strict adherence to the new Supreme Headquarters Allied Expeditionary Forces (SHAEF) regulations and no more than that. We are all in beds in civilian homes, and I am enjoying the profound contentment of just being alive." (10 May 1945)

"Ausleben, Germany. Censorship has been lifted. These Krauts were swept off their feet by an eloquent demagogue, with tremendous military power behind him. They refused, a majority anyway, to admit that the path of violence would lead them nowhere. They worshiped everything that signified power. They adored the military and the show of might. I am in charge of this town and three others. I have a platoon in each. The civilian males are either very young or very old, or disabled veterans without arms, legs, or suffering from blindness. Food is rationed. The women have lined and haunted faces. We are working hard and swiftly to screen all in order to uncover those who were hardcore Nazis."[1] (16 May 1945)

Bob L'Herreux, a young man in the Fox Company Headquarters group, was fast proving to be of inestimable value to me. He first came up as a replacement in the Bulge. They had scraped the bottom of the barrel again, and this particular buck private had been a clerk-typist in an air base in England. He hadn't fired a rifle since his basic training in the States. In disgust, I sent him to the weapons platoon where he became an ammunition bearer in one of the mortar sections. I forgot all about him. Three or four days later, as I recall, Pierce reported this same chap as missing in action (MIA).

I hated to report MIAs, for they presented a mystery. Why? Where were they? What happened? Did they deliberately just wander away? Is some native family harboring them? Did they run in the face of the enemy? And so on. There were, as a rule, few answers. Just MIA. Anyway, a few days went by, and Pierce reported that our MIA was back with his platoon. He had become lost in the darkness of night, and strayed from the area. His confused wanderings took him to another company's sector. During a counterattack, I was able to confirm, he had grabbed a machine gun and made a darned good account of himself.

It was my pleasure to discover that my one-time yardbird could speak French, German, and some Italian. He had a law degree from Georgetown University and was already an accomplished lawyer before entering the service. After the "shooting war" was over, I had him transferred to my headquarters group where his many talents could be used to the best advantage. Bob performed all sorts of important tasks: straightened out the company records, coordinated with our two top kicks in a variety of ways, acted as an interpreter time and time again, assisted and frequently wrote the company valor awards, and even

Second Lieutenant Robert D. L'Herreux (right) receives his officer's commission.

proved helpful in our brief exposure to the pitfalls of city government in our occupied towns.

For example, one morning the burgomaster (mayor) of Ausleben, a distraught girl, and an upset, anguished couple appeared at my headquarters asking for me. The girl's head and face were wrapped in bandages. I motioned to L'Herreux to find out what they wanted. The story was not a pleasant one. One of my own men had spent a part of the previous night with the girl. After he had satisfied his physical needs, according to the victim, he had simply tried to put his big, heavy GI combat boot, with his foot in it, right through her face. Her nose and jaw were broken and she had a deep cut under one eye that had required stitches. Her whole face was bruised and swollen. She gave Bob a description, and I knew at once who the culprit was, one of my best combat people. I sent for him. Confronted by his playmate of the night, he admitted he had administered the punishment. When I asked him why, he replied almost indifferently: "Well, sir, after I was through with her I got to thinking of all the guys in this company who aren't going home with us because of these damned Krauts. It made me so angry, I lost my head. So, I pushed her face in."

Even though I could understand his mental reaction, the act itself was inexcusable. I had to show these people that I could control my soldiers as well as the Germans. I had Bob inform the family that the offending soldier would be confined to quarters for one week, with only the despised K-Rations for food. I also made arrangements for the girl to be examined and treated by our own army doctors. Damned funny thing when I think about it, but I can't recall the girl or her parents complaining that she was raped. The protests were about the injuries she received.

[Two other members of Fox Company were equally helpful to Arn.] My executive officer was First Lieutenant George Fischer of Baltimore. A good soldier. He had been First Platoon leader in the Bulge and the Rhineland. Pfc. Louis C. Cullen proved a person of considerable note over in Ottleben. We called him "Doc." The village was crowded with all sorts of Displaced Persons (DPs). Doc was a platoon medic. He had acquired certain basic skills as a result of much time in combat. He became the town doctor for most minor problems. The villagers loved him. Cullen was from Missouri.

Soon after that, I received a complaint that one of our men had stolen considerable jewelry from a German family. An investigation revealed the loot in the bottom of one of my men's barracks bag. The young man confessed, but explained his act by saying that he thought conquering soldiers were allowed to plunder the enemy, including civilians. History books prove the guy had a point. However, I had the stolen property restored to the rightful owners. Nor did I punish the soldier.

The military "wheels" now began to make preparations for the invasion of Japan, the final submersion of the "Rising Sun." It promised to be

Ausleben, Germany. My headquarters while we were there. (Author on left, First Lieutenant George E. Fischer on right.)

a costly maneuver, but it had to be done now that Hitler was through in Europe and Mussolini's ambitions had been snuffed out. A point system was established. So many points for each dependent, so many for each decoration, for each month of service, for each month overseas, etc.[2]

"I have lots of points but officers of my background will probably be given three choices: occupational work here in Europe; transfer to the China/Burma/India (CBI) Theater by way of the States; direct assignment to the CBI from Europe. There is also a rumor going around that if one has *x* number of points consideration will be given for an honorable discharge. I am so grateful to be alive that I haven't given much thought to the future, in the service or out.

"We are now trying to process Hitler's 'slave laborers' for return to their own countries. Germans who have been bombed out have to be clothed and fed and sheltered, too. My towns are: Ausleben, Ottleben, Beckendorf, and Warsleben. They are in an area about twenty miles west of Magdeburg. If you're checking your map look for Oschersleben; my towns are not too far away. I have a civilian car and a Swiss driver. Organization, responsibility, and proper delegation are the keys to success in any venture. I have learned about the importance of those three in the army. By the way, it's amazing how much better one can sleep when one takes some clothes off." (20 May 1945)

We were all pleased and proud when Undersecretary of War Robert Patterson visited our area. He proved to be a pleasant guy. Later, he sent General Hobbs a note thanking him for the courtesy extended to him while in Old Hickory's domain.[3]

A few more words about my Mercedes-Benz in Ausleben. My Swiss driver kept the old jalopy washed and polished until it shown with elderly pride. One day the motor stalled. The driver persuaded a nearby farmer friend to pull the dying vehicle into town with his horse. My driver steered, and I stayed in the car enjoying the leisurely pace. Back in town my driver got the car going again only to have it catch fire, a short or something. Willie Jones, one of the company jeep drivers, happened to be in the vicinity. Grabbing his jeep fire extinguisher, he managed to put out the blaze. The Mercedes-Benz had had it. I went back to riding in the jeep with Willie, who was from Alabama and had joined the 30th in the States in August 1942.

During this time about ten of my men were taken on a tour of the infamous Buchenwald Camp, which was in the vicinity of Weimar, Germany. Heinrich Himmler, the Nazi head of the SS and minister of the interior, and his colleagues had created this awful place, one of several. When they came back, my kids told me that a normal day for an unfortunate inmate would begin at 0400 in the morning and end at 2000 at night. Sixty thousand slept on four by six shelves of wood. Each shelf accommodated three men. There were two latrines for the sixty thousand. Often they were clubbed and hung up on meat hooks like butchered cattle, and then the crematorium. One hundred-twenty per day died that way. In what was called a hospital, six patients were assigned to a six by six bed. One SS doctor murdered seventeen thousand persons in two years by injecting poison in their systems. The skin of the victims was often used to make "parchment" lampshades. Buchenwald was active for eight years, a never-to-be-forgotten symbol of man's inhumanity to man.[4]

Then Fox Company received a wonderful tribute. An American infantry division held three regiments. Each regiment consisted of twelve companies, or thirty-six companies in a division. Imagine my surprise and elation when our Fox Company was selected, out of these thirty-six, to furnish fifty men to act as a special honor guard for a ceremonial meeting with the Russians on the east bank of the Elbe River, in the vicinity of Magdeburg.

We had about a week to get ready. I issued orders in the manner of a machine gun spitting bullets. I selected Lieutenant Victor Simone to pick the men and drill them. I asked him to pick the tallest and most soldierly-looking people in the outfit. He did. Lieutenant Fischer was given the job of properly equipping the men: new uniforms; cleaned and painted helmets; freshly-shined shoes, new issue, if needed; and polished insignia. In short, these people were to look like soldiers, spelled with big "S"! All of the chosen men were ordered to get haircuts, somehow, somewhere, and to make sure their worn and beat-up rifles were as clean as humanly possible. And so on.

Knowing their captain was a perfectionist, everyone worked like beavers. Simone drilled the men at close order drill, several hours a day, out in a level pasture. This took some doing because combat personnel do not have occasion to resort to the training of barracks life. To say the least, most of the men were quite rusty, and some of the replacements we had acquired made me wonder as to the quality of their basic training. Under Simone's expert leadership, it wasn't long until all began to shape up. Pride in being selected had its effect also. They made solid progress. My selection of Igor Karpenko as official interpreter met with the grateful approval of Colonel Russell Baker, who had succeeded Colonel Sutherland as 119th Regiment CO several weeks before.

On 28 May 1945 we loaded the men on trucks and crossed the Elbe River at Magdeburg. As I recall, the place for the ceremonies was in a clearing among some trees. The Russians had covered the area, for reasons unknown, with white sand that gave the ground a smooth and neat appearance.

Simone had drilled our lads, so I chose him to bring them into the area. He did so, and, gosh, did they look sharp. In fact they looked

Awaiting Major General Leland S. Hobbs. Note the Russian Honor Guard in the background.

GREAT. Carried themselves magnificently. I watched with pride. The Russian Honor Guard in their three-quarter length tunics, wide belts and high boots, were smaller than my lads. Simone had chosen well. Simone formed our men facing the open, sanded area. The Russians drew up opposite the Americans. Previously, I had been selected by General Hobbs to hand him the medals he would pin on the chests of the Russian soldiers. I was given this interesting assignment because I was the CO of the company furnishing the American Honor Guard. Hobbs decorated their people. A Russian general placed medals on our division staff officers. Both Russian and American flags were on display. The ceremony ended with the playing of the national anthems of both countries. It was indeed impressive, and I was proud to be a part of it all. Many pictures were taken at the scene. There were probably similar such events all along the Elbe, but this one was the one close to my heart.

The ceremony was not the end of things. That evening in a grove near the place of ceremony, the Russians entertained the 30th's brass. Igor, who had been busy all day, and I were invited to attend to the fes-

Left to Right: Major General Leland S. Hobbs, Russian colonel, Lieutenant Colonel John W. Dandridge.

tivities. He, because of his knowledge of the language, and I, because I was the CO of the company that furnished the American Honor Guard. I can still see tall, clean-cut Karpenko standing among all that rank, interpreting with all his might. He was conscientious anyway, and he performed beautifully that night.

There was tons of food. Fish of all kinds, caviar, pastries, and other items I can't remember, let alone describe. The vodka flowed to the complete oblivion of many of the Americans. The Russians drank their vodka straight, out of tall tumblers, much as we consume iced tea. Now and then I noticed that some kept a glass of water nearby and used it as a chaser, but only now and then.

Our hosts drank toasts to anything and everything. It was a rugged ball game for which most of us were ill prepared, but we could not lose face, not in front of those two-fisted guzzlers. The Russian females present were obviously available for whatever purpose one might wish. But, again, the overpowering vodka didn't help. Broad shouldered, squat, muscular gals of the peasant variety; to say they were ugly would be a compliment. One wag indicated their faces reminded him of an abandoned "artillery impact area."

During the course of the evening, I noticed that one of our high-ranking officers was becoming increasingly unsteady on his feet. I asked Igor, who had been almost glued to General Hobbs all evening, to keep a watchful eye on the inebriated "wheel." Later, Igor came to me, and suggested that we get the high-ranking party lover back to his quarters. With the help of the officer's aide, driver, and command car we did just that. Igor contributed some much-needed muscle. By the time we got him in his bunk, he was out of it. I am certain that Igor never forgot that memorable day and night, an American enlisted man mingling with all that rank. In turn, it is more than obvious that I haven't forgotten.[5]

So ends the story of Fox Company's rise to the zenith of glorious recognition. Both Hobbs and Baker sent me warm messages of commendation that I passed on quickly to Simone, Fischer, and the members of the honor guard. In particular, Simone deserves proper acknowledgment. He landed on Omaha Beach in June 1944, holding the rank of sergeant, and saw plenty of action with Fox Company. Twice wounded, Simone was battlefield promoted to second lieutenant by CO Arn. At the time he was so helpful in the honor guard affair, he commanded our First Platoon in one of the towns we were occupying.

I received special orders from battalion headquarters to set up a reception center for processing Displaced Persons somewhere in my area of control. There was a former Junkers plant in Simone's town of Dessau.[6] I ordered Simone to make it into the necessary facility, start-

First Lieutenant Victor J. Simone.

ing with cleaning the building. Simone used former Nazi party members for most of the hard labor. Then he organized the processing and feeding programs. Eventually, he handled a thousand Displaced Persons a day. German prisoners of war were his dishwashers, he used some fifty of them for that purpose. Many of our own Fox Company people helped him with interpretation. The Displaced Persons usually stayed in Simone's building about twenty-four hours, and then were taken by truck bound for localities all over Europe. It was a remarkable job performed by a most able officer. Simone received a fine commendation from Colonel McCown.[7]

Soon, we received moving orders. "We have moved south about 150 miles, to a town called Hirschberg. It's on the Saale River, fifteen miles from the Czech border, to the west and seventy-five miles west of Pilsen, Czechoslovakia, deep in the Thuringian Forest. This is in the heart of Bavaria. Munich, Hitler's center of activity once, is only fifty miles to the south. My own quarters are on the east bank of the river overlooking the town. Lieutenant Fischer, Benny, and my two top kicks are in this lovely chateau with me. My own room has a private bath with

There I sit in all the splendor of a king. Ain't right is it?

a shower. The view from my window is breathtaking. The war was scarcely noticed in this place. I have found and taken over a mess hall for the whole company. We all eat together now, and Sgt. Riley Jones is having a ball.

"Old Man Arn has seventy-three points now. Here's how they're figured: thirty-two months service, thirty-two points; eleven months overseas, eleven; Purple Heart with Cluster, ten; Silver Star, five; three Battle Stars, fifteen. Total: Seventy-three. There is an outside chance that I may get another award and perhaps two more Battle Stars, which would bring my total to eighty-eight points, three more than the minimum. That should be enough for me to make a decision as to whether I should transfer out of the 30th Division into another outfit and stay in Europe indefinitely, or remain with the 30th and end up fighting the Japs in the CBI. We are back in garrison life again: saluting officers, wearing insignia, standing for reveille and retreat, inspections, etc. They have even issued GI pajamas which I can't get used to."[8] (31 May 1945)

We were trucked into Hirschberg late at night. I had no other instructions than to house the men somehow, as well as possible. I decided to wait out the night in the trucks, muttering to myself about the stupidity of the men above me. At dawn, my officers and I took a look around. We found an abandoned factory. I had visions of a barracks.

I issued orders to each platoon leader to secure a bed for each of his men, regardless of how it was to be done, together with suitable bedding, from the town's homes; and to move the equipment into the second and third floor of the factory, one half of each floor per platoon. I have never seen men work so hard and yet have so much fun. All civilians were told that their beds would be available to them, in good shape, after we left town. Everybody cooperated in good spirit, and there was no trouble. By nightfall we had created an army barracks of a sort, only more comfortable.

The next day, wandering about, I found a kind of town social hall with a kitchen. I ordered Sgt. Jones to convert the place into a mess hall for Fox Company. He did just that, complete with plates, cups, silverware, tablecloths, for nearly two hundred men. I never asked Jones where he got all that equipment, but that evening we all sat down together and ate like human beings in quiet, clean comfort. Jones was an absolute genius.

Late that night, Benny came dashing into the factory to inform me that he had found an ideal quarters for the captain. He would show me in the morning. It was a lovely chateau, high on a hill. There was one problem: it was owned and occupied by a family whose head was an irate, aristocratic old gentleman. He met me at the door with flashing eyes and obvious disdain. His military bearing told me that he had been a German officer at one time, perhaps in World War I. One of my boys came forward as an interpreter. It was explained that the American officer wanted to move his headquarters people into the home. His heated reply needed no interpretation.

"Soldier," said I coldly, "you tell that old fool unless he removes his family and servants to the basement, I'll bring in a squad of soldiers and we'll put everybody down there bodily. Remind him also that his beloved military establishment has been eradicated, and that he is in no position to argue with me." I thought the old boy was going to have apoplexy. I turned to issue an order. He looked at me and raised his hand in resignation. He would comply at once. Davis, Kirkman, Fischer, Benny, and Montalvo moved in with me. It was scrumptious, but I made it clear to everyone that there would be no damage to anything. There wasn't. I didn't want the unhappy master of the house to get the impression that we were animals. I now ascertained that the factory where I had the men housed was a leather factory at one time, and our "landlord" had made a fortune out of the business. He was a "wheel" in the town, as his family had been for many years before him. He never came near us, and I only saw him once or twice after that.

I had promoted several NCOs to second lieutenants during combat. Now, we were back in garrison life. All the regulations were in effect and would be enforced; orders from the higher-ups. I recall walking down the street one day with Second Lieutenant Kenneth A. Austin of Jacksonville, Florida, one of my promoted people. One of the men from his platoon approached us. He saluted me smartly, but turned to Austin and said "Hi, Ken." I had a lesson to teach. I stopped the soldier dead in his tracks. "Have you forgotten, soldier, that Sgt. Austin is now Lieutenant Austin, and, therefore, you will give him the respect he deserves by saluting him according to army regulations?" Flustered, our man snapped to attention and threw Austin a highball that he brought up from below the sidewalk. I motioned him to pass on.

Austin started to protest. I raised my hand for silence. "Ken, I'm as anxious as you are to get back home and out of this monkey suit, and even forget, someday, all of this if that's possible. But as long as we are here and still in the service, we'll act like soldiers, particularly in front of these goddamned Krauts. Therefore, I am going to insist on, among other things, military courtesy and discipline. I believe you'll agree that Fox Company has accomplished convincing achievements during and since the fighting ceased, which makes our outfit continue to be an outstanding one. Let's keep it that way." "Yes, sir." Austin replied, and that was that.

To add to the problem of reestablishing discipline where combat discipline existed before, a stupid order came down from Eisenhower's SHAEF. "There will be no fraternization." Colonel McCown told his officers that the 2nd Battalion would enforce the order to the letter. I wasn't quite that gung ho. To me, that damned fool order meant that none of my people could even so much as wink at a girl, stoop to help a child, or lend a hand to a feeble old person, let alone give a cheery "hello" to some of the bedraggled, worn-out non-combatants. I was right. That's exactly what the order meant. Someone didn't know American GIs as well as I did.

For example, I was well aware that the men of Fox Company, for the most part, had had nothing to do with women for many long months. I sensed that some foolish incidents might take place created by the rigidity of the SHAEF order. I also knew that venereal disease (VD) was rampant all over Europe. I came to a decision. I would interpret the SHAEF mandate in my own way.

I assembled the entire company in our mess hall. "Men, SHAEF has issued an order that there will be no fraternization with anyone, male, female, even the kids, and they insist that the order be enforced." Groans went up all over the hall. My language then became salty, and to the point, in the colorful gutter talk of the GI Joe.

I will clean it up. I probably said something like this: "On the other hand, I have a plan for Fox Company which includes our own interpretation of the order and our own enforcement of the interpretation. I have a pretty good idea as to how long it's been since most of you have had anything to do with a woman. The temptation to do something about that is everywhere. I also know, and if you don't know you do

2nd Battalion staff officers and company COs: Left to right (back row): Captain Corby L. Hart, author (F CO), First Lieutenant Ralph G. Nelson, First Lieutenant Eric A. Johnson, Captain Robert J. Henglein (E CO), (front row): unidentified, First Lieutenant Lehmann, Captain Cagliano (H CO), Captain Charles N. Blodgett, First Lieutenant Richard W. Earll, First Lieutenant Harness. Absent: First Lieutenant Murray Chase, First Lieutenant Harold H. Huston, and First Lieutenant T. F. Brooks.

now, that VD is running wild all over Europe and infecting a discouraging number of U.S. troops. For certain, you have no wish to return home infected with VD. Since you will be tempted, and because many of you will be unable to resist, I have asked the top kicks to order an ample supply of condoms and 'pro kits.' They will be available in the orderly room. No names will be taken, and no questions asked. You may secure as much protection as you wish. There will be no bed check either."[9]

I paused. The men looked at me in disbelief. At long last, the Old Man had finally flipped his lid. "Now, in exchange for these liberties," I continued firmly, "we will hold reveille every morning, without fail, and a careful roll call will be taken, I can assure you. You'd better be in that formation, or I'll throw the whole damned book at you. Neither will I tolerate any

The author inspects Company F.

brutality. There'll be no rape and no stealing. During the daylight hours if I or any of the company's officers see a single man jack of you fraternizing, you'll get it. Do I make myself clear? Are there any questions?"

I couldn't accept the "no fraternization" concept. But I was definitely worried about VD and how not to increase the epidemic. The incidence of VD in Fox Company was minimal. In other companies, the results were far different. Some companies not only had bed checks, but would even conduct search procedures of civilian homes looking for wayward GIs. No protection was offered at all, because it seemed to recognize fraternization in its most intimate dimension. We were realists in Fox Company, and our top kicks were amazed at how quickly our supplies dwindled.

One day Colonel McCown journeyed into our area. He was impressed with our adaptation to Hirschberg, particularly with my headquarters abode. Turning away, he paused. "Arn, I want to congratulate you on your low VD incidence. How do you explain it?" "Just a group of fine, moral young men, colonel." He drove away, shaking his head.

F Company throws a farewell party for the CO. He leaves for rehabilitation leave in Riviera, June 1945. Left to Right: (back row) S/Sgt. Riley Jones, First Lieutenant William A. Glatzmeyer, author, First Lieutenant Neal M. Bertelson, First Lieutenant Kenneth F. Austin, (front row) First Lieutenant George E. Fischer, First Lieutenant Victor J. Simone, unidentified, Lieutenant Charles B. Miner.

One evening, I walked into our mess hall and noted a tone of celebration in the air. Someone had "requisitioned" a cache of excellent champagne. In fact, there was enough for two companies. I didn't ask any questions. Just indulged. Before sitting down to eat, I proposed this toast. "May you and your dog tags never part, and may you never, ever, see anymore combat." The cheers were louder than the scraping chairs.[10]

"I am getting a real break. The Army has set up a rehabilitation center in the French Riviera down on the shores of the Mediterranean Sea. I will leave soon for a seven-day stay there. Will fly. Four-and-a-half-hour flight. Will visit Cannes and Nice." (15 June 1945)

"When an Army is ordered home, it usually means an Army Headquarters only, 1,000 to 1,500 men, not the divisions within the Army. The 30th is now one of several divisions within the Seventh Army. People seem to think that because the war is over in Europe, we'll be coming home soon, all of us. 'Tis not so.' It'll take weeks to move all of the divisions home. Many ships will be filled up with either low-point men being assigned to the CBI or high-point men who have expressed a desire not to go to the CBI. There is uncertainty here about how many will stay here for occupational work. As much as I want to see both of you again, I'm just happy that I am out of the mess alive. Forgive me but nothing else matters for the moment. I leave for the Riviera on the 23rd." (21 June 1945)

"I arrived here in Cannes late today. Took a C-47 from Weimar, Germany to Nice, France. Trucks to here. My first experience in the air. The plane behaved fairly well. (Actually we hit an air pocket over the Alps and in the steep drop that followed, one nurse on the plane suffered a broken arm. We sat on our parachutes directly on the fuselage, as there were no seats). The snow-capped French Alps are beautiful. The Riviera is a fifty- to sixty-mile stretch along the French Mediterranean Coast. Cannes, Antibes, Nice, Monte Carlo, a Mecca for the wealthy and the curious for years. I am staying at the Mondial Hotel. I can see the blue sea from my window. Uncle Sam has taken over most of these places. What with the area teeming with Red Cross gals, nurses, WACs, French women, and what-have-you, there is no end to the excitement that prevails everywhere. Will go swimming at Eden Roc tomorrow. The nightclubs are flourishing. Dance bands have come out of the woodwork. GI Joe is spending money like there is no tomorrow." (23 June 1945)

It proved to be an exciting and an exhausting ten days instead of one week, because there weren't enough planes to get us back on schedule. To the uninitiated GI, the French version of what became known as the bikini, worn on the beaches, produced some real eye-popping as well as other impressions. Another diversion were the countless "pédalos" darting in all directions on the water. These were little two-seat boats, propelled by one person, pumping as one does on a bicycle. This maneuver turned a paddle wheel in the stern. The speed was usually judged by the strength and athletic ability of the peddler. Great fun. We got little sleep and less rest.

Once, several of us were lying on a raft in the sun offshore at Eden

Roc. An attractive, rather plain freckle-faced gal climbed on board. It was Dorothy McGuire, the movie star, who was twenty-five at that time. She sat there among us for about thirty minutes, asking questions of combat soldiers. Sensible questions, too. A fascinating woman. I have never forgotten her.

"Still at the Riviera. The 30th Division should be on its way home around July 15. Will go to the Pacific, after more training, for the invasion of Japan. High-point men will be given the opportunity to transfer from the division and stay in Europe on occupational work. The 30th was awarded two more battle stars, making five in all, and since I qualified for both, I now have eighty-three points. I think that may be enough to allow me to decide whether I want to return to the States with the 30th and maybe become involved in more combat, or be transferred to another division and stay in Europe a while longer. I have found out that my efficiency rating as an officer is very high. Because of that rating, they say I could be considered as 'essential.' I am also eligible for a twenty-one day furlough." (29 June 1945)

"Excelsior Hotel, Frankfurt, Germany. I am waiting for ground transportation to take me back to Old Hickory. When we landed in Weimar the place was in the hands of the Russians. The city is about fifty miles west of the Elbe. The "Russkys" have come a long way west. In Weimar, each of us was interrogated at some length. It was ridiculous. We're supposed to be on the same side. They finally decided that we could proceed to Frankfurt. From there we would have to find our own way back to our respective outfits. Bavaria seems a long way from here. No matter; no one is firing at me."[11] (4 July 1945)

We lounged around Frankfurt for a day or two. The city had taken a severe beating from Allied bombing. The huge railroad station in the heart of the city was just a mass of twisted steel girders and rubble. Here, the famed I. G. Farben Industries had a plant. Ike's SHAEF Headquarters, in due time, was established in it.[12]

Rumors were tossed about. All officers in Old Hickory with seventy-eight points or more would be transferred to the 75th Division, unless they wished to remain with the 30th and participate in the invasion of Japan. The 75th was doing occupational work in France. Quite frankly at this point, I was leaning toward the idea of remaining in Europe rather than face more combat in the CBI. I guess I had had it.

One day, a friendly voice hailed me. It was my old buddy, Lieutenant Chuck Reilly, from the days and weeks at Ft. McClellan. We celebrated, in spades. He had survived many experiences also, and had been transferred to the 30th. It was quite a reunion. One of my favorite people, he would ship home with the division.

"I have been recommended for a Bronze Star. If it is awarded I will have eighty-eight points. However, there is confusion here now. I suspect that if I would simply sign up for the CBI, it would clear the air. I know it would help me get home faster." (17 July 1945)

About this time, an interesting session with Colonel McCown took place. I was called to the battalion headquarters. His nibs gave me a tight-lipped smile, and even asked me to sit down. "Arn, why are you hesitating about coming back to the States with us? I'll even make you an offer. I will soon take over the 119th. Commanding Officer Colonel Baker is going on to other duties. I think you're capable of handling a battalion right now. That's a majority for you (Major) very soon, and a lieutenant colonelcy in the not-too-distant future. As you know, I am a career man, and I intend to go far in the military. Arn, I want you to come with me."

I was indeed impressed because I never thought McCown felt highly of me. His offer, be assured, was not to be treated lightly. "Sir, I am most grateful for what you have just said, but is the colonel aware that I am thirty-six years old, and I have only been in the service since the fall of '42?" "Of course I know that," said he not too patiently either. "It's all in your records. However, you can undoubtedly handle men. We have trouble finding officers with that essential trait. Take the twenty-year retirement option. You'll still be in your early fifties. Further, you have no idea what rank you will have attained by then. There is also an excellent retirement program. Incidentally, you have also demonstrated a knack for military administrative work. I repeat: I want you to stay with me."

"Sir, I'll think it over and get back to you in twenty-four hours." "Good." Boy, did I do some thinking. I compared a career in the service with what I had done and possibly could do in the business world. I had every reason to believe that with the start I had already made in sales, I could continue to do well. I admitted to myself that since I was now single, I had more flexibility to move around and do some experimenting. Either way, thirty-six wasn't terribly old. I admired McCown as a soldier. I knew that I would learn and develop while associated with him. And, of course, I was flattered that an honest-to-God soldier, such as he, had the high opinion of me.

I pondered. I reviewed the terrifying experiences of combat. I was fully aware there was no guarantee there would be no more conflicts. What would my chances be to survive further combat or even another war? Would my luck continue to hold out, or had I already run out of time? I also reasoned that the higher the rank, the less the danger. Thus the hours of the night wore on.

I came to a decision. Returning to the colonel the next day, I said: "Sir, I have spent most of the night thinking about your offer. I want you to know that I appreciate your opinion and confidence in me. But I have decided to return to civilian life and continue my career in business." "Okay, Arn, it's your decision. I think you're making a big mistake. However, I do want you to know you've served your country well." "Thank you, sir." That was the end of that.[13]

Another pass to Paris. There was a hotel in Paris, for officers only, the Mayflower, which possessed a nightclub with good American dance music. A live place to say the least. I became attached to the Mayflower. Upon my return to camp, I was informed that I had been awarded another Silver Star. This one would be referred to as a "cluster" to my first Silver Star. Old Hickory was making a complete review of its combat history. In the review, it was discovered that there were many people worthy of recognition who had been hitherto overlooked.

This award was for the time on 25 July 1944 in the St.-Lô battle zone, where I could no longer tolerate the desperation of the men about me. I guess I must have forgotten my own harrowing fear in my concern for the men. Our position was no longer tenable. Anyway, I managed somehow to bring some order out of chaos and to get our dwindling personnel out of the hotspot we were in. Later, we were able to hold on and even manage a faint semblance of an offense. Once men in the ranks sense leadership, it's amazing how well they perform. The citation reads that I was a captain when the incident occurred. I was a second lieutenant. I didn't argue with anybody about the mistake in rank. I accepted the award during a modest ceremony in Camp Oklahoma City from Brigadier General James M. Lewis, the new CO of the 30th.

"We are still living in this tent city. It is really hot. I shall be transferred out of the 30th soon." (24 July 1945) I was right, for it became evident that I was leaving. One afternoon Sgt. Kirkman came to my tent. "Sir," he said, and he cleared his throat, which was a habit of his when he had something important on his mind. "You know that I am a career man, so you'll be surprised when you hear what I am about to propose. My suggestion involves a violation of an army code."

I was all attention now, for I recalled another Kirkman proposition way back in a small German one-street town. Once again, I had no idea what he had in mind. "What's up, Top?" "We have a real nice NCO Club here in a building. Well, it's really part tent, part building. We constructed it ourselves; has a bar, makeshift kitchen, etc. Now that we know you're leaving us, we would like to have you join us tonight for a farewell drink." He seemed relieved. He had said it.

I was just as surprised as I was that time in Germany. "Top, you know an officer is not allowed in an NCO Club for social purposes. We would all get into trouble if we were caught." "Yes, sir, we know that. But we're willing to take that chance. The men and I just want to show what a helluva man we think you are."

I was so pleased and proud, I decided to accept. To hell with the rules. "Well, thank you, how do you propose to do this?" "Well, sir, we'd like to have you be at the rear door of our club, after dark, say about 2200. I'll be there to meet you." Believe me, I was there on time, but not without misgivings.

I'll never forget that evening. The men had a place for me at one of the tables. The beer was excellent. The stories were colorful and, as always, exaggerated. For the first time, my kids could level with me. Many of the incidents, recalled by relaxation and loosened tongues, had been long forgotten by the Old Man. I would be dishonest if I didn't admit that a guy named Arn didn't always come out smelling like a rose. It was that kind of delightful affair. We were really with one or two exceptions civilians once again. Face to face, and even. If I had objected it would have ruined the evening.

So it went. For purposes of caution, they had placed a lookout at the door, outside. An excited NCO almost tore the door down and rushed inside. "The Officer-of-the-Day (OD) is coming straight for us. I can see his flashlight." Top Kick was prepared. "Alright, men, when the officer walks in, I'll snap everyone to attention, which means ON YOUR FEET. We'll thus screen Captain Arn from his view. He won't stay long: it's just a routine check." In a moment, the Officer-of-the-Day was at the door.

"TEN-SHUN!" yelled Kirkman. To a man they rose, shuffled about, closing up a bit, and snapped to attention. The Officer-of-the-Day couldn't have seen me with an X-ray machine. "Having a good time, Men?" "Yes, sir," was the ear-shattering reply in chorus. "Okay, remember lights out at 2400, and hit those sacks." And he was gone. It was a heartwarming, never-to-be-forgotten night.

"Top has placed a pad on the Fox Company bulletin board, near the headquarters' tent. It is for any of the men who wish for me to have their names and addresses at home. Seventy-five have already signed up. Isn't that something?" (27 July 1945)

"I will be transferred to the 75th Division. Their headquarters is on the Marne River, Châlon-sur-Marne, France, about forty miles southeast of Rheims. I made a farewell speech this morning to the entire company. It was emotional as hell. Afterward, every man came up and shook hands with me. The 75th is running all sorts of 'tent cities': Camp Cleveland, Camp Boston, Camp New York City, etc. Passes are being issued for travel almost anywhere. The fighting days are over for the high-point men, if they so desire. As you know, it means staying over here for some time." (28 July 1945)

That night the officers of Fox Company held one helluva party for me. Our company mess sergeant, Riley Jones, planned the whole affair. We had steak, french fries, wine, cake, cheese, cognac: the works. I marveled, as always, at Jones' ability. I recall crawling into my bedroll about dawn, thinking I would report to the 75th on a stretcher.[14]

9. A Finale Immersed in Pondering

29 July 1945–2 February 1946

*With deep reluctance, Arn left Old Hickory for the 75th
Infantry Division, which administered a number of redeployment centers. Eager to resume civilian life, he took command of
a large company of like-minded former combat troops just as
anxious to return home. The Department of War tried to comply, but shortages of ships and rumors of political favoritism
toward different units created growing animosity. Many enlisted men, bored, homesick, and resentful, often vented their
frustration in petty crimes amongst themselves or in more
serious offenses against local residents. Officers tried to restore
order and instill military protocol, but often succumbed to the
same restlessness. Such emotions also affected Arn. He missed
the familiar faces of Fox Company and felt uncertain about his
postwar career when he finally left active service. Arn's day
came on 2 February 1946, after a two-month terminal leave.
Even then, the war never ended for Arn. In retrospect, he realized that he had participated in a turning point in human
history. He was clearly proud to have been associated with the
men of the 30th Division and especially those in Fox Company.
But like other combat infantrymen, Arn was too busy fighting
the war and trying to survive to understand the meaning of
this experience. He pondered that issue over the rest of his life.*

Currently, the 75th Division was managing seventeen redeployment areas in the Rheims area.[1] I cannot recall the
name of the commanding officer of the 75th's 291st Regi-

ment. I do remember that he was either old beyond his years or just plain elderly. I reached his headquarters, Camp Boston, Suippes, France, about thirty miles northeast of Châlon in midmorning, 29 July 1945. The colonel was studying my records. After a bit of small talk, I decided to take the bull by the horns. "Sir, if the colonel doesn't mind, I've worked with troops for a long time, in training, in combat, and in occupational work, at least it seems that way to me. Isn't there something I can do for you around headquarters here for the duration of our stay over here? Quite frankly, I respectfully request to be relieved of troop responsibility."

My voice trailed off. Fox Company was all I ever wanted. "Arn, these rifle companies of mine are swollen far beyond the normal Table of Organization (TO). I am delighted to get my hands on an officer with a record like yours. You're just the man to handle a bunch of highly decorated prima donnas who have set their sights for home. Also remember they are from many different outfits. You are, therefore, the CO of A Company, 1st Battalion. Right Now! Any questions?" "No, sir," I saluted and left. What the hell was the use of making an issue out of anything at this stage of the game?

A Company's CO, First Lieutenant A. D. Zahnizer, was not at all pleased when I arrived in the company area. He had been CO for some time and was certain that his captaincy was coming soon. I felt sorry for the guy, but I outranked him and he was now the executive officer of the company. Victor Binter was the 1st Sergeant and he proved to be a good one. Thank God.

Once I got my feet on the ground, and with the reputation that Old Hickory had everywhere, it wasn't long until we had things moving along. I insisted on certain military procedures and their enforcement, which delighted Binter. He was almost as GI as Kirkman. Zahnizer soon realized that I was all business and quickly adapted himself to my way of doing things. We became good friends. It wasn't easy. Able Company was now composed of men from all sorts of outfits who had had good and bad officers. I had lots of NCOs also. All had little or nothing to do.

The 75th had been baptized in combat in the Battle of the Bulge. I don't remember where now, but I had been close to them before. It was in the middle of the night. The snow was waist deep. I had been attempting to consolidate the Fox Company positions. Several of my people were with me. Up ahead we noticed a light through the trees from a farmhouse. I couldn't imagine who would be showing a light so foolishly. With our weapons at the ready, we approached the building with caution. No one challenged us. There was no evidence of outpost security. Nothing.

Voices in English could be heard. I simply opened the door and walked in, my men right on my heels. Such a scene of utter confusion I had seldom witnessed. The place was crammed to the rafters with 75th Division "doughs." "Who's in command here?" I roared. "I am," replied a very young lieutenant from a remote corner. "Well, what in the hell is going on here? Can you explain, lieutenant?" "Frankly, sir, I don't know where I really am or what I am supposed to be doing. We've only just arrived from the States. I would appreciate some help." "First of all, for God's sakes, get some men outside and in a security perimeter, or else the Krauts will chew you up alive. Right in here, douse those goddamned lights." They were in a real mess. It took me the rest of the night to get the situation straightened out and to send the lieutenant on toward what we figured out as his objective. Then I recalled my own inexperience earlier, and my impatience melted away.[2]

"I am being sent to Information and Education School (IES) at the Cité Universitaire in Paris, 5–12 August 1945. The 30th Division is on its way to Le Havre, France. Should be on the high seas by 15 August." (1 August 1945) "Paris. I went to the Folies-Bergère last evening. The nudity is prevalent. A long line of bare-breasted girls is certainly a lesson in body rhythm, and, additionally, a sight to see. I shall return, as MacArthur once said upon another occasion. Will go on a sightseeing tour tomorrow. This time I will look for more historical places. Back to Camp Boston next Sunday. I have heard that there are two thousand nurses, American, at Camp Carlisle, three miles from Camp Boston. I will be careful and will watch out for snares." (7 August 1945)

"The Truman bomb has been dropped on Japan. We have no news as to whether the Japs have surrendered or not. The 30th left for home earlier than expected, and is now in America. Ironically, if Japan surrenders the men of the 30th will all be civilians before Arn." (13 August 1945) "Japan has surrendered." (15 August 1945) [Later Arn observed,] "Those who went home with outfits which were slated for the CBI were lucky. The bomb helped to get all of them out of the service sooner than they ever dreamed of."[3]

Over the next months, nothing but confusion and uncertainty reigned at every level, all of the time. A tug of war existed between the military and Congress. Influential relatives were placing all sorts of pressure on their congressmen to get the boys home. We officers knew that the main problem was simply a shortage of ships. It took all we had to convince homesick and bored troops that such was the case. There was an alarming increase in GI robberies, rapes, and even murders.

I could not tell my parents everything that happened. Numerous events kept me busy. I was routed out of my bedroll one night by the officer in charge of the guard for the nearby German prisoner of war compound. Able Company personnel had the guard detail. "Sir, one of your men has apparently committed suicide while on guard duty." I ordered a jeep and rushed to the scene. My GI had placed the butt of his rifle on a board on the ground. He had placed the muzzle of the rifle inside his mouth. Using a small sapling, long enough to reach that far, he had pushed the trigger. His helmet was found over fifty feet from the body. The entire back of his head was blown off. If memory serves me correctly, a bullet leaves the muzzle of an M-1 rifle with the velocity of 2,800 feet per second. Our soldier had assured himself of instant death.

In the investigation that followed, which was required by regulations, a "Dear John" letter was found at the bottom of his barracks bag from a girl back home in New Mexico. She had jilted him for another. I uncovered evidence also that he had been drinking heavily. It was all tragic. If the Good Lord will again forgive me, the suicide aspect was deliberately avoided and other important people went along with me. I will never know what was done with insurance.[4]

At another time, the provost marshal of Camp Boston, a friend of mine, routed me out one night with: "Wanna see some fun, captain?" Knowing the man as I did, I decided to dress and climb in his jeep. We approached a wooded hillside some distance from Camp Boston. He ordered his driver to turn off his lights and turn into an almost hidden dirt road at the foot of the rise. I had yet to ask any questions. We got out and proceeded silently up the hill. A moon, partially obscured by the trees, provided ample light. Parting some bushes, the provost marshal motioned me forward to take a look.

A large tent greeted my eyes. Stretching from it and down the hill was a long line of GIs. As a matter of fact the end of the line was out of sight. I could see only a dim lantern light through the thin tent wall. "What the hell goes on, major?" I queried in a puzzled tone. "We have been combating the VD incidence, captain, and trying to find the source. There are French prostitutes operating in that tent. They must be in bad shape. We are going to raid that tent right now, as I have men deployed all around this spot for that purpose. They will move in on my signal. I want the women and their accomplices, not those damned stupid GI yardbirds. The medics will get them later." The operation was successful. The provost marshal did nothing about the lined-up soldiers. They just melted away into the darkness. We entered that filthy tent, and were confronted by four of the most repulsive women I have ever seen before or since. The whole sordid affair made me sick, but the provost marshal's slick handling of the situation eliminated at least that one source of deadly and crippling VD.

"The men are getting more restless every day. No AWOLs (Absent without Leave), but we're worried about it. It could develop into a serious situation. If they had allowed the army people to handle the evacuation, we would all be home by now. No, the politicians must meddle. They have fouled it all up. By the way, I really resent the wholesale criticisms of officers by returning soldiers back home. The guys who have never heard a shot fired in anger will blab the most.[5] I have written President Jim Ver Meulen of The American Seating Company and asked for a sales assignment in the Cleveland area." (24 August 1945)

"We should be on our way by 15 October, they tell us. Brother Jack is now on Okinawa. How far apart we are. We live in two-man tents. Cement floors with wooden sides. Saw Betty Hutton, the Hollywood musical star, the other evening. She worked so hard her dress was soaked with sweat. A great performer, a GI's gal. Old Hickory shipped home on the

Queen Mary and engaged in a ticker tape parade up Broadway. I missed all of that, didn't I? I ran into Sgt. Guy Bates the other evening. He left us on Christmas Eve during the Bulge. He has fully recovered which pleases me very much. He was an excellent soldier."[6] (25 August 1945)

"I can wear a five-battle star ribbon on my chest now. The 30th fought in Normandy, North France, Rhineland, Central Germany, and the Ardennes. That is all the big campaigns there were in Europe, and we were in them all." (28 August 1945)

"This is some life. Officers' Clubs are teeming with all sorts of social programs. I can scarcely believe it. Even have planned picnics. I assume that officers will be the last to get out. Everybody drinks in Europe, but only the Americans seem to get drunk. Often I am ashamed of the way our soldiers carry on. I hope that everyone is sent home soon." (4 September 1945) "The 75th, they tell us, may be on the way home in early October, but more likely between the 1st and 15th of November. Gosh, maybe I'll be home for Thanksgiving but don't bet on it." (5 September 1945) "All captains with eighty-five points or more will be alerted for the States in sixty days, they say. I hope so." (7 September 1945) "We move now on 15 October 1945, but it's all rumor and conjecture. Honestly. No one seems to know. Strangely, I can't seem to make up my mind as to where I want to live and/or work." (17 September 1945) "Got a letter from Jim Ver Meulen. There are no openings in the Cleveland area. But there are many territories with equal or better opportunities." (18 September 1945) "With Cleveland out of the picture, I will take my time about returning to the American Seating Company."[7] (22 September 1945)

Presently, another trip to Paris. An American nurse wanted to see the seamy side of Parisian nightlife. I made some inquiries, and a particular den of iniquity was recommended. It was off the Champs Elysées and down a flight of stairs, into a sort of dark hole. A real "gin mill," as the GIs called them.

We settled into a corner and ordered a drink and waited. A young American lieutenant was hanging on the bar, obviously inebriated. He leered at everybody, lost in a sort of blowsy cynicism. After an interval or two, I heard high heels on the stairway. A buxom lass, a real "femme de la rue," sauntered up to the tipsy officer. She gave him an enticing smile and a hip sway that would have troubled the most resistant of men. The girl greeted the inebriate as alluringly as she knew how, and this one knew how. The officer blinked at her. I nudged my companion. Craftily the girl placed a hand in her blouse and drew out one well-rounded breast. She grinned. The blotto lieutenant took one look, leaned forward and snapped the middle finger of his hand against the healthy nipple pointed in his direction. It hurt, of course, and even a professional has a right to resent that sort of an affront. Haughtily, she retreated back up the stairs with her shapely derrière flaunting her disgust. Our soused American officer watched her go moving his eyes and head as he coordinated with the movement of her body. That was all; end of that phase of this caper. "Well, I never saw anything like that before, captain," commented the nurse nervously. "You asked for it, nurse," I replied in a sophisticated fashion. Actually, I hadn't seen anything like it either.

A few minutes later, a masculine-looking female clumped down the stairs. Spotting the nurse, she came over and in a chair close to my friend, sat down with evidence of considerable interest. The nurse and I continued to sip our drinks and chat. Abruptly, the nurse stiffened, her eyes wide. "Captain, let's get out of here," she whispered hoarsely. "This, this person, has 'her' hand on my leg." We got out. Her glimpse of the seamy side of Paris had been accomplished. But it was really only that: a glimpse.

"I am wondering now if my suits will fit me. As you know I am somewhat thinner now than when I entered the service. But it's glorious to be in a position to think about such things. Right? I have sixty days of terminal leave coming to me at full pay when I get home, leave I have never taken. I am supposed to wear my uniform during that period. Right now it looks like we'll go to Camp Pittsburgh first, between 4–8 October. Le Havre by the 15th of October." (2 October 1945)

"We have moved to Camp Pittsburgh. It is near Mourmelon-le-Grand, France. We should be ready for Le Havre by the 17th. Sailing dates, however, have been changed to 21 or 23 October 1945. We should arrive in an American port by 2 or 3 November." (10 October 1945) "The 75th is still 'sweating it out'. There is an acute shortage of ships. Camp

Atterbury may be my separation center. Because I have been so busy handling troops, I've had little opportunity to take advantage of the tours that were offered around Europe. I will return some day and see what I want to see. I now have 211 men and seven officers in Able Company. It's a real headache, but no one's firing at me." (19 October 1945)

"We're still in Camp Pittsburgh. We are even issuing passes to the men for Brussels, Paris, and Luxembourg. The 66th Division is in Le Havre. They are now using a great many of the available ships to bring the men home from the Pacific Theater. I guess I won't make it for Thanksgiving." (22 October 1945)

"Guess what? We are now headed for Marseilles in a day or two. Will go through Gibraltar on our way home. Takes longer, twelve to fourteen days. Indiantown Gap, Pennsylvania, will be the separation center. The entire division will move into a staging area near Marseilles. We will probably be on our way home during the first ten days of November." (24 October 1945)

"We are now thirteen miles from Marseilles. This is called the Delta Base Section. We are really on the alert now. We also know that we will sail on one of the famous 'Victory Ships.'[8] Our destination will be Hampton Roads, Virginia. We should be there about 20 or 22 November. Again, I'm afraid that Thanksgiving is out of the question. This camp is deep in the foothills north of Marseilles. I have had a chance to visit that ancient seaport. Every night there are stabbings and shootings. The Military Police use armored scout cars." (4 November 1945)

Before sailing, one of my GIs came to me with a problem. He had been rolling the dice with considerable success, having accumulated over $2,500. What to do with it? How to get it home? I was allowed to approve money orders destined for home in amounts not to exceed fifty dollars. The soldier had determined that such a procedure would call for all sorts of bother. I agreed. He also felt that if we had any luggage inspection before sailing, serious questions might be asked about his having that much money in his possession. I suggested that he distribute the money in small amounts among his buddies, keep a careful account of the people who had the money, and then collect at our destination when we landed. He left, and I had forgotten the matter.

I was quickly reminded of it several days later. Sgt. Binter and I were checking the men against the company roster as they came down the gangplank in Newport News, Virginia. People were beginning to congregate in a sizeable crowd at the foot of the gangplank. To determine what was going on, I moved into the congestion only to find my gambling soldier standing in the midst of the group, with a big cigar in his mouth and clipboard in hands just like mine. He, too, was checking names, but for the purpose of collecting his money. I got the impression that he collected every dollar owed him. He seemed to be that kind of a guy.

On the morning of 16 November 1945, after a series of silly rumors and more delays, we boarded trucks and headed for the pier in the harbor of Marseilles. By coincidence, another ship had docked on the other side of the same pier. We were boarding the *Central Falls Victory*. The other ship was in the process of unloading German prisoners of war, who had been enjoying the good life back in the United States. Well-fed, tanned, they came off the boat in an exuberant mood. Then one prisoner of war made a mistake. He walked up to one of my GIs, grinned, and asked him for a light for his cigarette. The Kraut was standing near the edge of the pier. I am certain that he had had little to do with combat GIs since he had been captured, maybe years before. Anyway, an American hard fist came up and a bona fide Kraut found himself in the Mediterranean. The Military Police had to fish him out. Officers and NCOs moved fast, or we might have had a real donnybrook right there on the dock. It was difficult for many combat people to forget. After talking with me, the Military Police lieutenant decided that the incident was closed.[9]

The *Central Falls Victory* had been launched 17 April 1945 at a cost of $3.5 million. The ship was built to accommodate 1,500 men. We had 1,954 on board. She was making her third round trip voyage from Newport News to Marseilles. We would take the southern course of 4,160 miles. All of our personnel had eighty points or more, and 90 percent had seen a great deal of combat warfare.[10]

Down in the lower regions of the ship, bunks had been constructed in tiers of eight bunks per tier, one above the other. When we hit rough weather, many of the men became seasick. One can well imagine the conditions existing in the sleeping areas, if one was occupying the lowest bunk with seven seasick soldiers above one. It did happen. A strange trait of seasickness is that fresh air and food will hasten the cure, but those two remedies are the least desired by the ill person. "Just leave me alone and let me die," is the usual attitude. The sleeping areas soon became a shambles, and the smell was nauseating. I wasn't ill a single minute during the voyage. A cartoon appeared in the ship's newspaper with this caption "No, I'm not seasick, but I'd sure hate to yawn." The war had not destroyed the American sense of humor.

On 27 November 1945 we sailed into the harbor at Newport News, Virginia. I had been away from my beloved United States for almost eighteen months. I can recall vividly my feeling of pride as I stood at the rail and gazed upon my revered country, the broad sweep of the Chesapeake Bay off our starboard, Hampton Roads, Old Point Comfort, Fort Monroe, Fort Eustis, and just a few miles to the north, the historic trio: Jamestown, Williamsburg, and Yorktown. I could feel and see the evidence of the strength and faith of our early forefathers all around me.

And I had participated in the making of more history, Normandy, Mortain, the Siegfried Line, the Battle of the Bulge, the Elbe and the Russians, and the demise of Hitler. Had I not had other things to do, I would have loved to have lingered and explored this glorious past of a remarkable human experiment. That time was to come, but many years later.

Trucks were ready. Late on the 27th, we billeted in Camp Patrick Henry. I wired my parents as quickly as possible to the effect that I had arrived safely. I would let them know when to expect me in Cleveland. The next day, a troop train took me to Indiantown Gap, Pennsylvania. Processing continued. Papers were filled out, and my current active duty career in the military service was terminated. Special Order No. 307 awarded me a Terminal Leave of sixty days with date of discharge, 2 February 1946.[11]

On 2 December 1945 I left by train for Cleveland. It was an inconspicuous homecoming. No people to greet me at the 55th Street Station of the Pennsylvania Railroad. I have forgotten why. Maybe I failed to

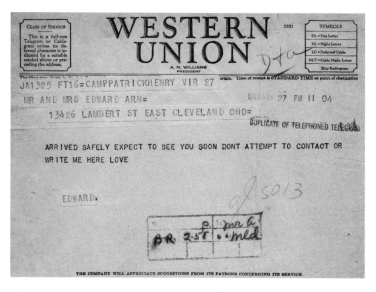

The author wires his parents upon his stateside arrival.

give my family specific instructions. I really don't know. I took a cab to the home of my parents on Lambert Street in East Cleveland, the town in which I had grown up. To describe the emotion of that reunion would be futile. I will just say that I was made much aware of family love, once again. Fanfare was only a temporary need, buried in that moment of sincere devotion. I suspect that when a civilian in uniform returns to communal life, he should reenter as unobtrusively as possible.

The service left me with habits and emotions, little ones and big ones, that are with me to this day. For example, all the hooks on the clothes hangers in my closet are in one direction on the closet bar; shoes are always positioned in neat rows; jackets and suit coats face in one direction; towels folded neatly on the rack after use; a hatred for small, thin used bars of soap, but real respect for soap generally that will never leave me; near indifference toward rain at a football game: what the hell, I used to live in it; a dislike for snow and cold; a tolerance for heat, because, for me, it was easier to get used to than cold; impatience with people who cannot make a decision fast in an emergency; a general dislike for small men (physically) because they remind me of the pompous, inefficient little guys who somehow managed to get a commission in the service and had never had that much authority before; intolerance toward people who scoff at the military service even though they've never served, nor do they know anything about the service; a groin rash that breaks out if I miss a daily shower; a healthy, normal liking for young men, because they remind me of the many fine young men I used to know in the military and still respect, many of whom did not come home; antipathy toward unnecessary noise; a competitive spirit which almost worships winning even though men's lives are no longer at stake anymore; a love of flag and country in spite of the stupid mistakes we Americans manage to make in wholesale quantities; a waning tendency to bark at people when asking them to do something; a quiet, lonely wish for a return to the old swashbuckling days—with combat deleted; a sense of urgency about everything, so that even minor details are checked to make certain all will go well, no matter how trivial the project may be; a hesitant approach to some matters because of lack of knowledge of the situations.

Be that as it may, I still hear the cries of the wounded; the almost incessant uproar followed by eerie periods of utter silence; the mangled bodies often in grotesque postures, bloodied faces chalk-white, open eyes staring, rotting flesh with its peculiar odor; degrading filth; abominable weather while living in the habitats of the animals; in short, the miserable existence of the infantry soldier. I remembered it all as I greeted my loved ones.

I shall always ponder over the horrible futility of it all. Millions of lives snuffed out. Billions of dollars worth of devastating destruction and billions more lost in useless armaments.

WHY?

᪥ Notes

Preface

1. For representative examples of this debate, see Russell F. Weigley, *Eisenhower's Lieutenants: The Campaign of France and Germany, 1944–1945* (Bloomington: Indiana University Press, 1981); Martin L. Van Creveld, *Fighting Power: German and U.S. Army Performance, 1939–1945* (Westport, CT.: Greenwood Press, 1982); Roger A. Beaumont, "On the Wehrmacht Mystique," *Military Review* 66 (July 1986): 45–55; Lee B. Kennett, *G.I.: The American Soldier in World War II* (New York: Scribner, 1987); Michael D. Doubler, *Closing with the Enemy: How GIs Fought the War in Europe, 1944–1945* (Lawrence: University Press of Kansas, 1994); Colin F. Baxter, "Did the Nazis Fight Better than Democrats: Historical Writing on the Combat Performance of the Allied Soldier in Normandy," *Parameters* 25 (Autumn 1995): 113–18; Richard Overy, *Why the Allies Won* (New York: W. W. Norton, 1996); Stephen E. Ambrose, *Citizen Soldiers: The U.S. Army from the Normandy Beaches to the Bulge to the Surrender of Germany, June 7, 1944–May 7, 1945* (New York: Simon and Schuster, 1997); Peter R. Mansoor, *The GI Offensive in Europe: The Triumph of American Divisions, 1941–1945* (Lawrence: University Press of Kansas, 1999); Peter S. Kindsvatter, *American Soldiers: Ground Combat in the World Wars, Korea, & Vietnam* (Lawrence: University Press of Kansas, 2003); Paul Fussell, *The Boys' Crusade* (New York: Random House, 2003).

2. Robert L. Hewitt, *Work Horse of the Western Front: The Story of the 30th Infantry Division* (Washington, D.C.: Infantry Journal Press, 1946), 282; Mansoor, *GI Offensive*, 265.

Introduction

1. Edward C. Arn, "Service Experience Questionnaire," 18. Edward C. Arn Collection, Wooster, Ohio. Arn's responses are the source of the direct quotes in this introduction.

2. During basic training, Arn wrote a brief autobiography about his life prior to induction. The cadre required this exercise to judge a potential officer's ability to express clear thoughts. The editor has incorporated that information in this section.

3. Edward Arn married Emma E. Irons in Cleveland, Ohio, 27 November 1892. They had one child, Helen I. Arn (1893–1991).

Emma Irons Arn died, 2 August 1903. "Arn/Conelly Family History," 1992, 9, Arn Collection.

4. Robert R. Palmer and William R. Keast, "The Procurement of Officers," in Robert R. Palmer, Bell I. Wiley, and William R. Keast, *The Procurement and Training of Ground Combat Troops. United States Army in World War II, The Ground Forces*, (Washington, D.C.: Department of the Army, 1948), 108. Originally prepared by the Historical Division, War Department Special Staff, this official series became known as "Green Books" because of the color of their hardback covers. Kent R. Greenfield, *The Historian and the Army* (Port Washington, N.Y.: Kennikat Press, 1970); Robert F. Coakley, "Reflections on Writing the Green Books," *Army History: The Professional Bulletin of Army History*, 25 (Summer 1993): 37–39.

5. The AUS's anticipation of taking high casualties in the coming Normandy invasion and the need for replacements proved true. Combat riflemen and their company officers from 6 June 1944 through the following eight weeks constituted about 83 percent of these losses. Doubler, *Closing*, 27–28, 60, 239–40; Samuel Stouffer, Arthur A. Lumsdaine, and Marian Harper Lumsdaine, "Attitude before Combat and Behavior in Combat," in Studies in Social Psychology in World War II, Samuel Stouffer et al., *The American Soldier: Combat and Its Aftermath* (Princeton: Princeton University Press, 1949), 2: 8–9. Hereafter cited as SSP.

6. Hewitt, *Work Horse*, 1–25. This work is the basic source for the history of "Old Hickory." Numerous studies are available about the Normandy invasion. Stephen E. Ambrose, *D-Day, June 6, 1944: The Climactic Battle of World War II* (New York: Simon & Schuster, 1994) presents the basic story. Additional information can be found in Colin F. Baxter, *The Normandy Campaign, 1944: A Selected Bibliography* (Westport, CT.: Greenwood Press, 1992) and David Chandler, ed., *The D-Day Encyclopedia* (New York: Simon & Schuster, 1994).

7. James J. Carafano, *After D-Day: Operation Cobra and the Normandy Breakout* (Boulder, CO.: Lynne Rienner Publishers, 2000), 133–35.

8. Martin Blumenson, *Breakout and Pursuit. United States in Army in World War II. The European Theater of Operations.* (Washington, D.C.: Department of the Army, 1961), 305–22. Arn's commendation for the Silver Star noted that on 25 July 1944 he left a safe "shelter in the height of a fierce bombing and strafing raid" to give "aid and comfort" to "numerous" wounded men. When the raid ceased, Arn "rallied his company and led them in a fierce attack on the securely entrenched enemy." His actions "saved the lives of many men," and reflected "great credit upon himself and the Armed Forces." "Headquarters, 30th Infantry Division, Office of the Commanding General," Arn Collection.

9. Alwyn Featherston, *Saving the Breakout: The 30th Division's Heroic Stand at Mortain, August 7-12, 1944* (Novato, CA.: Presidio Press, 1993), 186–87.

10. Charles B. MacDonald, *The Siegfried Line Campaign. United States Army in World War II. The European Theater of Operations*, (Washington, D. C.: Department of the Army, 1963) details this operation.

11. Cornelius Ryan, *A Bridge Too Far* (New York: Simon & Schuster, 1974);

Robert J. Kershaw, *It Never Snows in September: The German View of Market Garden and the Battle of Arnhem* (Marlborough: Crowood Press, 1990). The Army Special Training Program (ASTP), sponsored by Secretary of War Henry Stimson, selected 150,000 of the brightest draftees to attend college at government expense, taking majors in specialties the AUS thought would be needed later in the war and during peacetime. Louis E. Keefer, *Scholars in Foxholes: The Story of the Army Specialized Training Program in World War II* (Jefferson, N.C.: McFarland, 1988); Louis E. Keefer, "The Birth and Death of the Army Specialized Training Program," *Army History 33* (Winter 1995): 1–7.

12. Germans called the city Aachen; the French, Aix-la-Chapelle.

13. *Combat History of the 119th Infantry Regiment* (Baton Rouge, LA.: Army and Navy Publishers, 1946), 56–76. Arn earned another Silver Star for rallying the "remainder" of his company at Aachen on 6 October 1944. "At the risk of his own life," he led his men into "defensive positions" where they remained "vulnerable" and "exposed to considerable fire, in order to direct artillery fire upon the enemy." The following day, his company counterattacked, recaptured "all lost ground," and assaulted "the Siegfried Line" with "fresh enthusiasm." "Headquarters 30th Infantry Division, Office of the Commanding General," Arn Collection.

14. Hewitt, *Work Horse*, 141; Mansoor, *GI Offensive*, 264–65.

15. John S. D. Eisenhower, *The Bitter Woods: The Battle of the Bulge* (New York: G.P. Putnam's Sons, 1969), 27–260 and John Pimlott, *Battle of the Bulge* (New York: Galahad Books, 1981) offer a general introduction to the Ardennes Campaign.

16. Charles B. MacDonald, *A Time for Trumpets: The Untold Story of The Battle of the Bulge* (New York: William Morrow and Company, 1985), 440–49.

17. Charles Whiting, *'44: In Combat from Normandy to the Ardennes* (New York: Stein and Day, 1984), 83–84, describes this incident.

18. *The Stars and Stripes*, 22, 23, 25, 29 December 1944, 10, 13 January 1945; Hanson W. Baldwin, *Battles Lost and Won: Great Campaigns of World War II* (New York: Harper & Row, 1966), 315–67; Charles Whiting, *Massacre at Malmédy: The Story of Jochen Peiper's Battle Group, Ardennes, December, 1944* (New York: Stein and Day, 1971); Trevor N. Dupuy, *Hitler's Last Gamble: The Battle of the Bulge, December 1944–January 1945* (New York: HarperCollins, 1994).

19. Stephen E. Ambrose, *Eisenhower and Berlin: The Decision to Halt at the Elbe* (New York: W. W. Norton, 1967) explains General Dwight D. Eisenhower's reasoning.

20. Samuel Stouffer, "The Point System for Redeployment and Discharge," SSP, 2: 520–48.

21. Overall casualties in the ETO ran to 586,628, with 456,779 from combat divisions. Old Hickory, in combat for 282 days, had the ninth highest total casualty rate among the forty-two infantry combat divisions in the ETO, 26,038, or 185 percent. Of these, 4,731 were KIA or MIA. Some 12,960 suffered various wounds, many severe enough to result in 513 deaths and 4,245 discharges. 8,618, including Arn, were wounded but returned to duty. Under the

organization of a standard infantry division, the 30th's three infantry regiments, the 117th, 119th, and 120th, contained 9,000 men. These regiments lost 4,005 men killed or missing in action. The 119th had 1,025 KIA or MIA. Using Fox Company's Morning Reports, Arn and 1st Sgt. Thomas H. Kirkman compiled a list of 610 WIA and 128 KIA, the lowest casualty rate among the infantry companies in the 119th Regiment. Figures derived from: Hewitt, *Work Horse*, 333–56; *Order of Battle of the United States Army in World War II: European Theater of Operations. Divisions* (Washington, D.C.: Office of the Theater Historian, 1945); Adjutant General's Office, *Army Battle Casualties and Nonbattle Deaths in World War II. Final Report. 7 December 1941–December 1946* (Washington, D.C.: Department of the Army, 1953) 84–85; Ambrose, *Citizen Soldiers*, 276–86; Mansoor, *GI Offensive*, 252; Doubler, *Closing*, 239.

22. The following discuss the problems facing writers of such works, especially the nature and limitations of memory: William H. Woodward, "The Citizen-Soldier Historian and the 'New Military History,'" *The Army Historian* 9 (Fall 1985): 13–15; Paul Fussell, *Wartime: Understanding and Behavior in the Second World War* (New York: Oxford University Press, 1989), 267–97; Peter S. Kindsvatter, "Cowards, Comrades, and Killer Angels," *Parameters* 20 (June 1990): 31–49; Alice M. Hoffman, *Archives of Memory: A Soldier Recalls World War II* (Lexington: University Press of Kentucky, 1990), 9–23, 144–54; Mark E. Clark, "Military Memoirs of World War II: Is It Too Late?" *Army History* 35 (Fall 1995): 28–31; Barry S. Strauss, "Reflections on the Citizen-Soldier," *Parameters* 33 (Summer 2003): 66–67, Tom Mathews, *Our Fathers' War: Growing Up in the Shadow of the Greatest Generation* (New York: Broadway Books, 2005).

Chapter 1

1. President Franklin D. Roosevelt signed *The Selective Training and Service Act*, the nation's first peacetime conscription, 16 September 1940. John J. O'Sullivan, *From Voluntarism to Conscription: Congress and Selective Service, 1940–1945* (New York: Garland, 1982); J. Garry Clifford and Samuel R. Spencer Jr., *The First Peacetime Draft* (Lawrence: University Press of Kansas, 1986).

2. Prior to December 1941, monthly draft quotas were small, averaging about ten men for each of the nation's 6,500 local boards. A married man with a dependent was designated 3-A. Men immediately eligible for induction were designated 1-A. Arn remained 3-A until 19 August 1942, when his draft board reclassified him 1-A. John W. Chambers II, *To Raise an Army: The Draft Comes to Modern America* (New York: Free Press, 1978), 254–55; Kennett, *G.I.*, 9; George Q. Flynn, *The Draft, 1940–1973* (Lawrence: University Press of Kansas, 1993), 18, 34–52.

3. Twenty thousand dollars in 2003 dollars came to $225,276.07. Figure based on a conversion formula developed by the *Bureau of Statistics*.

4. John Toland, *Infamy: Pearl Harbor and Its Aftermath* (Garden City: Doubleday, 1982); Wayne S. Cole, *Roosevelt and the Isolationists, 1932–45* (Lincoln: University of Nebraska Press, 1983) analyze the prewar period and the impact of the Japanese attack on public attitudes.

5. A shortage of officers created the need for the VOC program. Palmer and Keast, *Procurement and Training*, 104, 108, 117, 347; Edwin P. Hoyt, *The GI's War: The Story of American Soldiers in Europe in World War II* (New York: McGraw-Hill, 1988), 45–59. Potential officers needed a score of 110 on the Army General Classification Test (AGCT) to qualify for OCS.

6. Military manpower shortages forced draft officials to reconsider earlier deferments. The changes caused uncertainty among men 3-A, like Arn, who did not hold jobs draft officials deemed essential. "Numbers Game," *Business Week* (7 March 1942), 72; "Draft and Deferments," *Newsweek* 19 (13 April 1942), 31; "Dependency no Deferment," *Business Week* (27 April 1942): 15–16.

7. Arn's draft board ordered him to report 6 August 1942 for a "Qualifying Examination" for admission into the VOC program. Bess H. Moon to Arn, 1 August 1942, Arn Collection.

8. Captain Michael C. Burgan informed Arn that the "Commanding General" had approved his "induction" into the VOC plan. Burgan to Arn, 11 August 1942, Arn Collection. Arn's draft board changed his classification to 1-A on 19 August 1942 following his admission to the VOC program.

9. Ennis P. Whitley to Arn, 3 September 1942, Arn Collection.

Chapter 2

1. Military slang for a malingerer, an untrained and inept military recruit, or a soldier assigned to menial duties. These terms, idioms, and anagrams can be found in A. Marjorie Taylor, *The Language of World War II: Abbreviations, Captions, Quotations, Slogans, Titles and Other Terms and Phases* (New York: H. W. Wilson, 1944); Frederick Elkin, "The Soldier's Language," *American Journal of Sociology* 51 (March 1946): 414–22; John R. Elting, Dan Cragg, and Ernest Deal, *A Dictionary of Soldier Talk* (New York: Charles Scribner's Sons, 1984).

2. Begun in December 1940 and completed at a cost of $12 million by May 1941, Camp Croft housed 16,500 troops and covered 21,000 acres. "The 32nd Informer," 2 (6 September 1942), Arn Collection; Martin A. Kreidberg and Merton G. Henry, *History of Military Mobilization in the United States Army, 1775–1945* (Washington, D.C.: Department of the Army, 1955), 598.

3. John A. English, *A Perspective on Infantry* (New York: Praeger, 1981), 165–68, lists the organization of a typical AUS infantry regiment as of 1942.

4. For similar descriptions of basic training, see "The Making of an Infantryman," *American Journal of Sociology* 51 (March 1946): 367–79; Keast, "The Training of Officer Candidates," *Procurement and Training*, 325–64; Keast, "The Training of Enlisted Replacements," ibid., 369–429; Edward A. Suchman, Samuel A. Stouffer, and LeLand C. DeVinney, "Attitudes toward Leadership and Social Control," SSP, 1: 410–15; Arthur J. Vidich and Maurice R. Stein, "The Dissolved Identity in Military Life," in *Identity and Anxiety: Survival of the Person in Mass Society*, ed. by Maurice R. Stein, Arthur J. Vidich, and David M. White (New York: Free Press, 1960), 493–506; Joanna Bourke, *An Intimate History of Killing: Face-to-Face Killing in Twentieth-Century Warfare* (New York: Basic Books, 1999), 57–90.

5. AUS physicians noted on 27 March 1942 that Arn weighed 167 pounds, stood slightly under six feet, had 20/20 vision, and was in "excellent" health. "The Report of Physical Examination, 27 March 1942," Arn Collection.

6. The editor incorporated Arn's autobiographic material in the introduction.

7. Arn's proficiency in the BAR was no accident. He made extensive notes on the weapon's construction, functions, assembly, and disassembly, firing positions, methods to set a field of fire and sighting, and adjustments for windage and elevation. Arn, "Fort Benning Notebook," 3 March 1942, Arn Collection.

8. Arn paid particular attention to the manual on this subject: Training Bulletin No. GT-1, *Organization of the Infantry Regiment* (Washington, D.C.: Department of the Army, 1942).

9. Receiving mail from home was a major morale builder, even letters with complaints or news about sickness or death. Frank F. Mathias, *G.I. Jive: An American Bandsman in World War II* (Lexington: The University Press of Kentucky, 1982), 22–28; Keith F. Somerville, *Dear Boys: World War Letters from a Woman Back Home*, ed. by Judy B. Litoff and David C. Smith (Jackson: University Press of Mississippi, 1991), 1–16.

10. Arn's fellow trainees were correct. He made extensive notations in his "Notebook" about every aspect of military life an officer might encounter.

11. Someone scribbled a line on Arn's graduation program that testified to his intensity. "Dear me, what does the schedule say for tomorrow." "Graduation Program," 27 May 1943, Arn Collection.

12. Arn took justifiable pride in achieving the goals Fort Benning's cadre set to develop the qualities the AUS deemed vital for future officers: "Morale. Discipline. Health. Strength. Endurance. Technical Proficiency. Initiative. Leadership. Teamwork. Tactical Proficiency." *Fort Benning on Parade* (1943). Leon C. Standifer, *Not in Vain: A Rifleman Remembers World War II* (Baton Rouge: Louisiana State University Press, 1992), 41–75, supplements Arn's description.

13. Cora May Conelly Arn was East Cleveland, Ohio's Production Chairman for the American Red Cross. Arn/Conelly Family History, 12.

Chapter 3

1. "Headquarters Second Training Regiment, IRTC, Fort McClellan, Alabama, 7 June 1943," Arn Collection. Wiley, "Building and Training of Infantry Division," *Procurement and Training*, 433–69, mentions the background of Arn's assignment.

2. Gung ho, a purportedly Chinese term American troops adopted, had two definitions: working together; or a person who acted with zealous military enthusiasm.

3. By 1943, Fort McClellan spread across forty thousand acres. Unmarried officers, like Arn, lived in Bachelor Officers Quarters (BOQ) on base. Charles J. Sullivan, *Army Posts and Towns: The Baedeker of the Army* (Los Angeles, CA.: Haynes, 1942), 96–97.

4. Some young troops freed from the restraints exerted by families and

community became sexual predators. Henry Elkin, "Aggressive and Erotic Tendencies in Army Life," *American Journal of Sociology* 51 (March 1946): 408–14; Kennett, *G.I.*, 76–78; Harold Pagliaro, *Naked Heart: A Soldier's Journey to the Front* (Kirksville: Thomas Jefferson University Press, 1996), 12–13; Peter Schrijvers, *The Crash of Ruins: American Combat Soldiers in Europe During World War II* (New York: New York University Press, 1998), 171.

5. Talladega National Forest lies east of Fort McClellan.

6. Major General Ludwig W. Conelly joined the Ohio National Guard in 1929 and retired in 1945. The 37th "Buckeye" Infantry Division, organized from the Ohio National Guard, mustered into service in October 1940. Stanley A. Frankel, *The 37th Infantry Divison in World War II* (Washington, D.C.: Infantry Journal Press, 1948).

7. About sixty thousand conscientious objectors served in the military during World War II. Some civilian officials and AUS officers did fail to make a distinction between cowards, slackers, and legitimate conscientious objectors. Often these officials and officers allowed conscientious objectors to suffer physical punishment and psychological humiliation. Mulford Q. Silbey and Philip E. Jacobs, *Conscription of Conscience: The American State and the Conscientious Objector, 1940–1947* (Ithaca: Cornell University Press, 1952), 86, 95–107; Rachel Baker, *Conscience, Government and the War* (London: Routledge and Kegan Paul, 1982), 91–92; George Q. Flynn, "Lewis Hershey and the Conscientious Objector: The World War II Experience," *Military Affairs* 48 (February 1983): 1–6; Cynthia Eller, *Conscientious Objectors and the Second World War: Moral and Religious Arguments in Support of Pacifism* (New York: Praeger, 1991), 173–77.

8. Roscoe C. Blunt Jr., *Foot Soldier: A Combat Infantryman's War in Europe* (Rockville Center, NY.: Sarpedon, 2001), 1, verifies Arn's observations about Talladega National Forest.

9. Geoffrey Perret, *There's a War to Be Won: The United States Army in World War II* (New York: Random House, 1991), 127–297; Williamson Murray and Allan R. Millett, *A War to Be Won: Fighting the Second World War* (Cambridge: Harvard University Press, 2000), 196–410, expand on this military situation.

10. Fort Meade served as a staging area for overseas embarkation to the ETO.

11. *The Infantry Lieutenant and His Platoon* (Washington, D.C.: Department of the Army, 1944), 8.

12. Arn's CO had a variety of options for presenting charges and specifications against him, especially Article 92, "Conduct Unbecoming An Officer"; or Article 134, "General Article" for conduct prejudicial to good order. Lee S. Tillotson, *Index-Digest and Annotations to the Uniform Code of Military Justice* (Harrisburg, PA.: Military Service Publishing Company, 1952), 293–96.

13. Charles Whiting, *Death of a Division* (New York: Stein and Day, 1981); Robert P. Kissel, "Death of a Division in the Schnee Eifel," *World War II* (January 2000): 46–52, also discuss the 106th Division.

14. Arn had been in combat for nearly six months before the 106th arrived in the ETO.

15. Military slang denoting someone who does not know what he is doing.

16. For projected casualty rates among combat riflemen in the coming cross-channel invasion, see Russell Weigley, *The American Way of War: A History of United States Military Strategy and Policy* (Bloomington: Indiana University Press, 1977), 312–46; Max Hastings, *Overlord: D-Day and the Battle for Normandy* (New York: Simon and Schuster, 1984), 210. The War Department had transferred almost 60 percent of the 106th's original strength, including Arn, as replacements to other units before the division rotated overseas. Reconstituted with green troops, the inexperienced division, which had the youngest average troops (twenty-two) of any army combat division in the ETO, went on-line 11 December 1944, east of St. Vith, Belgium, in an area the army considered quiet. Taking the position held by the 2nd Division, the 106th bore the initial brunt of the German counterattack in the opening round of the Ardennes Campaign. Robin Cross, *The Battle of the Bulge, 1944: Hitler's Last Hope* (Havertown, PA: Casemate, 2002), 73–74, 110–15, 122. William Wharton's novel, *A Midnight Clear* (New York: Knopf, 1982), deals with former members of the ASTP, who were probably combat infantrymen in this division.

17. Arn followed directions listed in "Check List for Officers on Order to POE, 18 May 1944." Arn Collection.

Chapter 4

1. Fort George C. Meade, named for the Union Civil War general, is located south of Baltimore, Maryland, and southeast of Washington, D.C. Sullivan, *Army Posts and Towns*, 101.

2. Completed in May 1943 after hurried construction, and tainted by charges of corruption, Camp Shanks, some twenty miles north of New York City, processed 1.3 million troops to the ETO until its demobilization in 1946. *New York Times*, 18 January, 22 July 1946.

3. Most replacements underwent such anxieties. M. Brewster Smith, "The Combat Replacement," SSP, 2: 196–97, 203–204, 272–76; Kennett, *G.I.*, 134–35; Robert Kotlowitz, *Before Their Time: A Memoir* (New York: Alfred A. Knopf, 1997), 57–62, 83–85; Doubler, *Closing*, 253–56.

4. Samuel E. Morison, *The Battle of the Atlantic, September 1939–May 1943. History of the United States Naval Operations in World War II* (Boston: Little, Brown and Company, 1947); Edwin P. Hoyt, *The Death of the U-Boats* (New York: Warner Books, Inc., 1988); Clay Blair, *Hitler's U-Boat War: The Hunters, 1939–1942* (New York: Random House, 1996); Blunt, *Foot Soldier*, 4–11, discuss submarine warfare and such troop convoys.

5. Foster R. Dulles, *The American Red Cross: A History* (New York: Harper & Brothers, 1950), 445–49, covers the Red Cross' support of American troops in Great Britain. Patrick F. Gilbo, *The American Red Cross: The First Century* (New York: Harper & Row, 1981), 142–72, presents a general history of the wartime Red Cross. Combat medics most valued the Red Cross' role in securing blood for the wounded. Keith Winston, *V-Mail: Letters of a World War II Combat Medic*, ed. by Sarah Winston (Chapel Hill, NC.: Algonquin Books, 1985), 154.

6. Blumenson, *Breakout and Pursuit*, 36–180. Field Marshal Erwin Rommel had prepared the German defenses against an Allied invasion in his "Atlantic Wall." Friedrich Kuge, *Rommel in Normandy* (Navato, CA.: Presido Press 1979), 88–171; Samuel W. Mitcham Jr., *The Desert Fox in Normandy: Rommel's Defense of Fortress Europe* (Westport, CT.: Praeger, 1997), 1–55.

7. Allied infantrymen ran a casualty rate of 63 percent. Hastings, *Overlord*, 210–20.

8. Bruce C. Zorns, *I Walk Through the Valley: A World War II Infantryman's Memoir of War, Imprisonment and Love* (Jefferson, NC.: McFarland & Company, 1991), 72–73; Robert Kotlowitz, *Before Their Time: A Memoir* (New York: Alfred A. Knopf, 1997), 58–63, offer similar views. See also S. Kirson Weinberg, "Problems of Adjustment in Army Units," *American Journal of Sociology* 50 (January 1945): 271–78; Fred V. Flynn, "Preparing the 'Self' for Combat," *Military Review* 71 (August 1991): 77–87.

9. *Utah Beach to Cherbourg 6–27 June 1944* (Washington, D.C.: Department of the Army, 1947), 74–93; Hastings, *Overlord*, 196–210; Donald J. Willis, *The Incredible Year* (Ames: Iowa State University Press, 1988), 10–11; Max Hastings and Gerald Astor, *June 6, 1944: The Voices of D-Day* (New York: St. Martin's Press, 1994) depict the invasion's physical and material aftermath in Normandy. Months later, D+146 days, the area remained basically the same. Roscoe C. Blunt Jr., *Inside the Battle of the Bulge: A Private Comes of Age* (Westport, CT.: Praeger, 1994), 5–6. Walter S. Dunn Jr., *Second Front Now—1943* (University: The University of Alabama Press, 1980), 58–74, lists the various types of Allied landing crafts available for the invasion. Pagliaro, *Naked Heart*, 97–98, covers a comparable seaborne transfer. Russell F. Weigley, "From the Normandy Beaches to the Falaise-Argentan Pocket," *Military Review* 70 (September 1995): 45–64 is a critique of AUS efforts.

10. Arn's reaction to the "repple depple" was typical. Smith, "Combat Replacement," 2: 272–73; John P. Irwin, *Another River, Another Town: A Teenage Tank Gunner Comes of Age in Combat, 1945* (New York: Random House, 2002), 4–5, 127.

11. Edward J. Brennan Jr., *The Lion's Pride: Theodore Roosevelt and His Family in Peace and War* (New York: Oxford University Press, 1998), 238–39.

12. Patton and Roosevelt had been friends before the war. Ladislas Farago, *Patton: Ordeal and Triumph* (New York: Ivan Obolensky, Inc., 1963), 437.

13. For more information on Old Hickory, see "Leland S. Hobbs, Major General, U.S. Army Commanding, 25 May 1944, to Officers and Men of the 30th Infantry Division, Headquarters 30th Infantry Division, APO 30," Arn Collection; Henry D. Russell, *The Purge of the Thirtieth Division* (Macon, GA.: Lyon, Marshall & Brooks, 1949); Keith Todd, *Old Hickory: 30th Infantry Division* (Paducah, KY.: Turner, 1990), 9–21; Bruce Jacobs, "Tensions Between the Army National Guard and the Regular Army," *Military Affairs* 73 (October 1993): 12–17, Mansoor, *GI Offensive*, 67–71. Specialists can follow the 30th Division's combat activities in the primary documents housed in Section 330, Record Group 407, Modern Military History Records Branch, National Archives. Record Group 332 contains information on unit citations the 30th

Division earned. To consult these records, see James G. Bradsher, "Practicing the Historian's Craft: The Army Historian and the Army Records," *The Army Historian* 8 (Summer 1985), 10–11. The United States Army Military History Institute, Carlisle Barracks, Pennsylvania, contains the 30th Division's World War II Survey Collection. Prior to the United States' entry into World War II, General George C. Marshall had reorganized the composition of army divisions. Maurice Matloff, "The 90 Division Gamble," in *Command Decisions*, ed. by Kent R. Greenberg (Washington, D.C.: Department of the Army, 1960), 365–81.

14. *Combat History*, 8–13; Hewitt, *Work Horse*, 1–7. Field Marshal Gerd von Runstedt had clashed with Chancellor Adolf Hitler over strategy and tactics in Normandy, particularly Hitler's refusal to release critical Panzer divisions. On 2 July 1944, Hitler relieved von Runstedt, replacing him with Field Marshal Günther von Kluge as commander-in-chief of German forces in the west. Blumenson, *Breakout and Pursuit*, 17–47; Kenneth Macksey, *Why the Germans Lose at War: The Myth of German Military Superiority* (London: Greenhill Books, 1996), 204–205. The obstacles that hedgerows presented are explained in Glover S. Johns Jr., *The Clay Pigeons of St. Lô* (Harrisburg, PA.: The Military Service Publishing Company, 1958), 1–177; Balkoski, *Beyond the Beachhead*, 175–235; Charles R. Cawthon, *Other Clay: A Remembrance of the World War II Infantry* (Niwot: University Press of Colorado, 1990), 75–76; Mansoor, *GI Offensive*, 150–59.

15. *Combat History*, 20–21; Hewitt, *Work Horse*, 25–33; Blumenson, *Breakout and Pursuit*, 92–93, 106–108.

16. John Keegan, *Six Armies in Normandy: From D-Day to the Liberation of Paris, June 6th–August 25th, 1944* (New York: Viking Press, 1982), 61–63, 128–31, 241–43, 249–50, expands on Arn's comments about German firepower.

17. *Combat History*, 22–23; Mansoor, *GI Offensive*, 153–55; Doubler, *Closing*, 31–60.

18. Hewitt, *Work Horse*, 7–33; Doubler, *Closing*, 20, 236–38.

19. Shirley A. Star, "Psychoneurotic Symptoms in the Army," SSR, 2: 445–55; Doubler, *Closing*, 27–28, 246–47, elaborate on the range of emotions replacements felt.

20. Beaudoin's helpfulness contradicted the assumption that veteran combat troops did little to acclimate replacements. Ambrose, *Citizen Soldiers*, 277–78.

21. Training Bulletin No. GT-1. *Organization of the Infantry Brigade* (Washington, D.C.: Department of the Army, 1942), 22–24; Hewitt, *Work Horse*, 273.

22. Hastings, *Overlord*, 186–95; Kenneth Macksey, *Tank Force: Allied Armor in World War II* (New York: Ballantine, 197), 138–45, compare AUS and German weapons, armor, and firepower in Normandy. Philip D. Jones, "U.S. Antitank Doctrine in World War II," *Military Affairs* 60 (March 1980): 62–66; Mark E. Clark, "Infantry Defending Against Armored and Mechanical Attacks: A Historical Review," *Military Review* 71 (July 1999): 56–57; Doubler, *Closing*, 31–60, discuss the relationship between armor and infantry.

23. On combat stress and exhaustion, see Robin M. Williams Jr. and M. Brewster Smith, "General Characteristics of Ground Combat," SSR, 2: 59–104; John C. McManus, *The Deadly Brotherhood: The American Combat Soldier in World War II* (Novato, CA.: Presidio Press, 1998), 166–67; Doubler, *Closing*, 242–44. Other infantrymen's experiences duplicated Arn's first taste of battle. Cawthon, *Other Clay*, 54–55, 57–58. For more on fear, see John Keegan, *The Face of Battle* (New York: The Viking Press, 1976), 71–74.

24. The 30th Division contained an artillery unit with a "Long Tom," the standard heavy 155-mm caliber gun of AUS forces in the ETO, capable of firing a "95-pound projectile about 14,000 yards." Hewitt, *Work Horse*, 273.

25. Operation Cobra, devised by Lieutenant General Omar Bradley, began with saturation carpetbombing to break the stalemate the hedgerows had caused. Infantry and armor would then penetrate German lines, prevent their reformation, power a breakout from the hedgerows, and lead to a war of mobility and pursuit to encircle the enemy. *The Stars and Stripes*, 31 July 1944; Blumenson, *Breakout and Pursuit*, 198–304; Charles B. MacDonald, *The Mighty Endeavor: The American War in Europe* (New York: Da Capo Press, 1992), 331–57.

26. S/Sgt. Jack R. Beatty later won the Silver Star. Hewitt, *Work Horse*, 285. Arn, as a means to further instill morale in Fox Company, acted quickly "to have unusual deeds properly recognized" through the awarding of appropriate medals. Arn to David Bailey, 9 May 2002, Arn Collection.

27. Carafano, *After D-Day*, 71–257.

28. Thomas A. Hughes, *Over Lord: General Pete Quesada and the Triumph of Tactical Air Power in World War II* (New York: The Free Press, 1995), 205–22; Doubler, *Closing*, 63–86, 233–35, 295–96, reviews the tactics used in Operation Cobra.

29. *New York Times*, 25 July 1944; Hewitt, *Work Horse*, 34–35; Kennett, *G.I.*, 175–76; Fussell, *Wartime*, 17–18. Newspaper reports downplayed the human costs of these mistakes and glossed over the incidents. Charles R. Shrader, "Friendly Fire: The Inevitable Price," *Paramaters* 22 (Autumn 1992): 32–35, 40–42; Cawthon, *Other Clay*, 110–11, add additional information.

30. While Arn minimized his efforts, his conduct earned a Silver Star for "gallantry in action."

31. *Combat History*, 23–26; Hewitt, *Work Horse*, 36–37, 348; Blumenson, *Breakout and Pursuit*, 224–335; Carafano, *After D-Day*, 114–21. For the hostility between enlisted men and officers, see Suchman, Stouffer, and DeVinney, "Attitudes toward Leadership and Social Control," SSR, 1: 381–82, 391–401; Gerald F. Linderman, *The World within War: America's Combat Experience in World War II* (New York: The Free Press, 1997), 187–234.

32. Arn received his first Purple Heart for this wound, 3 August 1944. "Headquarters Sixty-Second Medical Battalion, APO 270," Arn Collection. About twenty thousand members of the 30th Division gained Purple Hearts. Hewitt, *Work Horse*, 282; *The Medal of Honor* (Washington, D.C.: Government Printing Office, 1948), 461.

33. Front-line troops felt assured by having medical aid men attached to

their units. Smith, "Combat Motivation," SSR, 2: 144–214; Graham A. Cosmas and Albert E. Cowdrey, *Medical Service in the European Theater of Operations* (Washington, D.C.: Center for Military History, 1992); Albert E. Cowdrey, *Fighting for Life: American Military Medicine in World War II* (New York: The Free Press, 1994) offer insights into the Medical Department's efforts in the ETO.

34. By 2 August 1944, Operation Cobra was a clear success. The Allies had achieved their breakout from Normandy, avoided the costly trench warfare that inflicted so many deaths in World War I, gave the AUS the mobility sought for Lieutenant General Patton's armored forces, captured over twenty thousand prisoners, and shoved German troops into a headlong retreat. Blumenson, *Breakout and Pursuit*, 305–22; Weigley, *Eisenhower's Lieutenants*, 136–38, 145, 147–69; Jon Guttman, "Closing the Falaise Pocket," *World War II* (September 2001): 34–40.

35. Blumenson, *Breakout and Pursuit*, 457–75; Featherston, *Saving the Breakout*, 40–97. The disintegrating German Army risked much to achieve much at Mortain. Their objectives were to split Allied forces, drive them back to the Normandy beaches, stop an Allied encirclement, close the route to Paris, and prevent a retreat from France that would force the Wehrmacht to fight on its own soil.

36. By defeating the best the Wehrmacht could offer, the Allied victory at Mortain proved a critical morale booster for the AUS generally and the 30th Division specifically. "Leland S. Hobbs, Major General, U.S. Army Commanding, Headquarters 30th Infantry Division, APO 30, 12 August 1944, to The Soldiers of the 30th Infantry Division," Arn Collection; *Combat History*, 29–38; Hewitt, *Work Horse*, 48–77; Omar Bradley, *A Soldiers Life* (New York: Henry Holt and Company, 1951), 371–76, 398; Allyn R. Vannoy and Jay Karamales, *Against the Panzers: United States Infantry versus German Tanks, 1944–1945* (Jefferson, N.C.: McFarland, 1996), 19–41; Reardon, *Victory at Mortain*, 86–87, 92–117, 139, 165–66, 202, 218, 220, 267–68.

37. Hewitt, *Work Horse*, 61–77; Featherston, *Saving the Breakout*, 209–10; 225, 240; Mansoor, *GI Offensive*, 169–70.

38. *Combat History*, 35.

39. Featherston, *Saving the Breakout*, 186–87; Reardon, *Victory at Mortain*, 205, 328n23, treat Arn's role in the Battle of Mortain.

40. *Combat History*, 37–46; Blumenson, *Breakout and Pursuit*, 559–711.

41. Military historians consider Confederate Major General Thomas "Stonewall" Jackson's 1862 Shenandoah Valley campaign a model of how an undermanned army, using mobility and geography, could defeat a numerically larger but less efficient enemy. Robert G. Tanner, *Stonewall in the Valley: Thomas J. "Stonewall" Jackson's Shenandoah Valley Campaign, Spring 1862* (Garden City, N.Y.: Doubleday, 1976); Robert R. Krick, *Conquering the Valley: Stonewall Jackson at Port Republic* (New York: William Morrow, 1996).

42. *Combat History*, 45–46.

43. By this time, many members of the "outnumbered and outclassed" Luftwaffe had lost confidence and were demoralized. John Killen, *A History of*

the Luftwaffe (Garden City, N.Y.: Doubleday & Company, 1968), 260–62; E. R. Hooton, *Eagles in Flames: The Fall of the Luftwaffe* (London: Arms & Armour, 1997), 279. For the disillusionment of ordinary Wehrmacht troops with the Luftwaffe, see Paul Carell, *Invasion–They're Coming!: The German Account of the Allied Landings and the 80 Days' Battle for France*, 163–65 (New York: Dutton, 1963).

44. D. Bruce Lockerbie, *A Man under Orders: Lieutenant General William K. Harrison, Jr.* (New York: Harper & Row, 1979).

45. Alcohol usage among front-line troops served as an antidote to fear and was far more widespread than Arn suggested. Kindsvatter, *American Soldiers*, 96–97; Fussell, *Boys' Crusade*, 103–4.

46. For the French "cleansing" of women who collaborated with Germans, see Margaret C. Weitz, *Sisters in the Resistance: How Women Fought to Free France, 1940–1945* (New York: John Wiley & Sons, 1995), 268, 276–81; Kotlowitz, *Before Their Time*, 75–77.

47. The relationship between combat exhaustion, premonitions of dying, and death can be found in M. Brewster Smith, "Combat Motivations among Ground Troops," SSR, 2: 188–89; James Jones, *WW II: A Chronicle of Soldiering* (New York: Grosset & Dunlap, 1975), 86–91, 196.

48. *Combat History*, 17.

49. *The Stars and Stripes*, 11, 18 November 1944; *Combat History*, 46–51; Hewitt, *Work Horse*, 78–99; Dunn, *Second Front*, 151–245; Keegan, *Six Armies*, 238–312.

50. Toland, *Bridge Too Far*, and Kershaw, *Never Snows in September* discuss this failure. William B. Breuer, *Feuding Allies: The Private Wars of the High Command* (New York: Wiley, 1995); G. E. Patrick Murray, *Eisenhower Versus Montgomery: The Continuing Debate* (Westport, CT.: Praeger, 1996); Ronald Andidora, *Home by Christmas: The Illusion of Victory in 1944* (Westport, CT.: Greenwood Press, 2002) study the conflict among Allied leaders.

Chapter 5

1. Hewitt, *Work Horse*, 98–110; MacDonald, *Siegfried Line Campaign*, 39–206; Blunt, *Foot Soldier*, 79–97.

2. Baird was wounded in October and evacuated. The point that Arn did not recall his first name, and the lack of Baird's record in Hewitt and *Combat History*, illustrates the high casualty rate among replacements in rifle companies. Some commentators estimate that a typical infantry company needed up to six weeks to integrate replacements, including junior officers, and have them adjust to battlefield conditions. Kotlowitz, *Before Their Time*, 76–77; Doubler, *Closing*, 27–28; Fussell, *Boys' Crusade*, 77. A Bailey Bridge, devised by Sir Donald Bailey, consisted of prefabricated, standardized parts of various dimensions and strengths, mounted on lateral rollers, that engineers could assemble as circumstances dictated. Readers can follow Arn's Aachen account in H. R. Knickerbocker et al., *Danger Forward: The Story of the First Division in World War II, United States Army, World War II* (Washington, D.C.: Society of the

First Division, 1947), 265–83; Weigley, *Eisenhower's Lieutenants*, 357–64; Doubler, *Closing*, 98–105, 118–22.

3. *Combat History*, 56–57; MacDonald, *Siegfried Line*, 256–57, 264, 268; Charles Whiting, *Bloody Aachen* (New York: Stein and Day, 1976), 81–82; Alan J. Levine, *From the Normandy Beaches to the Baltic Sea: The Northwest Europe Campaign, 1944–1945* (Westport, CT.: Praeger, 2000), 132–33. Rimberg Castle, a high-walled, turreted structure, surrounded by a moat and pillboxes, lay east of the Wurm River.

4. For a comparison of the weight, armor, and firepower of the Panzer VI (Tiger) and AUS M4 (Sherman), see Hugh M. Cole, *The Lorraine Campaign. United States Army in World War II. The European Theater of Operations*, (Washington, D.C.: Department of the Army, 1950), 603–604; Vannoy and Karamales, *Panzers*, 189–323; Blunt, *Comes of Age*, 68; Roman J. Jarymowycz, *Tank Tactics from Normandy to Lorraine* (London: Lynne Rienner Publishers, Inc., 2001), 207–344.

5. *Combat History*, 59; Hewitt, *Work Horse*, 104–25, 320; MacDonald, *Siegfried Line*, 252–80.

6. McManus, *Deadly Brotherhood*, 76–77; Schrijvers, *Crash of Ruins*, 202–206; Richard D. Courtney, *Normandy to the Bulge: An American Infantry GI in Europe during World War II* (Carbondale: Southern Illinois University Press, 1997), 56–96, detail similar instances of looting, souvenir collecting, and destruction of civilian property. *The Spoils of War: World War II and Its Aftermath: The Loss, Reappearance, and Recovery of Cultural Property*, ed. by Elizabeth Simpson (New York: H. N. Abrams, 1997) is a full treatment of more systematic thievery.

7. MacDonald, *Siegfried Line Campaign*, 275–79. Doubler, *Closing*, 118–22, elaborates on the new techniques the 30th Division devised to reduce and destroy pillboxes. Merkstein, a coalmining area, contained showers and hygienic facilities that the men of Old Hickory appreciated.

8. *Combat History*, 63 states that sixty-five men were "trapped."

9. Hewitt estimates Fox Company's remaining effective manpower at forty. Hewitt, *Work Horse*, 123.

10. *Combat History*, 63, 85.

11. "General Order Number 106, 25 November 1944, Headquarters 30th Infantry, APO 30" answered Arn's questions by awarding him the Silver Star for "gallantry in action." Arn Collection.

12. Hewitt, *Work Horse*, 136; Weigley, *Eisenhower's Lieutenants*, 358.

13. Read Fussell, *Wartime*, 96–114; Zorn, *Walk*, 95–96; Schrijvers, *Crash of Ruins*, 177–90 for the sexual deprivation Arn described.

14. "Million dollar wounds" are explained in Samuel A. Stouffer, Arthur A. Lumsdaine, and Marion H. Lumsdaine, "Attitudes Before Combat and Behavior in Battle," SSR, 2: 6–8; Irvin, *Another River*, 64.

15. Kennett, *G.I.*, 161–62; Blunt, *Comes of Age*, 84–86, 177–79; Blunt, *Foot Soldier*, 142–46; Edwin P. Hoyt, *The GI's War*, 524–25; Bourke, *Killing*, 344–48, explore the growing American brutalization toward the enemy in response to actions outside established "rules" of warfare.

16. *Combat History*, 69–74; MacDonald, *Siegfried Line*, 301–304.

17. A report in the *Chicago Tribune* noted that the "30th closed the pocket." *Chicago Tribune*, 30 October 1944, Arn Collection. MacDonald, *Siegfried Line*, 305; Whiting, *Bloody Aachen*, 131–32 also notes Fox Company's achievement. Jack Moore to Edward Arn, 15 September 1994, further details this event, Arn Collection.

18. Discussions of wartime leaves appear in Brian H. Chermol, "Wounds without Scars: Treatment of Battle Fatigue in the U.S. Armed Forces in the Second World War," *Military Affairs* 49 (January 1985): 9–12; Doubler, *Closing*, 22–23, 242–44, 258, 262.

19. Leslie W. Bailey, *Through Hell and High Water: The Wartime Memoirs of a Junior Combat Officer* (New York: Vantage Press, 1994), 142–43; Klaus H. Heubner, *Long Walk through War: A Combat Doctor's Diary* (College Station: Texas A & M Press, 1987), 99–104, 118–20, 157, 164–65, expand on this policy.

20. For a psychological study of Hitler, see Walter C. Langer, *The Mind of Adolf Hitler: The Secret Wartime Report* (New York, Basic Books, 1972). Matthew Cooper, *The German Army, 1933–1945* (New York: Stein and Day, 1978), 528–44 explains the plot to assassinate Hitler. Studs Terkel, *"The Good War": An Oral History of World War II* (New York: Pantheon Books, 1984) studies the war from the perspective of ordinary and not-so-ordinary Americans.

21. In commenting on this instance of battle fatigue, Arn added that "Kirklin's name was never mentioned. We had work to do. Years later while on a business trip in West Texas, I saw Kirklin again. He had created quite a legend in Odessa about his exodus from combat. I didn't disturb or contract his history at all. I would assume he must be grateful."

22. *Combat History*, 76–82, 85; Hewitt, *Work Horse*, 147–51, 288; MacDonald, *Siegfried Line*, 499–503, 560–666.

23. For German destruction of Roer River dams, see *The Stars and Stripes*, 30 November 1944; Bradley, *Soldier's Story*, 456–57, 499–500; MacDonald, *Siegfried Line*, 574; Willis, *Incredible Year*, 109–13. The resultant floods, further fed by an unseasonable winter thaw, delayed invasion plans of the First and Ninth armies.

24. The 30th Division established a recreation center near Kerkrade, in the buildings that housed Rolduc College, formed in 1106. Hewitt, *Work Horse*, 165–66.

25. An American citizen, Mildred E. Gillars, nicknamed "Axis Sally," played popular music and broadcast propaganda on German radio. John C. Edwards, *Berlin Calling: American Broadcasters in Service to the Third Reich* (New York: Praeger, 1991), 88–98.

26. *Chicago Sun*, 3 December 1944, Arn Collection.

27. Arn's duties as company commander including censoring mail. "Higher-ups," he reminisced, believed that uncensored mail would "reveal military knowledge of value to the enemy." Even so, Arn confessed that he "always had an uncomfortable feeling" prying "into the private aspects of the lives of my lads." Arn to Institute of World War II and the Human Experience, 19 March 2003, Arn Collection.

28. Arn's comments underscored the resentment rife among combat troops

toward Air Force personnel. M. Brewster Smith, "Attitudes of Ground Combat Troops toward Rear Echelons and the Home Front," SSR, 2:290–91; Kennett, *G.I.*, 86; Schrijvers, *Crash of Ruins*, 200–201.

29. On wartime newspaper reporting, see Joseph J. Matthews, *Reporting the Wars* (Westport, CT.: Greenwood Press, 1972), 174–258; Frederick S. Voss, *Reporting the War: The Journalistic Coverage of World War II* (Washington, D.C.: Smithsonian Institution Press, 1994); Fussell, *Wartime*, 154–58, 287–88.

30. These conditions existed despite the Medical Corps' hygienic efforts. Richard V. N. Ginn, *The History of the U.S. Army Medical Service Corps* (Washington, D.C.: Office of the Surgeon General and Center of Military History, 1997), 162–65; Schrijvers, *Crash of Ruin*, 13–14.

Chapter 6

1. Hewitt, *Work Horse*, 173; Charles Whiting, *Ardennes: The Secret War* (New York: Stein and Day, 1985), 9–105; Willis, *Incredible Year*, 86–87.

2. David P. Colley, *The Road to Victory: The Untold Story of World War II's Red Ball Express* (Washington, D.C.: Brassey's, 2000), 135, 184, 190, 193; David P. Colley, "The Red Ball Express," *World War II* (March 1997): 35–40, emphasize the contributions African-American soldiers made in the "Red Ball Express."

3. Eisenhower, *Bitter Woods*, 105–238; Blunt, *Comes of Age*, 43–93; Don Smart, "Terror at Honsfeld," *World War II* (November 2001): 50–56; Blunt, *Foot Soldier*, 95–103; Doubler, *Closing*, 198–205.

4. Hewitt, *Work Horse*, 173.

5. *Combat History*, 86; Michael Reynolds, *The Devil's Adjutant: Jochen Peiper, Panzer Leader* (London: Spellmount Limited, 1995), 86, 104.

6. Arn later recommended a battlefield field promotion for S/Sgt. Kenneth F. Austin to Second Lieutenant. Austin further earned a Silver Star. Hewitt, *Work Horse*, 284.

7. Hugh M. Cole, *The Ardennes: Battle of the Bulge. The United States Army in World War II. The European Theater of Operations.* (Washington, D.C.: Department of the Army, 1965), 75–106, dissects this intelligence breakdown and the resultant confusion among American troops.

8. Estimates vary about the size and composition of these forces. Consult for instance, Reynolds, *Devil's Advocate*, 45, 49, 273–80; Ambrose, *Citizen Soldiers*, 189.

9. MacDonald, *A Time for Trumpets*, 160–223.

10. *Combat History*, 86–87; Hewitt, *Work Horse*, 174–76, 284; Cole, *Ardennes*, 260–69; Reynolds, *Devil's Advocate*, 88–97, 114.

11. Weigley, *Eisenhower's Lieutenants*, 495–96; James M. Gavin, *On to Berlin: Battles of an Airborne Commander, 1943–1946* (New York: Viking Press, 1978), 216–19, 229, 240–41; MacDonald, *Time for Trumpets*, 423; Arn to Gavin, 10 August 1978, Gavin to Arn, 30 August, 1978, Arn Collection. Few if any other generals took such risks like Gavin. Ambrose, *Citizen Soldiers*, 121–22. See also Marvin R. Cain, "The Military Memoir as Critical History: The Case of James M. Gavin," *Military Affairs* 44 (December 1990): 177–80.

12. *Combat History*, 88–89; Hewitt, *Work Horse*, 174–76; Cole, *Ardennes*, 335–46; Reynolds, *Devil's Advocate*, 127–28.

13. Clay Blair, *Ridgway's Paratroopers: The American Airborne in World War II* (Garden City, NY.: The Dial Press, 1985), 358–74.

14. *Combat History*, 88–89; John Toland, *Battle: The Story of the Bulge* (New York: Random House, 1959), 134; Reynolds, *Devil's Advocate*, 182–88.

15. Discussions of trench foot can be found in Cowdrey, *Fighting for Life*, 266–67; Courtney, *Normandy to the Bulge*, 60–61. On the AUS' logistic approach to this problem, see William F. Ross and Charles F. Romanus, *The Quartermaster Corps: Operations in the War against Germany. United States Army in World War II. The Technical Services.* (Washington, D.C.: 1965), 599–614. Standifer, *Not in Vain*, 196–215; Blunt, *Foot Soldier*, 121–24, 128, 141 describe the wintry weather and its affect on American troops.

16. Reynolds, *Devil's Advocate*, 218; Kennett, *G.I.*, 165–66; Ambrose, *Citizen Soldiers*, 351–54, deal with the shooting of POWs.

17. Cole, *Ardennes*, 366–67; John Strawson, *The Battle for the Ardennes* (New York: Charles Scribner's Sons, 1972), 103–4, 169, 175; Toland, *Battle*, 193; Peter Elstob, *Hitler's Last Offensive* (London: Secker & Warburg, 1971), 284–86; Reynolds, *Devil's Advocate*, 235, 239, 243–44.

18. Hewitt, *Work Horse*, 182–88; *Combat History*, 89; Toland, *Battle*, 166; Reynolds, *Devil's Advocate*, 222–24; Ambrose, *Citizen Soldiers*, 213–18.

19. *Combat History*, 88–89; Cole, *Ardennes*, 341–51.

20. Hewitt, *Work Horse*, 186; Cole, *Ardennes*, 349–51. Herlong or McCown, if they desired, had sufficient grounds to press charges against Arn: Disrespect to a superior officer, (Article 89); "willfully disobeying" a superior officer, (Article 90); failure to obey an order, (Article 92). Tillotson, *Uniform Code*, 266–67, 269–70.

21. *Combat History*, 89–90; Cole, *Ardennes*, 365.

22. "Annex No.1 to G-2 Periodic Report No. 192, Observations of an American Field Officer who Escaped from the 1st SS Panzer Division of Adolf Hitler," Unclassified Document, Arn Collection; Hewitt, *Work Horse*, 186–88; Toland, *Battle*, 175–76, 194–95, 230, 263, 266, 382.

23. Eisenhower, *Bitter Woods*, 274–79; Reynolds, *Devil's Advocate*, 231–35, 240, 245.

24. Hewitt, *Work Horse*, 188–89; Whiting, *Ardennes*, 182–83; Reynolds, *Devil's Advocate*, 212. Such incidents led troops in Old Hickory to vilify the Army Air Force as "the American Luftwaffe." Toland, *Battle*, 231.

25. Dupuy, *Hitler's Last Gamble*, 273, 277; Reynolds, *Devil's Advocate*, 213–46.

26. Hewitt estimates that the 1st SS Panzer Division (*Leibstandarte Adolf Hitler*) lost "two-thirds" of its equipment and "one-third" of its manpower. Reynolds put total AUS casualties against Peiper's force at 487, plus 170 POWs. Most were freed after AUS capture of La Gleize. Hewitt, *Work Horse*, 190, 285; Reynolds, *Devil's Advocate*, 237, 247–51; Levine, *Normandy Beaches*, 157–58.

27. Samuel L. A. Marshall, *Bastogne: The Story of the First Eight Days in*

Which the 101st Airborne Division Was Closed within the Ring of German
Forces (Washington, D.C.: Infantry Journal Press, 1946); Dupuy, *Hitler's Last Gamble*, 175–97, 211–31, 282–311; Donald M. Goldstein, Katherine V. Dillon, and J. Michael Wenger, *Nuts! The Battle of the Bulge: The Story and the Photographs* (London, Brassey's 1994); Albin F. Irzyk, "4th Armored Division Spearhead at Bastogne," *World War II* (November 1999): 34–40, 88–90.

28. This material, undated and from unknown sources, appears in Arn's Collection.

29. Charles Whiting, *Death of a Division* (New York: Stein and Day, 1981), 9–144.

30. Probably Pfc. James C. Bennett, Camden, South Carolina.

31. Arn's anticipation proved correct. Weigley, *Eisenhower's Lieutenants*, 546–47.

32. Suchman, "Social Mobility in the Army," SSR, 1: 271–83, covers such battlefield promotions.

33. *The Stars and Stripes*, 15, 20, 25 January 1945, Arn Collection.

34. Hewitt, *Work Horse*, 178; Charles Whiting, *Massacre at Malmédy: The Story of Jochen Peiper's Battle Group, Ardennes, December, 1944* (New York: Stein and Day, 1971); Dupuy, Bongard, and Anderson, *Hitler's Last Gamble*, 62–63, 366–67; Reynolds, *Devil's Advocate*, 252–63.

35. Whiting, *'44 In Combat*, 194.

36. T/Sgt. Hobdy Hayles had a Silver Star with Oak Leaf Cluster. Hewitt, *Work Horse*, 302; *Combat History*, 95–96.

37. Even the most conscientious field physicians had difficulty discerning if a self-inflicted wound was "intentional or accidental." Heubner, *Long Walk through War*, 50; Kennett, *G.I.*, 176–77; Mary Penick Motley, *The Invisible Soldier: The Experience of the Black Soldier in World War II* (Detroit: Wayne State University Press, 1975), 159.

38. *Combat History*, 98–99. An abatis consisted of felled trees with branches twisted, placed in front of entrenched works to form an obstacle to advancing enemy.

39. *Combat History*, 100. Pvt. Anthony F. Pistilli received the Distinguished Service Cross for this action. Hewitt, *Work Horse*, 318.

40. Ibid., 203–207; Toland, *Battle*, 273–358.

Chapter 7

1. *The Stars and Stripes*, 20 October 1944; John Costello, *Virtue under Fire: How World War II Changed Our Social and Sexual Attitudes* (Boston: Little, Brown and Company, 1985), 244–56; Willis, *Incredible Year*, 150; Winston, *Mail*, 196–97; Ambrose, *Citizen Soldiers*, 449–50; John Willoughby, "The Sexual Behavior of American GIs in the Early Years of the Occupation of Germany," *Journal of Military History* 62 (January 1998): 155–74, trace this non-fraternization policy's scope and failure.

2. Charles Whiting, *Hitler's Werewolves: The Story of the Nazi Resistance Movement* (New York: Stein and Day, 1972), 143–96; Gerhard Rempel, *Hitler's*

Children: The Hitler Youth and the SS (Chapel Hill: University of North Carolina Press, 1989), 219–64; David K. Yelton, " 'Ein Volk Steht Auf': The German Volkssturm and Nazi Strategy, 1944–45," *Journal of Military History* 64 (October 2000): 1061–83.

3. Reginald W. Thompson, *Battle for the Rhine* (New York: Ballantine, 1959), 123–37; John Toland, *The Last 100 Days* (New York: Random House, 1965), 171–74; Weigley, *Eisenhower's Lieutenants*, 606; Jon D. Latimer, " 'The Reichwald': Clearing a Path to the Rhine," *World War II* (March 1999): 22–28.

4. German V-1 Rockets had caused high casualties and physical damage to several hospitals in the Liège area. Comas and Cowdrey, *Medical Service*, 496–97. A description of the medical treatment Arn underwent can be found in Crowdrey, *Fighting for Life*, 247–71; Kotlowitz, *Before Their Time*, 149–88; Kathi Jackson, *They Called Them Angels: American Military Nurses of World War II* (Westport, CT.: Praeger, 2000), 76–80. Arn received his second Purple Heart 29 March 1945. "General Order # 11, 62nd Medical Battalion," Arn Collection. Wood, *On Being Wounded*, 74–185 explains the long-term affects of severe wounds.

5. *Combat History*, 102–4; Charles B. MacDonald, *The Last Offensive. United States Army in World War II. European Theater of Operations* (Washington, D.C.: Department of the Army, 1973), 163–84.

6. Stouffer, Arthur Lumsdale, and Marian H. Lumsdale, "Attitudes before Combat," SSR, 6–37; Linderman, *World within War,* 29–31, make similar points about caution.

7. *Combat History*, 102–9; Hewitt, *Work Horse*, 211–33; MacDonald, *Last Offensive*, 155–57; Peter Allen, *One More River: The Rhine Crossings of 1945* (New York: Scribner's, 1980), 136–38, 143, 145; Doubler, *Closing*, 168–71.

8. Allan Ecker, "The Escape-proof Prison: Breaking the Black Market in Paris," in *Close to Glory: The Untold Stories of World War II by the Soldiers Who Saw and Reported the War, Yank Magazine Correspondents*, ed. by Art Weithas (Austin, TX.: Eakin Press, 1991), 203; Antony Beevor and Artemis Cooper, *Paris After the Liberation, 1944–1949* (London: Hamish Hamilton, 1994), 115–20, 141–43, cover such black market activities.

9. Read why Paris remained untouched in Larry Collins and Dominique Lapierre, *Is Paris Burning?* (New York: Simon and Schuster, 1965).

10. Cosmas and Cowdrey, *Medical Service*, 541–42; Kennett, *G.I.*, 206–7; Zorn, *I Walk*, 176–77; Winston, *Mail*, 181–84; Beevor and Cooper, *Paris*, 85–87, 143–44, review the attractions and dangers liberated Paris held for Allied soldiers.

11. W. Denis Whitaker and Shelagh Whitaker, *Rhineland: The Battle to End the War* (New York: St. Martin's Press, 1989), 340–42; Allen, *One More River*, 210, 217, 221, 247–48.

12. Weitz, *Sisters in the Resistance*, 8–263.

13. "Headquarters 40th U.S. General Hospital, APO 350, U.S. Army, 29 March 1945, General Order: Number 69," Arn Collection.

14. *Combat History*, 110–12; Hewitt, *Work Horse*, 253–55; MacDonald, *Last*

Offensive, 303–19, 357, 384–86; Toland, *100 Days*, 268–69; Weigley, *Eisenhower's Lieutenants*, 649–51. Arn's determination to rejoin Fox Company reflected the cohesiveness and mutual loyalty front-line troops developed. Some wounded and hospitalized members of such units often felt torn by a sense of relief in being free from the daily threat of death and pangs of guilt for being away from their comrades. Kennett, *G.I.*, 139–40.

15. Blunt, *Come of Age*, 188–91; Willis, *Incredible Year*, 147, 149; Courtney, *From Normandy to the Bulge*, 123–24, deal with rumors about ETO troops being sent to the CBI.

16. President Roosevelt died at Warm Springs, Georgia, 12 April 1945. Secretary of War Edwin M. Stanton uttered that quote at Lincoln's death bed, 15 April 1865. David H. Donald, *Lincoln* (New York: Simon & Schuster, 1995), 599.

17. Probably Sgt. Louis S. Tavares, Company B, 120th Regiment, 30th Infantry.

18. Other American troops shared Arn's admiration for Dinah Shore, a popular singer and entertainment personality. Active in USO tours at home and overseas, she held an honorary rank of private first class and had a B-17 bomber named in her honor. *New York Times*, 25 February 1994. Julia M. Hicks, *Away from Home: The Story of the USO* (New York: Harper & Brothers, 1946); Fussell, *Wartime*, 143–64; Linderman, *World within War*, 315–16, notes such morale building.

19. *Combat History*, 123; *Medal of Honor*, 350–51.

20. Hewitt, *Work Horse*, 265–66; MacDonald, *Last Offensive*, 373–442; Ambrose, *Citizen Soldiers*, 439–64; Macksey, *Why the Germans Lose*, 209–21.

21. *Combat History*, 122–24; Joachim Schultz-Naumann, *The Last Thirty Days: The War Diary of the German Armed Forces High Command from April to May 1945. The Battle for Berlin. Reflections on the Events of 1945*, translated by D. G. Smith (New York: Madison Books, 1991), 3–202; Kelly Bell, "Bloody Battle for Berlin," *World War II* (March 1998): 22–28, 67; Antony Beevor, *The Fall of Berlin 1945* (New York: Viking, 2002), 173–205.

22. Jill Stephenson, *Women in Nazi Society* (New York: Harper & Row, 1975); Gisele Bock, "Racism and Sexism in Nazi Germany: Motherhood, Compulsory Sterilization and the State," in *When Biology Became Destiny: Women in Weimar and Nazi Germany*, ed. by Renate Bridenthal, Atina Grossman, and Marion Kaplan (New York: Monthly Review Press, 1984), 271–96.

23. Forrest C. Pogue, "The Decision to Halt on the Elbe," *Command Decisions*, 479–92.

24. Martha Gellhorn, *The Face of War* (New York: Atlantic Monthly Press, 1988), 171–78; Cawthon, *Other Clay*, 170–71; Blunt, *Foot Soldier*, 254–60, treat early encounters of American and Russian troops.

25. Charles Whiting, *The End of the War: Europe: April 15–May 23, 1945* (New York: Stein and Day, 1973), 28–35, 49–76, 105–106; Martin Gilbert, *The Day the War Ended, May 8, 1945—Victory in Europe* (New York: Henry Holt and Company, 1995), 243–67, 355–78; Peter Padfield, *Dönitz, the Last Führer: Portrait of a Nazi War Leader* (New York: Harper & Row, 1984), 405–22; Rus-

sell Miller with Renate Miller, *Ten Days in May: The People's History of VE Day* (London: Michael Joseph, 1995), 48–232; Beevor, *Berlin*, 339–420. Brian Jewel, *"Over the Rhine": The Last Days of War in Europe* (New York: Hippocrene Books, Inc., 1985), 45–57, presents a chronology of the events Arn mentions.

Chapter 8

1. Gilbert, *Day War Ended*, 355–78; Earl F. Ziemke, *The U.S. Army in the Occupation of Germany, 1944–1946* (Washington, D.C.: Center of Military History, 1975), 269–341; Joseph R. Starr, *Denazification, Occupation & Control of Germany, March–July 1945* (Salisbury, N.C.: Documentary Publications, 1977), 81–162; Kenneth O. McCreedy, "Planning the Peace: Operation Eclipse and the Occupation of Germany," *Journal of Military History* 65 (July 2001): 713–39; Irwin, *Another River*, 155–56.

2. Stouffer, "The Point System for Redeployment and Discharge," SSR, 2: 520–48; Leonard Cottrell Jr., "The Aftermath of Hostilities," ibid., 549–95; Glen C. H. Perry, *"Dear Bart": Washington Views of World War II* (Westport, CT.: Greenwood Press, 1982), 310–15; Sy M. Kahn, *Between Tedium and Terror: A Soldier's World War II Diary, 1943–1945* (Urbana: University of Illinois Press, 1993), 266–70, 277–78; Harold Freedlander, *I'll Be Back: World War II Letters to the Home Front*, ed. by Lois Freedlander, Ann F. Hunt, and Mimi F. McCain (Wooster, OH.: Wooster Book Company, 2002), 117.

3. Keith E. Eiler, *Mobilizing America: Robert P. Patterson and the War Effort, 1940–1945* (Ithaca: Cornell University Press, 1997), 429–31.

4. "Buchenwald Concentration Camp, 2 June 1944," Arn Collection. Willis, *Incredible Year*, 136–41; Edward J. Drea, "Recognizing the Liberators: U.S. Army Divisions Enter the Concentration Camps," *Army History* 24 (Winter 1993): 1–5; Ambrose, *Citizen Soldiers*, 461–64, cover other reactions to these death camps.

5. *Yanks Meet Reds: Recollections of the U.S. and Soviet Vets from the Linkup in World War II*, ed. by Mark Scott and Semoya Krasilhshchik (Santa Barbara, CA.: Capra Press, 1988), 17–179; Helene Keyssar and Vladimir Pozner, *Remembering the War: A U.S.-Soviet Dialogue* (New York: Oxford University Press, 1990), 189–207, recall such encounters between American and Soviet troops.

6. Charles G. Grey, *The Luftwaffe* (London: Farber and Farber, 1944), 148; E. R. Hooton, *Phoenix Triumphant: The Rise and Rise of the Luftwaffe* (London: Arms & Armour, 1994), 102–103; Ferenc A. Vajda and Peter G. Dancey, *German Aircraft Industry and Production, 1933–1945* (London: Airlife Publishing Ltd., 1998), 210–19.

7. Estimates place as many as 12 million Germans who fled before the Soviet Army. Added to these were freed Allied POWs, concentration camp survivors, and slave laborers. Hewitt judged that the 30th Division handled, at the minimum, "2,207 Allied prisoners of war and 4,719 displaced" western Europeans in the "first eight days of May." By 8 May 1945, the total swelled to

47,690 "displaced persons" and 15,926 Allied former POWs. Hewitt, *Work Horse*, 267–70. Earnest N. Harmon, *Combat Commander: Autobiography of a Soldier*, with Milton MacKaye and William R. MacKaye (Englewood Cliffs, N.J.: Prentice-Hall, 1970), 256–63, treats the earliest AUS approach to such problems.

8. Many troops and their families complained that discharges under the point system were too slow and discriminatory. Responding to demands to "bring the boys home," the Department of War reduced the total from 85 points to 60 by December 1945. Stouffer, "Point System," SSR, 2: 547; Kennett, *G.I.*, 224–25; Eiler, *Patterson*, 434–35, 439, 449–50.

9. A typical World War II "Pro Kit" for prophylactic use against venereal disease consisted of a soap-impregnated cloth, a cleansing tissue, a tube containing a five gram ointment compounded with calomel and sulfathiazole, and an individual medical prophylactic or condom. Stouffer and DeVinney, "How Personal Adjustment Varied in the Army–By Type of Experience in the Army," SSR, 1: 177–78; Heubner, *Long Walk*, 4, 102, 121, 167, 168; Cosmas, *Medical Service*, 142–46.

10. Removing a soldier's dog tags, his personal identification worn on a chain around the neck, signified his death. "The Finer Things," 18 May 1945, Arn Collection.

11. In hindsight, incidents such as these between Allied and Soviet troops foreshadowed the Cold War. Recalling those events, Arn wrote: "Anticipation of the Cold War never bothered me or my men very much *if at all.* We were thinking of home, women, good food, and sundry other mundane items. And living a part of our lives *under a good roof*, not one that had been blown to kingdom come. Our disdain for the rowdy Russians overwhelmed us at first. But we learned control." Arn to Mushkat, 13 August 2003, Arn Collection. Cottrell, "The Aftermath of Hostilities," SSP, 2: 554, 573–76, 627–30; Norman M. Naimark, *The Russians in Germany: A History of the Soviet Zone of Occupation, 1945–1949* (Cambridge, MA.: Belknap Press, 1995); David Pike, *The Politics of Culture in Soviet-Occupied Germany, 1945–1949* (Stanford: Stanford University Press, 1992), 3–135 analyze these issues.

12. See also Joseph Borkin, *The Crime and Punishment of I. G. Farben* (New York: Free Press, 1978).

13. Colonel McCown fulfilled his ambitions. Remaining in active service, he served in the Korean War and held various commands during the Vietnam War. He retired in 1972 at the rank of major general. *Arkansas Democrat Gazette*, 8 July 1999.

14. Arn and his wife returned to Hirschberg in 1998. He found the place much changed, but a few inhabitants remembered him from those "days in 1945." They now considered him "a friend who wants to make a personal contribution to change the world into a world of friends and peace." Ruth Japel to Arn, 2 April 1998, Arn Collection.

Chapter 9

1. About 550 officers and 4,500 enlisted men from Old Hickory who had sufficient points for discharge transferred to the 75th Division. Hewitt, *Work Horse*, 270. Mansoor, *GI Offensive*, 196, 229, 223, 252, presents background information on the 75th Division.

2. By the fall and winter of 1944, many replacements whom the AUS rushed into combat units during the Ardennes campaign were younger and less trained than their predecessors. About half of these unprepared reinforcements became casualties within their first three days of combat. Smith, "Combat Replacement," SSR, 2: 283–84; Wood Jr., *On Being Wounded*, 11–23; Bruce E. Egger and Lee M. Otts, *G Company's War: Two Personal Accounts of the Campaigns in Europe, 1944–1945*, ed. by Paul Roley (Tuscaloosa: The University of Alabama Press, 1992); Ambrose, *Citizen Soldiers*, 273–77; Fussell, *Boys' Crusade*, 6–12, 26–27, 95–104.

3. Like many World War II veterans, Arn had no sympathy for Truman's critics. Arn believed that the president's decision shortened the war and saved Allied and Japanese lives. A number of recent studies exist on this topic: Thomas B. Allen and Norman Polmar, *Code-Name Downfall: The Secret Plan to Invade Japan and Why Truman Dropped the Bomb* (New York: Simon & Schuster, 1995); Gar Alperovitz, *The Decision to Use the Atomic Bomb and the Architecture of an American Myth* (New York: Knopf, 1995); Robert Jay Lifton and Greg Mitchell, *Hiroshima in America: Fifty Years of Denial* (New York: Putnam's Sons, 1995); *Judgment at the Smithsonian*, ed. by Philip Noble (New York: Marlowe and Company, 1995); D. M. Giangreco, "Casualty Projections for the U.S. Invasion of Japan, 1945–1946: Planning and Policy Implementation," *Journal of Military History* 61 (July 1997): 531–53.

4. Lee Kennett, *G.I.*, 75–76; 87, 73; Chester G. Hearn, *The American Soldier in World War II* (London: Salamander Books, Inc., 2000), 25–26; Kindsvatter, *American Soldiers*, 110, 147, explore such "Dear John" letters and their affect on morale.

5. For the friction between officers and enlisted men, especially combat troops, see Ralph Lewis, "Officer-Enlisted Men's Relationships," *American Journal of Sociology* 52 (March 1947): 410–19; Suchman, Stouffer, and DeVinney, "Attitudes toward Leadership and Social Control," SSR, 2: 362–410.

6. S/Sgt. Guy C. Bates held the Silver Star. Hewitt, *Work Horse*, 285. Bates to Arn, 19 October 2002, Arn Collection.

7. James M. Ver Meulen to Arn, 13 September 1945, Arn Collection. Such uncertainty about the status of their prewar jobs and their "devolution" as soldiers typified the concerns of many returning men. Cottrell and Stouffer, "The Soldier Becomes a Veteran," SSR, 2: 596–613, 641–44; Jones, *A Chronicle*, 256–57; Henry J. Meyer and Erwin O. Smigel, "Job-Seeking and the Readjustment Allowance for Veterans," *American Journal of Sociology* 56 (January 1951): 341–47; Kevin Coyne, *Marching Home: To War and Back with the Men of One American Town* (New York: Viking Penguin, 2003), 199–375.

8. Samuel E. Morison, *The Two Ocean War: A Short History of the United*

States Navy in the Second World War (Boston: Little, Brown and Company, 1963), 132–33; Mark S. Foster, *Henry J. Kaiser: Builder in the Modern American West* (Austin: University of Texas Press, 1989), 82, describe such "Victory Ships." Victory Ships were powered by steam turbines and capable of cruising between fifteen to seventeen knots. They were named for various American cities and towns, followed by the suffix *Victory,* and could carry 4,555 net tons, which included a merchant marine crew, naval personnel, passengers, and cargo.

9. Arnold P. Krammer, *Nazi Prisoners of War in America* (New York: Stein and Day, 1979); Judith M. Gansberg, *Stalag, U.S.A.: The Remarkable Story of German POWs in America* (New York: Crowell, 1977); Robert D. Billinger Jr., *Hitler's Soldiers in the Sunshine State* (Gainesville: University of Florida Press, 2000) study German POWs in the United States.

10. Material about the *Central Falls Victory* derives from a "newsletter" supplied to the troops on board. Arn Collection. See also Roland C. Charles, *Troopships of World War II* (Washington, D.C.: Army Transportation Association, 1947), 356.

11. Camp Patrick Henry served as the staging area for the Hampton Roads POE. By December 1945, the camp processed returning troops. William R. Wheeler, *The Road to Victory: A History of Hampton Roads Port of Embarkation in World War II* (New Haven: Yale University Press, 1946); Edward F. Witsell, Major General, to Arn, 2 December 1945; Jacob L. Devers, Commanding, Headquarters Army Ground Forces, to Arn, 26 January 1946, Arn Collection.

Bibliography

Newspapers

New York Times, 1944–46.
The Stars and Stripes, 1944–45.

Manuscript Collections

Arn, Edward C. Collection. Private Collection.
Arn, Edward C. Collection. Wayne County Historical Society.

Books

Allen, Peter. *One More River: The Rhine Crossings of 1945.* New York: Scribner's, 1980.

Allen, Thomas B., and Norman Polmar. *Code-Name Downfall: The Secret Plan to Invade Japan and Why Truman Dropped the Bomb.* New York: Simon & Schuster, 1995.

Alperovitz, Gar. *The Decision to Use the Atomic Bomb and the Architecture of an American Myth.* New York: Knopf, 1995.

Ambrose, Stephen E. *Citizen Soldiers: The U.S. Army from the Normandy Beaches to the Bulge to the Surrender of Germany, June 7, 1944–May 7, 1945.* New York: Simon & Schuster, 1997.

———. *D-Day, June 6, 1944: The Climactic Battle of World War II.* New York: Simon & Schuster, 1994.

———. *Eisenhower and Berlin: The Decision to Halt at the Elbe.* New York: W. W. Norton, 1967.

Andidora, Ronald. *Home by Christmas: The Illusion of Victory in 1944.* Westport, CT.: Greenwood Press, 2002.

Army Battle Casualties and Nonbattle Deaths in World War II. Final Report. 7 December 1941–December 1946. Washington, D.C.: Department of the Army, 1953.

Astor, Gerald. *June 6, 1944: The Voices of D-Day.* New York: St. Martin's Press, 1994.

Bailey, Leslie W. *Through Hell and High Water: The Wartime Memoirs of a Junior Combat Officer.* New York: Vantage Press, 1994.

Baker, Rachel. *Conscience, Government and the War.* London: Routledge and Kegan Paul, 1982.

Baldwin, Hanson W. *Battles Lost and Won: Great Campaigns of World War II.* New York: Harper & Row, 1966.

Balkoski, Joseph. *Beyond the Beachhead: The 29th Infantry Division in Normandy*. Harrisburg, PA.: Stackpole Books, 1989.

Baxter, Colin F, ed. *The Normandy Campaign, 1944: A Selected Bibliography*. Westport, CT.: Greenwood Press, 1992.

Beevor, Antony, *The Fall of Berlin 1945*. New York: Viking, 2002.

Beevor, Antony, and Artemis Cooper. *Paris After the Liberation, 1944–1949*. London: Hamish Hamilton, 1994.

Billinger, Robert D. *Hitler's Soldiers in the Sunshine State*. Gainesville: University of Florida Press, 2000.

Blair, Clay. *Hitler's U-Boat War: The Hunted: 1942–1945*. New York: Random House, 1998.

———. *Ridgway's Paratroopers: The American Airborne in World War II*. New York: Garden City, NY.: The Dial Press, 1985.

Blumenson, Martin. *Breakout and Pursuit. United States in World War II. The European Theater of Operations*. Washington, D.C.: Department of the Army, 1961.

Blunt, Roscoe C. Jr. *Foot Soldier: A Combat Infantryman's War in Europe*. Rockville Center, NY.: Sarpedon, 2001.

———. *Inside the Battle of the Bulge: A Private Comes of Age*. Westport, CT.: Praeger, 1994.

Borkin, Joseph. *The Crime and Punishment of I. G. Farben*. New York: Free Press, 1978.

Bourke, Joanna. *A Intimate History of Killing: Face-to-Face Killing in Twentieth-Century Warfare*. New York: Basic Books, 1999.

Bradley, Omar. *A Soldier's Story*. New York: Henry Holt and Company, 1951.

Brennan, Edward J. *The Lion's Pride: Theodore Roosevelt and His Family in Peace and War*. New York: Oxford University Press, 1998.

Breuer, William B. *Feuding Allies: The Private Wars of the High Command*. New York: Wiley, 1995.

Bridenthal, Atina G., and Marion Kaplan, eds. *When Biology Became Destiny: Women in Weimar and Nazi Germany*. New York: Monthly Review Press, 1984.

Carafano, James J. *After D-Day: Operation Cobra and the Normandy Breakout*. Boulder, CO.: Lynne Rienner Publishers, 2000.

Carell, Paul. *Invasion–They're Coming!: The German Account of the Allied Landing and the 80 Days' Battle for France*. New York: Dutton, 1963.

Carson, Julia H. *Home Away from Home: The Story of the USO*. New York: Harper & Brothers, 1946.

Cawthon, Charles R. *Other Clay: A Remembrance of the World War II Infantry*. Niwot: University Press of Colorado, 1990.

Chambers, John W. *To Raise an Army: The Draft Comes to Modern America*. New York: Free Press, 1987.

Chandler, David, and James L. Collins, eds. *The D-Day Encyclopedia*. New York: Simon & Schuster, 1994.

Charles, Roland C. *Troopships of World War II*. Washington, D.C.: Army Transportation Association, 1947.

Clifford, J. Garry, and Samuel R. Spencer Jr. *The First Peacetime Draft.* Lawrence: University Press of Kansas, 1986.

Cole, Hugh. *The Ardennes: Battle of the Bulge. The United States Army in World War II: The European Theater of Operations.* Washington, D.C.: Department of the Army, 1965.

———. *The Lorraine Campaign. United States Army in World War II. The European Theater of Operations.* Washington, D.C.: Department of the Army, 1950.

———. *Roosevelt and the Isolationists, 1932–45.* Lincoln: University of Nebraska Press, 1983.

Colley, David P. *The Road to Victory: The Untold Story of World War II's Red Ball Express.* Washington, D.C.: Brassey's 2000.

Collins, Larry, and Dominique Lapierre. *Is Paris Burning?* New York: Simon & Schuster, 1965.

Combat History of the 119th Infantry Regiment. Baton Rouge: Army and Navy Publishers, 1946.

Cooper, Matthew. *The German Army, 1933–1945.* New York: Stein and Day, 1978.

Cosmas, Graham A., and Albert E Cowdrey. *Medical Service in the European Theater of Operations.* Washington, D.C.: Center for Military History, 1992.

Costello, John. *Virtue under Fire: How World War II Changed Our Social and Sexual Attitudes.* Boston: Little, Brown and Company, 1985.

Courtney, Richard D. *Normandy to the Bulge: An American Infantry GI in Europe during World War II.* Carbondale: Southern Illinois University Press, 1997.

Cowdrey, Albert E. *Fighting for Life: American Military Medicine in World War II.* New York: Free Press, 1994.

Coyne, Kevin. *Marching Home: To War and Back with the Men of One American Town.* New York: Viking Penguin, 2003.

Cragg, Dan. *The Guide to Military Installations.* Harrisburg, PA: Stackpole Books, 1983.

Cross, Robin. *The Battle of the Bulge, 1944: Hitler's Last Hope.* Havertown, PA.: Casemate, 2002.

Donald, David A. *Lincoln.* New York: Simon & Schuster, 1995.

Doubler, Michael. *Closing with the Enemy: How GIs Fought the War in Europe, 1944–1945.* Lawrence: University Press of Kansas, 1994.

Dulles, Foster R. *The American Red Cross: A History.* New York: Harper & Brothers, 1950.

Dunn, Walter S. *Second Front Now–1943.* University: The University of Alabama Press, 1980.

Dupuy, Trevor N. *Hitler's Last Gamble: The Battle of the Bulge, December 1944–January 1945.* New York: HarperCollins, 1994.

Edwards, John C. *Berlin Calling: American Broadcasters in Service to the Third Reich.* New York: Praeger, 1991.

Egger, Bruce E., and Lee M. Otts. *G Company's War: Two Personal Accounts of the Campaigns in Europe, 1944–1945.* Edited by Paul Roley. Tuscaloosa: The University of Alabama Press, 1992.

Eisenhower, John S. D. *The Bitter Woods: The Battle of the Bulge.* New York: G. P. Putnam's Sons, 1969.

Eller, Cynthia. *Conscientious Objectors and the Second World War: Moral and Religious Arguments in Support of Pacifism.* New York: Praeger, 1991.

Eller, Keith E. *Mobilizing America: Robert P. Patterson and the War Effort, 1940–1945.* Ithaca: Cornell University Press, 1997.

Elstob, Peter. *Hitler's Last Offensive.* London: Secker & Warburg, 1971.

Elting, John R., Dan Cragg, and Earnest Deal. *A Dictionary of Soldier Talk.* New York: Charles Scribner's Sons, 1984.

English, John A. *A Perspective on Infantry.* New York: Praeger, 1981.

Farago, Ladislas. *Patton: Ordeal and Triumph.* New York: Ivan Obolensky, Inc., 1963.

Featherston, Alwyn. *Saving the Breakout: The 30th Division's Heroic Stand at Mortain, August 7–12, 1944.* Novato, CA.: Presidio Press, 1993.

Feis, Herbert. *Japan Subdued: The Atomic Bomb and the End of the War in the Pacific.* Princeton: Princeton University Press, 1961.

Flynn, George Q. *The Draft, 1940–1973.* Lawrence: University Press of Kansas, 1993.

Foster, Mark S. *Henry J. Kaiser: Builder in the Modern American West.* Austin: University of Texas Press, 1989.

Frankel, Stanley A. *The 37th Infantry Division in World War II.* Washington, D.C.: Infantry Journal Press, 1948.

Freedlander, Harold. *I'll Be Back: World War II Letters to the Home Front.* Edited by Lois Freedlander, Ann F. Hunt, and Mimi F. McCain. Wooster, OH.: Wooster Book Company, 2002.

Fussell, Paul. *The Boys' Crusade.* New York: Random House, 2003.

———. *Wartime: Understanding and Behavior in the Second World War.* New York: Oxford University Press, 1989.

Gansberg, Judith M. *Stalag, U.S.A.: The Remarkable Story of German POWs in America.* New York: Crowell, 1977.

Gardiner, Juliet. *'Over Here': The GIs in Wartime Britain.* London: Collins & Brown, 1992.

Gavin, James M. *On to Berlin: Battles of an Airborne Commander, 1943–1945.* New York: Viking Press, 1978.

Gellhorn, Martha. *The Face of War.* New York: Atlantic Monthly Press, 1988.

Gilbert, Martin. *The Day the War Ended, May 8, 1945–Victory in Europe.* New York: Henry Holt and Company, 1995.

Gilbo, Patrick F. *The American Red Cross: The First Century.* New York: Harper & Row, 1981.

Ginn, Richard V. N. *The History of the U.S. Army Medical Service Corps.* Washington, D.C.: Office of the Surgeon General and Center History, United States Army, 1997.

Goldstein, Donald M., Katherine V. Dillon, and J. Michael Wenger. *Nuts! The Battle of the Bulge: The Story and the Photographs.* London: Brassey's, 1994.

Greenfield, Keith R., ed. *Command Decisions.* Washington, D.C.: Department of the Army, 1960.

——. *The Historian and the Army*. Port Washington, NY.: Kennikat Press, 1970.

Grey, Charles G. *The Luftwaffe*. London: Farber and Farber Ltd., 1944.

Harmon, Earnest N., with Milton MacKaye and William MacKaye. *Combat Commander: Autobiography of a Soldier*. Englewood Cliffs, NJ.: Prentice-Hall, 1970.

Hastings, Max. *Overlord: D-Day and the Battle for Normandy*. New York: Simon & Schuster, 1984.

Hearn, Chester G. *The American Soldier in World War II*. London: Salamander Books, Inc., 2000.

Heubner, Klaus H. *Long Walk through War: A Combat Doctor's Diary*. College Station: Texas A & M Press, 1987.

Hewitt, Robert L. *Work Horse of the Western Front: The Story of the 30th Infantry Division*. Washington, D.C.: Infantry Journal Press, 1946.

Hoffman, Alice M., and Howard S. Hoffman. *Archives of Memory: A Soldier Recalls World War II*. Lexington: University Press of Kentucky, 1990.

Hooton, E. R., *Eagles in Flames: The Fall of the Luftwaffe*. London: Arms & Armour, 1997.

——. *Phoenix Triumphant: The Rise and Fall of the Luftwaffe*. London: Arms & Armour, 1994.

Hoyt, Edwin P. *The Death of the U-Boats*. New York: Warner Books, Inc., 1988.

——. *The GI's War: The Story of American Soldiers in Europe in World War II*. New York: McGraw-Hill, 1988.

Hughes, Thomas A. *Over Lord: General Pete Quesada and The Triumph of Tactical Air Power in World War II*. New York: Free Press, 1995.

Irwin, John P. *Another River, Another Town: A Teenage Tank Gunner Comes of Age in Combat, 1945*. New York: Random House, 2002.

Jackson, Kathi. *They Called Them Angels: American Military Nurses of World War II*. Westport, CT.: Praeger, 2000.

Jarymowycz, Roman J. *Tank Tactics from Normandy to Lorraine*. London: Lynne Rienner Publishers, Inc., 2001.

Jewel, Brian. *"Over the Rhine": The Last Days of War in Europe*. New York: Hippocrene Books, Inc., 1985.

Johns, Glover. *The Clay Pigeons of St. Lô*. Harrisburg, PA.: The Military Service Publishing Company, 1958.

Jones, James. *WW II: A Chronicle of Soldiering*. New York: Grosset & Dunlap, 1975.

Kahn, Sy M. *Between Tedium and Terror: A Soldier's World War II Diary, 1943–1945*. Urbana: University of Illinois Press, 1993.

Keefer, Louis E. *Scholars in Foxholes: The Story of the Army Specialized Training Program in World War II*. Jefferson, NC.: McFarland, 1998.

Keegan, John. *Six Armies in Normandy: From D-Day to the Liberation of Paris, June 6th–August 25th, 1944*. New York: Penguin Books, 1982.

Kennett, Lee B. *G.I.: The American Soldier in World War II*. New York: Scribner, 1987.

Kershaw, Robert J. *It Never Snows in September: The German View of Market Garden and the Battle of Arnhem.* Marlborough: Crowood Press, 1990.

Keyssar, Helene, and Vladimir Pozner. *Remembering the War: A U.S.-Soviet Dialogue.* New York: Oxford University Press, 1990.

Killen, John. *A History of the Luftwaffe.* Garden City, NY.: Doubleday & Company, 1968.

Kindsvatter, Peter S. *American Soldiers: Ground Combat in the World Wars, Korea & Vietnam.* Lawrence: University Press of Kansas, 2003.

Knickerbocker, H. R. *Danger Forward: The Story of the First Division in World War II, United States Army.* Washington, D.C.: Society of the First Division, 1947.

Kotlowitz, Robert. *Before Their Time: A Memoir.* New York: Alfred A. Knopf, 1997.

Krammer, Arnold P. *Nazi Prisoners of War in America.* New York: Stein and Day, 1979.

Kreidberg, Martin A., and Merton G. Henry. *History of Military Mobilization in the United States Army, 1775–1945.* Washington, D.C.: Department of the Army, 1955.

Krick, Robert R. *Conquering the Valley: Stonewall Jackson at Port Republic.* New York: William Morrow, 1969.

Kuge, Friedrich. *Rommel in Normandy.* Novato, CA.: Presidio Press, 1979.

Langer, Walter C. *The Mind of Adolf Hitler: The Secret Wartime Record.* New York: Basic Books, 1972.

Lee, Ulysses. *The Employment of Negro Troops. United States Army in World War II.* Washington, D.C.: Office of the Chief of Military History, 1966.

Levine, Alan J. *From the Normandy Beaches to the Baltic Sea: The Northwest Europe Campaign, 1944–1945.* Westport, CT.: Praeger, 2000.

Lifton, Robert J., and Greg Mitchell. *Hiroshima in America: Fifty Years of Denial.* New York: Putnam's Sons, 1995.

Linderman, Gerald F. *The World Within War: America's Combat Experience in World War II.* New York: Free Press, 1997.

Lockerbie, D. Bruce. *A Man Under Orders: Lieutenant General William K. Harrison.* New York: Harper & Row, 1979.

MacDonald, Charles B. *The Last Offensive. United States Army in World War II. European Theater of Operations.* Washington, D.C.: Department of the Army, 1973.

———. *The Mighty Endeavor: The American War in Europe.* New York: Da Capo Press, 1992.

———. *The Siegfried Line Campaign. United States Army in World War II. The European Theater of Operations.* Washington, D.C.: Department of the Army, 1963.

———. *A Time for Trumpets: The Untold Story of the Battle of the Bulge.* New York: William Morrow and Company, 1985.

Macksey, Kenneth. *Tank Force: Allied Armor in World War II.* New York: Ballantine, 1970.

——. *Why the Germans Lose at War: The Myth of German Military Superiority*. London: Greenhill Books, 1996.

Mansoor, Peter R. *The GI Offensive in Europe: The Triumph of American Divisions, 1941–1945*. Lawrence: University Press of Kansas, 1999.

Marshall, Samuel S. L. A. *Bastogne: The Story of the First Eight Days in Which the 101st Airborne Division was Closed Within the German Ring*. Washington, D.C.: Infantry Journal Press, 1946

Mathais, Frank R. *G.I. Jive: An American Bandsman in World War II*. Lexington: The University Press of Kentucky, 1982.

Mathews, Tom. *Our Fathers' War: Growing Up in the Shadow of the Greatest Generation*. New York: Broadway Books, 2005.

Matthews, Joseph J. *Reporting the Wars*. Westport, CT.: Greenwood Press, 1972.

McManus, John C. *The Deadly Brotherhood: The American Combat Soldier in World War II*. Novato, CA.: Presidio Press, 1998.

Messenger, Charles. *The Last Prussian: A Biography of Field Marshal Gerd von Rundstedt, 1875–1953*. London: Brassey's, 1991.

Miller, Russell, and Renate Miller. *Ten Days in May: The People's History of VE Day*. London: Michael Joseph, 1995.

Mitcham, Samuel W. Jr. *The Desert Fox in Normandy: Rommel's Defense of Fortress Europe*. Westport, CT.: Praeger, 1997.

Morison, Samuel E. *The Battle of the Atlantic, September 1939–May 1943. History of the United States Naval Operations in World War II*. Boston: Little, Brown and Company, 1947.

——. *The Two Ocean War: A Short History of the United States Navy in the Second World War*. Boston: Little, Brown and Company, 1963.

Motley, Mary P. *The Invisible Soldier: The Experience of the Black Soldier in World War II*. Detroit: Wayne State University Press, 1975.

Murray, G. E. Patrick. *Eisenhower versus Montgomery: The Continuing Debate*. Westport, CT.: Praeger, 1996.

Murray, Williamson, and Allan Millett. *A War to Be Won: Fighting the Second World War*. Cambridge: Harvard University Press, 2000.

Naimark, Norman M. *The Russians in Germany: A History of the Soviet Zone of Occupation. 1945–1949*. Cambridge: Harvard University Press, 1995.

Noble, Philip, ed. *Judgment at the Smithsonian*. New York: Marlowe and Company, 1945.

Order of Battle of the United States Army in World War II: European Theater of Operations. Divisions. Washington, D.C.: Office of the Theater Historian, 1945.

Organization of the Infantry Brigade. Washington, D.C.: Department of the Army, 1942.

O'Sullivan, John J. *From Voluntarism to Conscription: Congress and Selective Service, 1940–1945*. New York: Garland, 1982.

Overy, Richard. *Why the Allies Won*. New York: W. W. Norton, 1996.

Padfield, Peter. *Dönitz, the Last Führer: Portrait of a Nazi War Leader*. New York: Harper & Row, 1984.

Pagliaro, Harold. *Naked Heart: A Soldier's Journey to the Front.* Kirksville: Thomas Jefferson University Press, 1996.

Palmer, Robert R., Bell I. Wiley, and William R. Keast. *The Procurement and Training of Ground Combat Troops. United States Army in World War II, The Ground Forces.* Washington, D.C.: Department of the Army, 1948.

Perret, Geoffrey. *There's a War to Be Won: The United States Army in World War II.* New York: Random House, 1991.

Perry, Glen C. H. *"Dear Bart": Washington Views of World War II.* Westport, CT.: Greenwood Press, 1982.

Pike, David. *The Politics of Culture in Soviet-Occupied Germany, 1945–1949.* Stanford: Stanford University Press, 1992.

Pimlott, John. *Battle of the Bulge.* New York: Galahad Books, 1981.

Reardon, Mark J. *Victory at Mortain: Stopping Hitler's Panzer Counteroffensive.* Lawrence: University Press of Kansas, 2002.

Rempel, Gerhard. *Hitler's Children: The Hitler Youth and the SS.* Chapel Hill: University of North Carolina Press, 1989.

Reynolds, Michael. *The Devil's Adjutant: Jochen Peiper, Panzer Leader.* London: Spellmount Limited, 1995.

Ross, William F., and Charles F. Romanus. *The Quartermaster Corps. Operations in the War against Germany. United States Army in World War II. The Technical Services.* Washington, D.C.: Department of the Army, 1965.

Russell, Henry D. *The Purge of the Thirtieth Division.* Macon, GA.: Lyon, Marshall & Brooks, 1949.

Ryan, Cornelius. *A Bridge Too Far.* Simon & Schuster, 1974.

Schrijvers, Peter. *The Crash of Ruins: American Combat Soldiers in Europe during World War II.* New York: New York University Press, 1998.

Schultz-Naumann, Joachim. *The Last Thirty Days: The War Diary of the German Armed Forces High Command from April to May 1945. The Battle for Berlin. Reflections on the Events of 1945,* trans. D. G. Smith. New York: Madison House, 1991.

Scott, Mark, and Semoya Krasilhshchik, eds. *Yanks Meet Reds: Recollections of the U.S. and Soviet Vets from the Linkup in World War II.* Santa Barbara, CA.: Capra Press, 1988.

Silbey, Mulford Q., and Philip E. Jacobs. *Conscription of Conscience: The American State and the Conscientious Objector, 1940–1947.* Ithaca: Cornell University Press, 1952.

Simpson, Elizabeth, ed. *The Spoils of War: World War II and Its Aftermath: The Loss, Reappearance, and Recovery of Cultural Property.* New York: H. N. Abrams, 1997.

Sligh, Robert B. *The National Guard and National Defense: The Mobilization of the Guard in World War II.* New York: Praeger, 1992.

Somerville, Keith F. *Dear Boys: World War Two Letters from a Woman Back Home.* Edited by Judy B. Litoff and David Smith. Jackson: University Press of Mississippi, 1991.

Standifer, Leon C. *Not in Vain: A Rifleman Remembers World War II.* Baton Rouge: Louisiana State University Press, 1992.

Starr, Joseph R. *Denazification, Occupation & Control of Germany, March–July 1945.* Salisbury, NC.: Documentary Publications, 1977.

Stein, Maurice, Arthur J. Vidich, and David M. White, eds. *Identify and Anxiety: Survival of the Person in Mass Society.* New York: Free Press, 1960.

Stephenson, Jill. *Women in Nazi Society.* New York: Harper & Row, 1975.

Stouffer, Samuel A., ed. *Studies in Social Psychology in World War II.* Samuel A. Stouffer, Edward A. Suchman, LeLand C. Devinney, Shirley A. Star, and Robin M. William Jr., *The American Soldier: Adjustment During Army Life,* Vol. 1, Samuel A. Stouffer, Arthur A. Lumsdaine, Robin M. Williams Jr., M. Brewster Smith, Irving L. Janis, Shirley A. Star, and Leonard S. Cottrell Jr., *The American Soldier: Combat and Its Aftermath,* Vol 2. Princeton: Princeton University Press, 1949.

Strawson, John. *The Battle for the Ardennes.* New York: Charles Scribner's Sons, 1972.

Sullivan, Charles J. *Army Posts and Towns: The Baedeker of the Army.* Los Angeles, CA.: Haynes, 1942.

Tanner, Robert G. *Stonewall in the Valley: Thomas J. "Stonewall" Jackson's Shenandoah Valley Campaign, Spring 1862.* Garden City, NY.: Doubleday, 1976.

Taylor, A. Marjorie. *The Language of World War II: Abbreviations, Captions, Quotations, Slogans, Titles and Other Terms and Phases.* New York: H. W. Wilson, 1944.

Terkel, Studs. *"The Good War": An Oral History of World War II.* New York: Pantheon Books, 1984.

Thompson, Reginald W. *Battle for the Rhine.* New York: Ballantine, 1959.

Tillotson, Lee S. *Index-Digest and Annotations to the Uniform Code of Military Justice.* Harrisburg, PA.: Military Service Publishing Company, 1952.

Todd, Keith. *Old Hickory: 30th Infantry Division.* Paducah, KY.: Turner, 1990.

Toland, John. *Battle: The Story of the Bulge.* New York: Random House, 1959.

———. *Infamy: Pearl Harbor and Its Aftermath.* Garden City, NY.: Doubleday, 1982.

———. *The Last 100 Days.* New York: Random House, 1966.

Treadwell, Mattie E. *The Women's Army Corps.* Washington, D.C.: Department of the Army, 1953.

Utah Beach to Cherbourg 6–27 June 1944. Washington, D.C.: Department of the Army, 1947.

Vajda, Ferenc A., and Peter G. Dancey. *German Aircraft Industry and Production, 1933–1945.* London: Airlife Publishing Ltd., 1998.

Van Creveld, Martin L. *Fighting Power: German and U.S. Army Performance, 1939–1945.* Westport, CT.: Greenwood Press, 1982.

Vannoy, Allyn R., and Jay Karamales. *Against the Panzers: United State Infantry versus German Tanks, 1944-1945: A History of Eight Battles Told through Diaries, Unit Histories, and Interviews.* Jefferson, NC.: McFarland, 1996.

Voss, Frederick S. *Reporting the War: The Journalistic Coverage of World War II.* Washington, D.C.: Smithsonian Institution Press, 1994.

Weigley, Russell F. *The American Way of War: A History of the United States Military Strategy and Policy.* Bloomington: Indiana University Press, 1977.

———. *Eisenhower Lieutenant's: The Campaign of France and Germany, 1944–1945* Bloomington: Indiana University Press, 1981.

Weithas, Art, ed. *Close to Glory: The Untold Stories of World War II by the Soldiers Who Saw and Reported the War, Yank Magazine Correspondents.* Austin, TX.: Eakin Press, 1991.

Weitz, Margaret C. *Sisters in the Resistance: How French Women Fought to Free France, 1940–1945.* New York: John Wiley & Sons, 1995.

Wharton, William. *A Midnight Clear.* New York: Knopf, 1982.

Wheeler, William R. *The Road to Victory: A History of Hampton Roads Port of Embarkation in World War II.* New Haven: Yale University Press, 1946.

Whitaker, Denis W., and Shelagh Whitaker. *Rhineland: The Battle to End the War.* New York: St. Martin's Press, 1989.

Whiting, Charles. *Ardennes: The Secret War.* New York: Stein and Day, 1985.

———. *Bloody Aachen.* New York: Stein and Day, 1976.

———. *Death of a Division.* New York: Stein and Day, 1981.

———. *The End of the War: Europe: April 15–May 23, 1945.* New York: Stein and Day, 1973.

———. *'44: In Combat from Normandy to the Ardennes.* New York: Stein and Day, 1984.

———. *Hitler's Werewolves: The Story of the Nazi Resistance Movement.* New York Stein and Day, 1972.

———. *Massacre at Malmédy: The Story of Jochen Peiper's Battle Group, Ardennes, December, 1944.* New York: Stein and Day, 1971.

Willis, Donald J. *The Incredible Year.* Ames: Iowa State University Press, 1988.

Winston, Keith. *V-Mail: Letters of a World War Combat Medic.* Edited by Sarah Winston. Chapel Hill, NC.: Algonquin Books of Chapel Hill, 1985.

Wood, Edward W. Jr. *On Being Wounded.* Golden, CO.: Fulcrum Publishers, 1991.

Ziemke, Earl F. *The U.S. Army in the Occupation of Germany, 1944–1946.* Washington, D.C.: Center of Military History, 1975.

Zorns, Bruce C. *I Walk through the Valley: A World War II Infantryman's Memoir of War, Imprisonment, and Love.* Jefferson, NC.: McFarland & Company, 1991.

Articles

Baxter, Colin F. "Did the Nazis Fight Better than Democrats: Historical Writing on the Combat Performance of the Allied Soldier in Normandy." *Parameters* 25 (Autumn 1995): 113–18.

Beaumont, Roger A. "On the Wehrmacht Mystique." *Military Review* 66 (July 1986): 45–55.

Bell, Kelly. "Bloody Battle for Berlin." *World War II* (March 1998): 22–28, 67.

Bradsher, James B. "Practicing the Historian's Craft: The Army Historian and the Army Records." *The Army Historian* 8 (Summer 1985): 10–11.

Cain, Marvin R. "The Military Memoir as Critical History: The Case of James M. Gavin." *Military Affairs* 44 (December 1990): 177–80.

Chermol, Brian H. "Wounds without Scars: Treatment of Battle Fatigue in the U.S. Armed Forces in the Second World War." *Military Affairs* 49 (January 1985): 9–12.

Clark, Mark E. "Infantry Defending against Armored and Mechanical Attacks: A Historical Review." *Military Review* 71 (July 1999): 56–57.

———. "Military Memoirs of World War II: Is It Too Late?" *Army History: The Professional Bulletin of Army History* 35 (Fall 1995): 28–31.

Coakley, Robert F. "Reflections on Writing the Green Books." *Army History: The Professional Bulletin of Army History* 25 (Summer 1993): 37–39.

Colley, David P. "The Red Ball Express." *World War II* (March 1997): 35–40.

"Dependency no Deferment." *Business Week* (27 April 1942): 15–16.

"Draft and Deferments." *Newsweek* 19 (13 April 1942): 31.

Drea, Edward J. "Recognizing the Liberators: U.S. Army Divisions Enter the Concentration Camps." *Army History: The Professional Bulletin of Army History* 24 (Winter 1993): 1–5.

Elkin, Frederick. "The Soldier's Language." *American Journal of Sociology* 51 (March 1946): 414–22.

Elkin, Henry. "Aggressive and Erotic Tendencies in Army Life." *American Journal of Sociology* 51 (March 1946): 408–14.

Flynn, Fred V. "Preparing the 'Self' for Combat." *Military Review* 71 (August 1991): 77–87.

Flynn, George Q. "Lewis Hershey and the Conscientious Objector: The World War II Experience." *Military Affairs* 48 (February 1983): 1–6.

Giangreco, D. M. "Casualty Projections for the U.S. Invasion of Japan, 1945–1946: Planning and Policy Implementation." *Journal of Military History* 61 (July 1997): 531–53.

Guttman, Jon. "Closing the Falaise Pocket." *World War II* (September 2001): 34–40.

Irzyk, Albin F. "4th Armored Division Spearhead at Bastogne." *World War II* (November 1999): 34–40, 88–90.

Jacobs, Bruce. "Tensions between the Army National Guard and the Regular Army." *Military Affairs* 73 (October 1993): 12–17.

Jones, Philip D. "U.S. Antitank Doctrine in World War II." *Military Affairs* 60 (March 1980): 62–66.

Keefer, Louis E. "The Birth and Death of the Army Specialized Training Program." *Army History: The Professional Bulletin of Army History* 33 (Winter 1995): 1–7.

Kindsvatter, Peter S. "Cowards, Comrades, and Killer Angels." *Parameters* 20 (June 1990): 31–49.

Kissel, Robert P. "Death of a Division in the Schnee Eifel." *World War II* (January 2000): 46–52.

Latimer, Jon D. " 'The Reichwald' ": Clearing a Path to the Rhine." *World War II* (March 1999): 22–28.

McCreedy, Kenneth O. "Planning the Peace: Operation Eclipse and the Occupation of Germany." *Journal of Military History* 65 (July 2001): 713–39.

Meyer, Henry J. and Erwin O. Smigel, "Job-Seeking and the Readjustment Allowance for Veterans." *American Journal of Sociology* 56 (January 1951): 341–47.

"Numbers Game." *Business Week* (7 March 1942): 72.

Shrader, Charles R. "Friendly Fire: The Inevitable Price." *Parameters* 22 (Autumn 1992): 29–44.

Strauss, Barry S. "Reflections on the Citizen-Soldier." *Parameters* 33 (Summer 2003): 66–77.

Weigley, Russell F. "From the Normandy Beaches to the Falaise-Argentan Pocket." *Military Review* 70 (September 1995): 45–64.

Weinberg, S. Kirson. "Problems of Adjustment in Army Units." *American Journal of Sociology* 50 (January 1945): 271–78.

Willoughby, John. "The Sexual Behavior of American GIs in the Early Days of the Occupation of Germany." *Journal of Military History* 62 (January 1998): 155–74.

Woodward, William H. "The Citizen-Soldier Historian and the 'New Military History.' " *The Army Historian* 9 (Fall 1985): 13–15.

Yelton, David K. " 'Ein Volk Steht Auf ': The German Volksstrum and Nazi Strategy, 1944–45." *Journal of Military History* 64 (October 2000): 1061–83.

ᴥ Index

Aachen, Battle of, 9–10, 102–19, 240n. 3
absence of field grade officers on front-
line, 141
African American soldiers, 132–33, 242n.
2
air-ground coordination. *See* ECA, observations during wartime on: "fly
boys," scorn for, and friendly fire
Akron, Ohio, 3
alcohol, use of in combat, 93–4, 109,
239n. 45. *See also* ECA, observations
during wartime on: Calvados
American Red Cross, 61, 95, 128, 208,
234n. 5
American Seating Company, 3–4, 14,
18–21, 22–24, 218, 219
antitank weaponry, 74. *See also* bazooka
apprehension and fear among replacements; 68–72, 74–75
Ardennes Campaign, 10–12, 131–60
Armstrong, Mason H., 140
Army Air Forces, 76–77, 88–89, 112. *See
also* ECA, observations during
wartime on: "fly boys," scorn for, and
friendly fire
Army Specialized Training Program
(ASTP), 9, 102, 114, 228n. 11
Arn, Cora C. (mother), 1–2, 22, 24, 40–41,
232n. 13
Arn, Edward (father), 1–2, 20, 24, 37–38,
73–74, 95, 96, 227–28n. 3
Arn, Edward C. (ECA)
    boyhood and early life of:
        ambitions, 3–4, 23; business ca-
        reer, 3–4, 14–15, 17–23, 42, 62,
        218, 219; description, 3–4;
        draft status, 3–4, 17, 18, 21–22,
        27, 230n. 3, 231n. 6; education,
        2–3; family, xiii, 14–15; mar-
        riages, 3, 4–5, 14–15, 17–22, 27,
        40, 46–47, 51, 55, 61, 95, 162,
        248n. 14; parents and child-
        hood, 1–2

characteristics and personal life of:
    caution, 10, 90–91, 92–93, 105,
    110–12, 134, 137, 146, 147,
    184–85, 243n. 20; characteris-
    tics, xiii, xiv–xvi, 2, 5–8, 9–10,
    11, 12, 14–15, 30, 57, 58, 69–70,
    73–74, 80–81, 92–93, 96,
    99–101, 115, 117, 129, 133,
    157–58, 159, 167–68, 171–73,
    195, 204, 206, 208, 216–17,
    219–20; conscientiousness,
    43–44, 46, 50; desensitization
    to death, 7, 52, 75, 115, 168,
    181; invisible scars, 224–25;
    leadership qualities, 6, 7, 8, 9,
    14, 39, 49–50, 52, 57, 106–7,
    113, 114, 116–17, 133, 158–59,
    209, 210, 215–16; motivation
    for writing memoir, xiii, 1, 15;
    patriotism, 3–4, 19; pride in
    30th Division, xv, 6–7, 64; re-
    action to attack on Pearl Har-
    bor, 4, 17, 19, 25; wartime
    personality changes, 14–15,
    224–25
military career of:
    Aachen, Battle of, and pillbox
    warfare, 107–19, 240n. 3;
    Aachen Gap, closing of,
    118–19; accomplishments,
    xiv–xv; administrative duties
    in 75th Division, 214–15; age as
    limit to combat, 5, 6, 17, 24, 25,
    28, 34, 42, 49, 55; Ardennes
    Campaign, 131–60; battlefield
    promotions, 114, 139, 154, 199,
    203; Belgium, reaches, 96;
    Bulge, Battle of, 136–52; as cit-
    izen-soldier, 1, comes of age
    as, 107, 126; company com-
    mand officer, becomes, 81;
    company commander, re-
    placed as, 120–21; company